MW01257656

Fifty Shades
of Gray Aliens

In Consideration of Aliens, UFOs, Abductees, Contactees, Experiencers, Channeling, and More

by Ken Ammi

One theory which can no longer be taken very seriously is that UFOs are interstellar spaceships
—Arthur C. Clarke

No End Books

"…of making many books there is no end;
and much study is a weariness of the flesh.
Let us hear the conclusion of the whole matter:
Fear God, and keep his commandments:
for this is the whole duty of man."
—Ecclesiastes 12

"I could actually borrow some of your work to answer some questions people have asked me. Kudos to what you did with this book"
—Joseph Jordan, president and co-founder of the CE4 Research Group and former investigator for MUFON

"Ken's work boldly considers all angles and perspectives to every aspect of this topic. He provokes the reader to consider all aspects of a situation that many may overlook because it may interfere with our preconceived ideas that, knowingly or not, we want to prove"
—Jim Wilhelmsen, MUFON research specialist and author of *Beyond Science Fiction!*

"This book is contains a great amount of research on the origins of gray aliens, extraterrestrials, dimensional travelers or demons. The research includes thorough examples...From Pop culture to the occult, the origins of the modern gray alien are pieced together"
—John Razimus, occult researcher and independent investigator

Introduction

Under consideration herein are some aspects and personages and beings involved in the fascinating, complicated, wacky, serious and all around flummoxing realm of the issues which hover around aliens and UFOs.

UFO literally simple means *U*nidentified *F*lying *O*bject and thus can be an airplane, a bird, a balloon, a satellite, etc.
This acronym has become synonymous with *a craft piloted by aliens,* which brings us to the next definition.
Incidentally, I do not know why alien fans correlate high tech with high spirituality.

As we shall see, the assumption seems to be that aliens employ high tech in order to reach the Earth and so this automatically means that we should convert to their alien theology.
Our human astronauts employ some of the highest tech as have: should we likewise consider them qualified to promulgate our theology?

By aliens, the reference is to claims of intelligent extra-terrestrial which is more and more so being thought of as actually being extra-dimensional life which we may also term *para-terrestrial.*

That is to say that initially UFOlogists speculated about life in other planets within our solar system, then beyond it and finally within realms to which we have no current access as we are separated not by mere distance but by lacking access to dimensions beyond three special plus time.

Obviously, this work's titled plays off of the book which is so indicative of the *pornification* of our culture: *Fifty Shades of Grey*. You will note that the title refers to gr<u>e</u>y yet, I chose to go with gr<u>a</u>y since it seems that when referring to aliens it is generally spelled with an "a"—grey or gray?

Now, I chose the title for the sake of parody and was not implying that within this work I will mostly focus upon the traditional small bodies, big headed, large almond eyed gray aliens.

Table of Contents

What are Aliens and UFOs?

There are many theories regarding what is variously referred to as aliens, extra-terrestrial, UFOs, flying saucers, etc. What is of interest is that there has been a point of convergence of sorts which has come about. This has occurred by people with very different theories somehow ending up with a theory of everything, as it were, pertaining to this particular topic.

In essence, there are three main categories into which all theories can be broken down:
1) *Extra-terrestrial aliens*
2) *Demons*
3) *Humans/governments*

In essence, these categories can be succinctly defined as follows.

Extra-terrestrial are just that, aliens from other parts of the universe regardless of how near or far.

Demons is in reference to disembodied malevolent beings which seek to delude, confuse and control people via being disguised as benevolent and/or malevolent extra-terrestrial aliens.

Humans/governments high tech projects/experiments which are behind literal UFOs—meaning literally **U**nidentified **F**lying **O**bject, objects that are flying but are not identified, with no further connotation.

With this last point we begin to see how these three main theories begin to meld into one and 3) and 1) get tied together. There are also sub-categories under each of these so let us consider some of these. Of course, the sub-categories also break down into more and more and more and yet, this would take us into the very many theories whereas our purpose is to get to the one which seems to bind them all.

Extra-terrestrial aliens are said to be from various places in the universe, to have been visiting Earth for millennia. The claim is that there are various species which have been doing this from the greys to the reptilians and from big foot to humanoids who look just like blond haired, blue eyed Scandinavians. These various species can be either benevolent or malevolent…or both.

Demons are meant to convey the fallen angels referenced in the Bible. Yet, sadly, in our (pseudo) syncretistic world some would say that the terms *demons, angels, aliens, higher beings, ascended masters*, etc. are interchangeable terms which simply get confused occasionally and yet, these terms are not interchangeable (for example, a disembodied angel who was created by God and rebelled is nothing like a physical being who was born and grew up in another sector of the universe—except, perhaps, in Mormon theology[1]).

In any case, some claim that malevolent aliens have been mistaken as demons. Some claim that benevolent aliens are mistaken as angels or gods. Some, that gods are mistaken as aliens. And on it goes.

Human/government high tech projects/experiments are either said to be purposefully attempting to fool people into thinking that they are seeing actual flying saucers piloted by aliens or are simply conducting experiments and have resulted in, as a mere byproduct/side effect, people mistake their high tech craft for alien vessels.

The point of convergence between the three main theories is occurring as those holding to them are coming to similar conclusions.

For example, the *extra-terrestrial aliens* camp came to consider that travel from such vast distances and at such speeds ranges from unlikely to impossible. Of course, anyone can simply say, "Well, the aliens have managed to do it…somehow" but that is another issue as anything can be *what if*-ed to death. In any case, the basic conclusion is that these beings are not traveling vast distances but are traveling inter-dimensionally: through dimensions (portals, worm holes, black holes, star gates, etc.). This is also seen via those who believe that aliens visit us from the future in which case, it is not about distance but solely about dimension.

Demons, and whatever other category of being people list herein, as noted above, falls within the inter-dimensional sphere.

Human/government technology may or may not be able to traverse dimension but that is irrelevant as if they are concocting illusion to cause delusion then they can make it appear as such via cloaking, holographic projections, etc. (see the *Will Yitzhaq Hayutman Reveal the Occult Holographic Third Temple?* chapter of my book *The Necronomiconjob, Liber III*).

Thus, the main convergence, the point of agreement between these varying theories is the concept of inter-dimensionality. However, there is a deeper point pertaining to the theory relating to human/government technology and yet, this ties in with the other two as well.

The deeper point is the question of whether humans/governments are interacting with and collaborating with aliens or demons. Some claim that aliens and demons have traded knowledge whereby to build high tech for whatever reasons: humans used for experimentations, *selling* souls, etc.

For example, some claim that via retrieval of downed alien craft and reverse engineering the Nazis were able to develop, for the time, very sophisticated weaponry. However, it is noteworthy that the highest tech of which the general populace knows is not the highest tech with which humans have come up since it is standard practice that governments keep the highest tech secretive.

Also, just prior to and during the Nazi regime Germany was a highly educated society and very involved in sciences such as engineering. Thus, the tech needs not be attributed to aliens or demons but to the human propensity towards creating—and destroying.

On Aliens and/or Demons

Perhaps the most interesting theory which unites them all is something to the likes of that influenced by inter-dimensional demons, fallen (employing a Christian term) humans/governments with power lust are developing high tech of which the populace gets, at best, mere glimpses.

Via this tech, people are made to believe that they are in contact with aliens. The aliens somehow always end up relating information regarding *spirituality* which is somehow always Pagan—the universe and Earth are living beings, humans are suck in a spiritual rut out of which the aliens can help us, Judeo-Christianity is fallacious, etc. New Age mysticism is the mythos of the aliens.

But why would human/governments do such things? Well, of what do alien contactees tell? Generally of being unwillingly abducted in a helpless waking coma type of state and undergoing various sorts of experiments which include DNA/gene related manipulations and some experiments are sexual in nature, deal with pregnancy, etc.

They also report being implanted with various devices which are claimed to do everything from tracking whereabouts to relaying instructions, thoughts, etc.

Some further claim that the goal is to develop human alien hybrids which in this scenario would actually mean human demon hybrids.

Some claim that the ultimate theory about this issue is that it is a part of the plans by what is known as the Illuminati to establish what is known as a *New World Order*. Thus, the Illuminati works within governments to develop high tech, they employ high tech to make people believe in aliens (and therefore, in most cases, to deny Judeo-Christianity).

These people are, from the earliest ages, visited by pseudo-aliens (some say that abductions run in families) which are a disguise via which the Illuminati cause multiple personality disorders/dissociative identity disorder (MPD/DID) so as to control people who can appear perfectly normal one minute but then be switched into someone they can use towards their ends.

This way, we end up with that about which I speculate in chapter *The Manchurian Messiah: Project Blue Beam, UFOs, Aliens & the NWO*. It amounts to a global event which is staged via high tech (involving audio visuals, etc.) which is fake alien invasion so as to allow human/governments to take total control (think of the freedoms that were sacrificed in order to protect us again terrorists) which will bring about a one world government.

Another scenario—actually an *either or*, or perhaps an *and/or* scenario—is a faked revelation of a messiah figure, most likely every messiah/gods in which humanity believes which will then reveal that every messiah/gods are all actually one and this will bring about the one world religion.

Note that Lynn Catoe, the senior bibliographer for the report titled *UFOs and Related Subjects: An Annotated Bibliography*, came to the following conclusion:
> A large part of the available UFO literature…deals with subjects like mental telepathy, automatic writing and invisible entities…poltergeist manifestations and "possession." Many…UFO reports…recount alleged incidents that are strikingly similar to demonic possession and psychic phenomena.[2]

John Keel, journalist, influential UFOlogist and author of the book *The Mothman Prophecies*, noted the following after having researched literature on demonology:
> The manifestations and occurrences described in this imposing literature are similar if not entirely identical to the UFO phenomenon itself.[3]

John Saliba, Jesuit priest, professor of religious studies and UFO researcher, notes:
> Many contactees…write about UFOs and space beings as if these were psychic phenomena, belonging to a different

time/space dimension that lies beyond the
scope…of modern science.[4]

What Whitley Strieber and Barbara Marciniak Do Not Know

Interestingly, some of the most well-known names within
UFO/alien circles, those have claim to have been having
interactions of various sorts with aliens for years, if not
decades, admit that even after having made a living
preaching the pseudo-gospel of the aliens, they still do not
know who or what the aliens are.

Consider one of the most famous contactees/abductees
Whitley Strieber from a Q&A session on *Barnes and Noble*
(April 12, 1997 AD):

Whitley Strieber: My whole experience is
still in question. There perhaps has been
some reincarnation-related material…Is
there such a thing as "greys"? I don't
know…

Question: Do you believe "the visitors' will
ever make themselves universally known to
us?

Whitley Strieber: I have no way of really
answering that question. I don't know what
"the visitors" are…

Question: What is your opinion on the
purpose of THE SECRET SCHOOL? Why
would the aliens care about illuminating
earthlings?

Whitley Strieber: Perhaps because we are
illuminating ourselves. I assume that aliens

are the answer when we actually don't know what is going on.

FYI: this refers both to Strieber's book "Secret School: Preparation for Contact" and to the *visitor*'s school to which he is referring.

> Question: Mr. Strieber, why do they interfere in our lives without obvious permission to do so?
>
> Whitley Strieber: We don't know what "they" are. Therefore we have no idea how issues like that actually relate to the experience. Next…
> The nature of what is real is fundamentally in question. We don't know who we are. We don't know what the universe is. And we don't know the relationship between ourselves and the universe, but we can find out.

Of particular interest may be the following:

> Question: Mr. Strieber, I wonder if you are as frightened of the inexplicable aspects of your experiences as you once were?
>
> Whitley Strieber: I'm not frightened anymore. I got used to being astonished, and bored with being scared of things that didn't hurt. I guess I lost interest in my fear. That doesn't mean that I have decided that the experience is benign or even positive. I don't know how to interpret it. I move ahead cautiously.

But to what frightening and scary experiences are they referring? In his book *Transformation* (1988 AD, ed. p. 181) Strieber writes:

> I felt an absolutely indescribable sense of menace. It was hell on earth to be there, and yet I couldn't move, couldn't cry out, couldn't get away…Whatever was there seemed so monstrously ugly, so filthy and dark and sinister. Of course they were demons. They had to be. And they were here and I couldn't get away.

Interestingly, whilst writing this section it was recalled that both Strieber and Barbara Marciniak (whose first book *Bringers of the Dawn* was published in 1992 AD) have both been dealing with aliens for decades and yet, both (and surely others) claim to not who with whom they are dealing, they still do not know who the aliens are even after having dealt with them for so very long and having spread their pseudo-gospel for so very long.

Well, lo and behold, it just so happens that in researching Strieber's statements in this regard, he mentions Marciniak:

> Question: Are you familiar with the work of Barbara Marciniak on/with the Pleiadians? If so, what do you think of it?
>
> Whitley Strieber: Channeled material is fascinating to me, because we don't know where it comes from. It would offer us rich new insight into the human mind, if we could understand this. I like Barbara very much and respect her integrity and effort.

But who is Barbara Marciniak? Both Strieber and Marciniak. Consider the following from *The Intuitive-*

Connections Network's "Conversation with Barbara Marciniak":

1) Will you tell us who the Pleiadians are?

That's the big mystery. I really don't know exactly who they are. They introduced themselves, when I first began to channel them, as a collective of multidimensional beings from the star system we call the Pleiades. They claim that they are kin to us, and that they have come back in time from their future to our present time...they've returned...to help us more clearly see our choices and possibly create an alternative probability based on personal empowerment and our connection to nature. Otherwise, we may end up as disempowered drones living a nightmare existence as half-human/half-machine beings [aka *transhumanism*].

2) How did you come to channel messages from them?

I was really captivated by the Seth material channeled by Jane Roberts. The main message was that your thoughts create your reality, and from my own experience I knew that to be true...In May of 1988, I followed an enticing impulse and went on a sacred journey tour to Egypt and Greece. While traveling to these ancient sites, I sensed a familiarity and felt that I had lived there in other times. The last stop was Delphi, where unbeknownst to me, female oracles in trance states had served as official soothsayers for centuries.

As I walked through the entrance to the temple, my body was hit with what I would now call cellular memories…I had a strong impulse to return to my room and practice channeling. I sat down on the floor, with my back up against the bed, recalled my visit to the King's Chamber of the Great Pyramid, and said out loud, "I intend to be a clear channel now." After a few minutes, I began to speak in a voice other than my own, and the source soon identified themselves as The Pleiadians…

7) You stress the importance of being immersed in nature. What is happening to our psyches as we shift from a nature-based society to an electronically entrained one?

…Being immersed in nature balances the mind and replenishes those codes ["genetic codes and energy frequencies from cosmic sources"] at every level; it refines and updates them, and makes us better equipped to manage our lives as co-creators.

The Pleiadians say that nature is a majestic program of energy, a force of consciousness, that we must learn how to consciously interact with…

Interestingly, within the Billy Meier section, we will learn that his alien contacts claim that anyone claiming to be in touch with *Pleiadians* is a fraud.

In other words, whatever the Pleiadians are, they are preaching a pseudo-gospel of neo-Pagan, nature worship, Gaia consciousness.

Also akin to neo-Pagan spirituality is the exploitation of sex disguised as spirituality—sexual devolution:

> 8) Will you explain how the proper use of sexual energy can restore all that is sacred and missing in our lives?

> ...the chief challenge to emotional balance is dealing with sexual energy, which is both the most difficult and dangerous of energies to understand. An open and honest exploration of sexual energy, in regards to what it is and how we use it, can restore the sacred in our lives...Sexuality is an essential aspect of our creativity; when founded upon worthy values, our sexual experiences will offer romance, excitement, trust, intimacy, passion, caring, love, and self-worth...Sexual energy is also a karmic opening...we may attract people from so-called past lives to recreate specific experiences for the purpose of healing unresolved issues...

Sex is wonderful when it is exercised in the God ordained manner as He did, after all, invent it. Yet, within "spirituality" movements sex is often turned into a styled temple prostitution, a means whereby to attract others to join the group, the movement, the belief. A means to have "fun" or even to engage in Tantric Yoga which is the epitome of sex disguised as spirituality.

In conclusion, some of the most famous contactees/abductees have been working as aliens to humans *go betweens* for decades. They have written books, given lectures, made videos, lead traveling groups to sacred or otherwise relevant sites in short, made their living promulgating alien messages. They do not even know who or what the aliens are but nevertheless, they preach messages of passively giving in to various abusive actions upon their persons, neo-Pagan spirituality and the fallacy of Judeo-Christian theology.

On Karla Turner's Conclusions

The late Karla Turner, Ph.D. had been involved in alien abduction work since 1988 AD and authored three relevant books on alien abductions from a non-Judeo-Christian perspective:

Into the Fringe wherein she recounts the 1988 AD abduction experienced by herself and some family members.

Taken retells the stories of eight female abductees.

Masquerade of Angels is "the biography of Louisiana psychic Ted Rice, who, used to channeling benevolent entities, then becoming aware of his alien abduction experiences, first believed the aliens were benign, then came to the conclusion that they were no more than remorseless predators."

The book *Evil Empire of the ETs and the Ultra-Terrestrials* edited together works by Karla Turner, Sean Casteel, Tim R. Swartz, Brad and Sherry Steiger and Timothy Green Beckley.

John Chambers wrote the article, "Karla Turner: A Tribute" which is subtitled, "A posthumous memorial to a special woman — an abductee unafraid to acknowledge alien terrorism."[5] The quotes which follow are from that article as his review of Karla Turner's views are in line with some of the points we have been making in this section.

For example, Chambers states that after the 1988 AD abduction experience, the Turner family, "were able to recall abduction events going back to their childhoods." Indeed, this is a common phenomenon, both that abductions run in families and begin a childhood.

There are perhaps three popular explanations for this—and perhaps they merge somehow.

Believers in actual extra-terrestrial aliens would say that this is due to the families having been used to produce human-alien hybrids.

Judeo-Christians who think that the aliens are demonic would appeal to the controversial issue of generational curses.

Some, of whichever camp, who see the alien phenomenon as being a twisted combination of the forces of dark/shadow governments and demons would claim that this is due to genetic traits such as the ability to develop multiple personalities or dissociative states (MPD and DID) and perhaps also generational curses.

As for Karla Turner:
> She was convinced that the aliens were here
> not to help us out, but to steal from us the
> sovereignty of our souls…
> Two traits, she had come to conclude,
> characterized alien behavior above all:
> deceitfulness and cruelty…
> the experiences were uniformly disturbing…
> often, they were cruel, inflicting physical
> and mental pain on the abductees…
> On account of a pulling action by the aliens,
> a third victim sustained a spinal injury so

severe that her doctor warned her it could
prove permanent...
traumatized...physical problems were
accompanied by the usual emotional trauma
of the abductee: confusion, terror, paranoia
and ambivalence...
the terrors of the abduction experience...

John Chambers also notes that "From beginning to end,
Turner had been struck by how contradictory the stories of
the aliens were." In fact, Karla Turner wrote an article for
UFO Magazine titled, "Abduction Phenomena Defy Set
Pattern: Only mythmakers say all abductions follow a
certain regimented pattern, says this author. Far too many
variables, too much high strangeness, toss all present
theories out the window":

> They would, she averred, say anything they
> wanted to attain their ends...the aliens
> insisted variously that they had come to help
> us cope with upcoming ecological disaster,
> interbreed for our good and theirs, help us
> evolve, take our genetic material to revivify
> their dying race. Sometimes they claimed
> they had outright created us; other times,
> that they were genetically altering us for our
> own good.[6]

He also provides two succinct and yet very telling
summaries:

> To audiences around the country she listed
> what she considered to be the only "facts"
> that might be construed about the alien
> invaders:
> * We do not know with any certainty what
> they are.
> * At least some of the aliens lie.

* During encounters, they control our perceptions.
* They can implant false memories.
* What we report about them is what they want us to report.
* The alien agenda has physical aims and procedures that have nothing to do with reproduction.
* From childhood, they manipulate us physically, spiritually, and sexually.
* They create virtual reality scenarios that are absolutely real to the abductees.
* They show an extraordinary interest in human souls and in our thoughts.
* There is some element of human involvement in UFO phenomenon.

The other pertained to the fact that she "maintained there were a number of steps abductees could take in the face of alien provocation":
* Educate themselves about the phenomenon; there is some control in knowledge.
* Let go of fear; it is through fear that negative entities maintain control. Anger is a more effective defense than fear.
* Abductees should be aware of how they're reacting; they should learn to step out of themselves, and to maintain perspective.
* Maintain a good quality of life.
* Be realistic about what can and cannot be done.
* Stay close to their families.
* Confide. "The hell with the results," says Turner. "You don't need the burden of carrying this around [without being able to

talk about it]." [Bracketed statement in original]

Chambers also notes that "Turner suspected the military sometimes harassed abductees after they had been harassed by the aliens" yet she "did not reveal facts for fear of endangering friends." Thus, it may be unclear what her view on this part of the issue was. Does the military involved and if so is it because they are, for whatever reason, keeping the extra-terrestrial alien phenomenon covered up or because they, themselves, are perpetrating the pseudo-abductions via demonic possessions?

Finally and ultimately, from her perspective and with her abilities Tuner concluded that "we should take into our own hands this appalling violation of our rights as human beings":

> This brave and defiant refusal, in the name
> of humanity, to countenance suffering from
> an alien tyrant masquerading as a
> benefactor, is Karla Turner's final legacy.

Aleister Crowley, Grays Aliens, and Demons

With regards to the correlation between the concept of inter-dimensional aliens and demons, it is very important to bring up Aleister Crowley who was perhaps the most infamous occultist.

Richelle Hawks notes:

> …in his brilliant and epic book,
> Supernatural, Graham Hancock makes an
> almost inarguable case that the traditional,
> psychedelic plant-induced shamanic visions
> and experiences, fairy lore, and now modern
> abduction/alien scenarios stem from and

share the same root, a kind of trance-induced, other channel of reality, in which these same grey-beings have won the starring roles...within the story of what could be the very first modern, recorded appearance of this same entity, he is clearly described as an interdimensional being, with no pretenses of alien origins. In this story, there are other ideas that fit within Hancock's theory, such as the use of a meditative trance, drug induced, for purposeful contact (as in shamanism) with the otherworld.[7]

It was between 1917-1919 AD when Aleister Crowley and one of his many sexual spirituality aids, Roddie Minor, conducted hashish and opium induced trances wherein she described her visions to Crowley who:

...decided to conduct more formalized, regular sessions with her, culminating in [the appearance of] a character within Minor's original visions, which became somewhat of an oracle channeled rather conversationally directly between Minor (and sometimes, others) and Crowley...

Crowley drew a portrait of an entity which tangibly appeared...[the] general narratives describing it generally follow the thought that Crowley opened up a magickal portal that allowed this entity...others like him and their representational consciousness into the modern world...

Aleister Crowley drew the portrait in 1918 AD and in 1945 AD gave it to Kenneth Grant who was heading the Ordo

Templis Orientis (*OTO*, the *Order of the Temple of the East* aka *Order of Oriental Templars* which was founded by Crowley). Grant subsequently referred to the portrait as not being a single being but as representing a class or species of being. Amongst the OTO the portrait came to be used as an icon for meditative purposes.

This developed into an *inner cult* which functioned via prescribed practices pertaining to meditation, rites, techniques all for the purposes of continuing the communication with the being(s).

As can be seen in the series of images below, the being is strikingly similar to what has come to be known as *grey aliens* or simply *greys*. The main difference is the eyes which in the portrait are small and squinted whilst in greys they are very large and higher up on the head.

However, in the original portrait, these large, higher up eyes are discernable or suggested, as it were. Also, the OTO had a practice of focused starring so that eventually the image would reveal the grey's eyes. Note the original portrait and with the eyes filled in.

As a side note, in one of his books Strieber noted that the symbolism of triangles and also eagles often accompanies abduction experiences. For whatever it is worth (during this author's life BC), the very night that passage was read and upon getting home it was noticed that the ginger beer that had become a favorite had the image of an eagle within a triangle watermarked into the glass of the bottle— something that had not at all been noticed before.

So in 1918 AD Crowley paints the portrait, the OTO receives it in 1945 AD, then in 1961 AD Betty and Barney Hill claimed to have been abducted by aliens which they described looking very much like *greys* (although at one point they claimed to have seen humans which appeared to be German Nazis and also Irish) and on it goes from there to the point that the *greys* have become the most recognizable alien face and is found absolutely everywhere.

While oddly shaped heads have been long depicted in ancient art and oddly shaped skull have been found (which are made by binding children's heads so as to elongate the skull as it grows) there does not seem to be anything quite like the *greys* depicted prior to 1918 AD.

Be aware that some claim that *grays* are found depicted in Egyptian hieroglyphs but these have been shown to be plants.

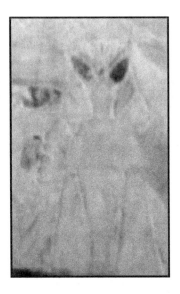

Here is a clear image of the same figure, note that now the alien appears to be wearing some fancy feathered head dress and has a cartoonish accordion elephantine trunk.

In the following images, we see what the grey alien is really—just a plant in a vase.

While we are at it, we might as well instantly debunk the claim that there are alien greys buried as mummies as is depicted in this image—after all, just look at the oh so very clear close-up. Clearly, this is simply a mummified human child.

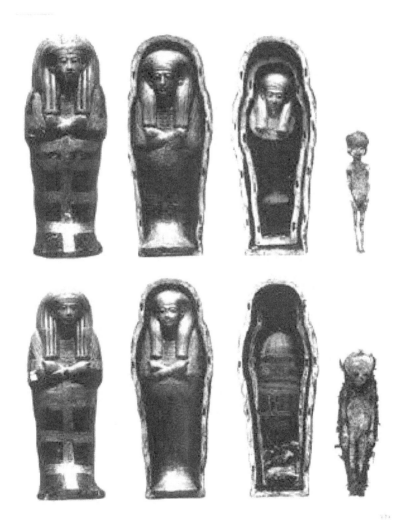

Demonology and Theosophical Aliens

One theory which can no longer be taken very seriously is that UFOs are interstellar spaceships.
—Arthur C. Clarke[8]

...any sufficiently advanced technology is indistinguishable from magic.
—one of Clarke's *three laws*

Herein we will consider the contents of an article by Christopher Partridge, Department of Theology and Religious Studies, University College Chester, "Alien demonology: the Christian roots of the malevolent extraterrestrial in UFO religions and abduction spiritualities."[9]

In this interesting article Christopher Partridge focuses on the Theosophical nature of what he terms "UFO religions" and also the shift from viewing "aliens" as extra-terrestrials to viewing them in the Judeo-Christian demonic context (what I term *extra-dimensionals*; E.D.s and not E.T.s).

Let us begin with his succinct definition or "Theosophy":
> Arguably, "Theosophy" can be traced back through Plotinus, Ammonius Saccas, and Plato to Pythagorean Greece. It has since surfaced periodically in Western esotericism, being, as Emily Seddon and Renee Weber point out, "most legitimately associated with figures such as Meister Eckhart, Giordano Bruno, Emanuel

Swedenborg, and Jacob Boehme" (Sellon
and Weber, 1992, p. 311).
Following a period of obscurity, it was then
revived at the end of the nineteenth century
by the Russian occultist Helena Petrovna
Blavatsky and an American, Henry Steel
Olcott, who in 1875 founded the
Theosophical Society in New York.

Thus, he notes:

...because UFO religions have their roots in
the Theosophical tradition, the religious
understanding of the extraterrestrial tended
to be fundamentally indebted to the concept
of the wise and benevolent ascended
master...the Theosophical tradition has
proved to be enormously significant in the
history of UFO religion...UFO religion has
been dominated by those from within the
Theosophical tradition...
Blavatsky...speculated about the Venusian
"Lords of the Flame", which, according to
Charles Leadbeater's interpretation of the
concept...were of the highest rank in the
hierarchy of ascended masters.

This is why there is such a long history of looking up to
(pun intended) "aliens" as higher beings; either
technologically, spiritually or some combination thereof.
They are anti-Christs in the sense of being replacements for
Christ Jesus, the savior, as the "aliens" can save humanity
from our violence towards each other and the Earth:

UFO groups and contactees of the 1950s
claimed to have received messages from
highly spiritually evolved, morally superior,

technologically advanced, benevolent beings with a deep salvific concern for a humanity.

The other side of the article's coin is stated as such:
>...in their construction of the malevolent alien, UFO religionists and abductees turn not to Theosophy and Eastern religious traditions but to the myths and symbols of Christian demonology.

These two extremes, as it were, come together in some personages' views:
>[David] Icke's relatively complex thesis is interesting in that, whilst it is highly critical of Christianity, its fundamental ideas demonstrate a dependence on Christian demonology.

Before continuing, note that Adolf Hitler himself was deeply into, and the Nazi Reich was premised upon, Theosophy. It is readily discernible how the concepts of Theosophy, which includes Eastern mysticism, were incorporated into Nazism where it was expressed by a frowny face and in the New Age movement where it is expressed by a happy face:

>The SS Ahnenerbe made a trip to Iceland and studied the ancient ruins and the Nordic Edda with a fine-tooth comb. The purpose was to discover the entrance to "Thule" (Mythical Aryan capital of the inner earth). This led them to an expedition to Tibet led by Dr. Ernst Schafer in 1934-36 and again in 1936-39.
>The Buddhist Monks received the Nazis with great joy. They saw the Nazis as a

prophetic fulfillment of the ones possessing the Shamballa power to complete the Dharma or cycle of the fifth root race, The Aryan. The monks accommodated them in every way.

They gave the Nazi expedition a 108 volume sacred text and allowed entrance into the cavernous systems sealed off from the rest of civilization for ages. This produced scientific studies in earth magnetism, and other geophysical experiments, as well as ethnological studies.

In their zeal to help fulfill the Nazi destiny over 200 monks were made SS officers and assigned to Himmler's staff as advisors at the Wewelsburg Castle. This was Himmler's occult center and think tank.

This was acceptable to Nazi ideology as they viewed the Hindu Indians and Tibetan Asians to be "spiritual Aryans". They believed that both groups were a connecting link to their own Aryan bloodline and descendants of the subterranean supermen. Their religions of Hinduism and Buddhism were a reflection of the religion of the Subterranean culture....

Just as Hitler described in "Mein Kamph", there is in a sense a Hierarchy of leadership within the New Age. They are all Globalist's as this is part of the Agenda. According to Alice Bailey's writings,

"The Plan is the organized program of the
spiritual Hierarchy to get a selected portion
of mankind to the next evolutionary level.
Since quality is vital for starting the next
"root- race", only selected "star seed"
people are designated to make the quantum
leap into the next level of human
transformation, but even these need careful
preparation by more advanced spirits lest
they "burnout" in the transition."[10]

Partridge refers to the fact that the occultist,
psychotherapist, and psychiatrist Carl Jung referred to
"aliens" as "technological angel."[11]
Based on this concept he states:

The alien as technological demon is popular
because it seems plausible, seems plausible
because it seems familiar, and seems
familiar because it has been constructed
from Western demonology.

Note that he implies that it is all a matter of interpretation
and we just so happen to be interpreting via a Judeo-
Christian worldview "Western demonology." However, the
question is: has it been "constructed from" or, rather,
actually "identified by" or "via" *Western demonology*?

Some interesting stats are presented by first setting a date
of June 24, 1947 AD which is when Kenneth Arnold
"reported sighting ten shining discs flying over the Cascade
Mountains when flying his private plane near Mount
Rainier in Western Washington":

"A Gallup poll taken on 19 August 1947,
revealed that…nine out of ten had heard
about the saucers"…By the end of that year
850 UFO sightings had been reported in

America alone….
Beginning in the early 1970s there was an exponential rise in reports of abductions.

The following is noted in relation to the 1487 AD text, *Malleus Maleficarum* which, or so it is claimed:

> …focused increasingly on obsession, possession and demonic alliances with humans…By the Middle Ages, learned magicians were suspected of summoning and using demons by their magic in order to exchange their souls for magical powers…it was only in the Middle Ages that…a new element was added to the European concept of witchcraft…This was the notion that the witch owed her powers to having made a deliberate pact with the Devil.

It *may perhaps* be accurate that in 1487 AD, by the Middle Ages, such pacts were "focused" upon. It *may, perhaps* also be true that it was "only in the Middle Ages" that this concept was added to (note the qualifier) *European concept of witchcraft.*

However, the concept itself, in general, has been known, noted, and understood since at least the time of the events recorded in the Bible's book 2 Kings 3:26-27 wherein the following is noted:

> When the king of Moab saw that the battle was too fierce for him, he took with him 700 men who drew swords, to break through to the king of Edom; but they could not. Then he took his oldest son who was to reign in his place, and offered him as a burnt offering on the wall. And there came great

wrath against Israel, and they departed from
him and returned to their own land.

In other words, when the battle was going against him, the
king of Moab conducted the ritual human sacrifice of his
son as a burnt offering to his false gods (true demons) who
responded by giving him the power "great wrath" to
prevail—for the time being.

Let us now get to some specific points about angels,
demons, the Genesis 6 Nephilim, etc.
The article noted the "relatively common narratives that
deal with the sexual union of deities and humans."
Historically what the article terms deities have been viewed
as angels, demons, fallen angels, aliens, etc.

Partridge notes the following with regards to the Nephilim:
> Justin Martyr, for example, is very clear that
> they were in fact "fallen angels" and that
> demons are the product of their unnatural
> union with human women....Martin Luther
> reiterates the early Christian belief that the
> "sons of the gods" are fallen angels and the
> *nephilim* demons.

Much could be said regarding the specifics here (see my
book *On the Genesis 6 Affair's Sons of God: Angels or
Not?*). For example, note that the referenced text is:
> ...that the sons of God saw that the
> daughters of men were beautiful; and they
> took wives for themselves, whomever they
> chose...
> The Nephilim were on the earth in those
> days, and also afterward, when the sons of
> God came in to the daughters of men, and
> they bore children to them. Those were the

mighty men who were of old, men of
renown.

There are, perhaps, three options about whom the Nephilim
were/are:
1) They are unrelated to Genesis 6 as they were already on
the Earth in those days.
2) They were the Sons of God who fell.
3) They were the offspring.

One must also ask whether the "Those" (or in some
translations "these") mighty men of renown were
themselves the Nephilim offspring or both, as per 3).

Another issue to consider is that it appears that the "product
of their unnatural union" are the demons but they did not
become demons until after they died—as it would have
been then that their bodies would decay and their spirits
would be left to roam the Earth.

Partridge notes that "Where in Genesis it is not clear that
these beings are particularly evil, in the apocalyptic
literature they reveal their evil nature." He references *1
Enoch* aka *Ethiopic Enoch* which notes that the:
> …archangels—Michael, Uriel, Raphael and
> Gabriel…slay the giants, although their
> malign spirits remain to "afflict, oppress,
> destroy, attack, do battle, and work
> destruction on earth" (1 En.15:1). Raphael is
> also instructed to bind Azazel and to cast
> him into an outer darkness, where he is to
> remain until the day of judgment, when he
> shall be "sent into the fire" (1 En 10:5e7).

Note that the term *archangel* is based on the concept of a
hierarchy of angels. The term appears in perhaps only one

text namely Dan 10:13 where Michael is referred to as one of the chief princes which are aka archangels in this context. In Hebrew this reads, "Miyka'el 'echad ri'shown sar" with *ri'shown* (Strong's H7223) being first, primary, etc. and *sar* (Strong's H8269) being a prince, ruler, leader, chief, chieftain, official, captain, etc.

Gabriel is referred to as "an angel of the Lord" (Luke 1:11). Uriel and Raphael are unknown in the Bible (for more details, see my book *In Consideration of the Book(s) of Enoch*).

In any case, Biblically the offspring of the *Sons of God* and *daughters of men* drowned in the great flood, the deluge (which was likely the reason for the flood in the first place).

If *1 Enoch* is to be taken as accurate in this regard; it may be referring to those who lived not only "on the earth in those days" but those who lived "also afterward." The biblical one can just as easily, and more in keeping with immediate as well as greater context, take "in those days" with a timeline beginning point which verse 1 has as "when men began to multiply on the face of the ground, and daughters were born unto them" which could be as early as when Adam and Eve's offspring first started having offspring, and "also after that" being just that: after that beginning point and yet, still pre-flood.

As to the reference to Aza'zel; *1 Enoch* personalizes this being as a condemned fallen angel.

In the Bible the term appears in Leviticus 16:8-10 which notes:

> Aaron shall cast lots for the two goats, one
> lot for the LORD and the other lot for the
> scapegoat. Then Aaron shall offer the goat
> on which the lot for the LORD fell, and
> make it a sin offering. But the goat on which

the lot for the scapegoat fell shall be
presented alive before the LORD, to make
atonement upon it, to send it into the
wilderness as the scapegoat.

Where is this being in the text? Well, *aza'zel* is or means
scapegoat, one of the two goats referenced. *Aza'zel*
(Strong's H5799) means, "1) entire removal, scapegoat a)
refers to the goat used for sacrifice for the sins of the
people b) meaning dubious" and comes from `*ez* (Strong's
H5795) meaning "1) female goat, she-goat, goat, kid"
which itself comes from the primitive root `*azaz* (Strong's
H5810) meaning "1) to be strong a) (Qal) to be strong,
prevail b) (Hiphil) to make firm, strengthen" and also
comes from the primitive root *'azal* (Strong's H235)
meaning "1) to go, to go away, to go about a) (Qal) 1) to go
away 2) to go about 3) to be used up, be exhausted, be
gone, evaporated b) (Pual) to go to and fro."

So, according to the Leviticus *aza'zel* is not a fallen angel,
demon or anything other than a goat. Yet, it is not
uncommon for an animal to come to be personified as a
being of some sort. Consider that *heylel* (aka *lucifer*) is
referred to a serpent and a dragon (see Revelation 12:9 and
20:2).

Also, in Job 41 *leviathan* is a water dwelling animal and yet
later becomes symbolic of a more general judgment:
        ...the LORD will punish Leviathan the
        fleeing serpent, With His fierce and great
        and mighty sword, Even Leviathan the
        twisted serpent; And He will kill the dragon
        who lives in the sea (Isaiah 27:1).

Partridge makes the following statement (citing the other works) that show who confusing some people make a non-issue:

> Certainly, in the Hebrew Bible Satan is not the demonic figure that he becomes in apocalyptic literature (see Kluger, 1967). Indeed, Satan is one of the 'members of the court of heaven', one of the bene 'elohim, a "son of God" (Job 1:6). The Book of Job in particular describes Satan as a being who works closely with Yahweh as his agent in the testing of Job (see Nielson, 1998, pp. 59e105).

According to Russell, Satan as a son of God has his origins in Canaanite religion:

> In Canaan these "sons" are gods, manifestations of the divine principle. Clearly, the original idea in Hebrew religion was that Yahweh was surrounded by a pantheon comparable to that of Zeus or Wotan. The idea of a pantheon was displeasing to strict monotheism, and the *banim* (*bene ha'elohim*) became shadowy figures. Yet they retained an important function of separating the evil aspect of the divine nature from the good. (Russell, 1977, p. 184)

Kirsten Nielsen explains the relationship between God and Satan more literally in terms of father and son:

> At the beginning father and son are together, but at a certain time their paths separate. Satan in the book of Job [is] the son of God who for some time roamed the earth. He lived among the other sons of God, close to

his father. There is nothing to indicate that
he was denied this position after he had
tested Job, neither was there a revolt against
his father or any fall from the heavenly to
the earthly. (Nielsen, 1998, p. 156) Only in
later Jewish legend do we find Satan
banished from heaven.

This all revolves around the Job text wherein, or so we are
told, "Satan is one of the 'members of the court of heaven',
one of the bene 'elohim, a 'son of God.'" He may very well
be able to be described as "a being who works closely with
Yahweh as his agent in the testing of Job" because
otherwise, Satan would have authority over God to do as he
pleases.

The claim was that Satan is one of the bene 'elohim/sons of
God but let us see what Job actually states:

Now there was a day when the sons of God
came to present themselves before the
LORD, and Satan came also among them.

So, the "sons of God" (one category of being) came to the
LORD and (besides them) Satan (another category of
being) came also among them. So the sons of God came
and Satan came with them. In other words, he is not
necessarily identified as being a son of God but as tagging
along, as it were, with them.

If you take the view that the sons of God here are "angles"
then you will further note the difference as Satan is not an
"angel" but a cherub (*angels* and *cherubim* are different
categories of beings).

But perhaps some will argue that all who came to God were
sons of God and Satan just happens to be mentioned by

name. In any case, it is inaccurate to state that "Satan is not the demonic figure" in the Hebrew Bible (the Tanakh aka Old Testament) especially when we note that *Satan* is aka *serpent* aka *heylel* aka *accuser* aka *adversary* (the literal meaning of *satan*), etc.

Nielsen seems to be, not surprisingly, elucidating a satanic doctrine (found in Mormonism) which is that Satan (and not Jesus?) is God the Father's son. He even singled out Satan as being "the son of God" in Job; this excludes the plural sons of God or includes Satan as being one of them (see above).

Jeffrey Burton Russell takes the satanic doctrine up (or is it *down*?) a notch by having "argued that Satan is 'the malignant, destructive aspect of Yahweh…subtracted from him and ascribed to a different spiritual power.'" So on this view; Satan is Yahweh but merely turned into another "person" to avoid theological embarrassment—or, something.

Even if we were to grant that Satan is "the son of God" (meaning something like a creation of His, which Satan, or rather heylel, is) the Hebrew Bible may not state that he "was denied this position after he had tested Job" but that something occurred before that which turned the ministering cherub heylel into Satan (see Isaiah 14 and Ezekiel 28). This was the time of his "revolt against his father" and is why in "later Jewish legend [historical records]…we find Satan banished from heaven."

Recall how above it was noted that David Icke's thesis is, both, "highly critical of Christianity" even while "its fundamental ideas demonstrate a dependence on Christian demonology." Well, the article also notes that, in short, many modern day views on aliens and UFOs are that:

The space gods may be Theosophical, but
the space demons are Christian.

Here is one such example as Partridge refers to
"Theologically positive, Theosophical streams of the
Ashtar Command" such as the "Ashtar Lightwork Centre"
which reported, "conscious contact with a so-called
Alien…Greys…a silver gray coloured lady stood at the
entrance, and asked politely if she could please come in."

Beings who stand at doorways asking permission to come
in is typical of the supposed litigious nature of demonic
activity; which must be allowed in by human permission
(conscious such as in a pact or unconscious such as in
messing around with Ouija boards). This is seen above with
regards to the grays pertaining to a gray colored lady and
more recently with regards to (mere) reports of black eyed
children who ask to be let into homes, cars, etc.

Note that:
>…the Ashtar movement explained a series
of failed prophecies regarding alien
intervention as well as the proliferation of
extraterrestrial messages that conflicted with
the earlier communications of Ashtar, in
terms spiritual warfare. As Christopher
Helland notes, "messages and practices from
a previous generation, which were thought
not to be consistent with current cosmology
and communications, were attributed to the
interference of negative space beings in the
upper atmosphere of the planet" (Helland,
2003, p. 174).

This led to the development of a
demonology in which "several young

members of Ashtar's training forces had
defected and become evil beings". This, we
are told, occurred decades ago when a group
of cadets rebelled from the Ashtar
Command and formed their own negative
extraterrestrial government. These beings
made alliances with "others of a similar
rebellious nature" and began operating upon
the "lowest planes closest to the Earth". Any
messages that had been channelled in the
past that contained overly negative
information or erroneous dates for landing
events were blamed upon these beings.
(Helland, 2003, p. 174)

This is basically the "satanic verses" of the Theosophical
Ashtar movement. You may be aware that in Islam there is
the concept of the satanic verses which is a way to explain
(explain away or, rather, excuse) heretical statements made
by Muhammad. They are said to have been satanic
deceptions which Allah then had to correct and replace.
In the case of the Ashtar movement, we have the *negative
space beings verses* excuse. The fact that the activities of
"fallen angels" (as they are known in common parlance)
and/or demons are the very same as those of "aliens" makes
one wonder about the being who brought revelation to
Muhammad (it was not Allah but "Gabriel").

From this concept of *negative space beings* who *defected
and become evil beings* comes elucidations such as that,
"some aliens fell by allying themselves with the reptilians
and 'functioning like the Borg in Star Trek.'" The Borg are
actually more akin to transhumans—biological organisms
melded with technology—but are likely referenced due to
their *hive* mind; common consciousness or literal group-
think.

It is also noted that:
> "some of the things that happened during
> that war" ["a great battle between good and
> evil aliens"], things that "were ten times
> worse than Roddenberry was allowed to
> show"…suggests that Star Trek is
> understood to have been used by
> extraterrestrials to reveal truth.

These references to science "fiction" are interesting for various reasons and actually come from the Ashtar Command claim that that "aliens" stated that:
> We will enter into a campaign of spreading
> our imagery through your media. So-called
> fictional sci-fi books, which will gain mass
> popularity, will actually be truth disguised
> as fiction. This will gently accustom humans
> to the concept.

Note that Phyllis Schlemmer was a trance medium who channeled a cosmic being named Tom who, in turn, claimed to be part of "the Nine" who were a group of beings from "Deep Space."

One person associated with Schlemmer was Gene Roddenberry:
> …the legendary creator of Star Trek, who,
> Schlemmer's website claims, was visiting
> the medium as part of his research for the
> sci-fi series. Hence *Star Trek: Deep Space
> Nine*. Maybe. The truth, as usual, appears to
> be even stranger.

> Roddenberry, a humanist who was deeply
> critical of religion but who was fascinated

by psi phenomena and altered states of consciousness (possibly stemming from a childhood out-of-body experience) and who accepted some measure of the "latent abilities" of telepathy, clairvoyance and psychokinesis, appears to have been recruited by a paranormal organization called Lab Nine to help prepare the public, via a film-script that he would write, for an impending first contact event.

Toward this end, he was given tours of parapsychological labs and introduced to Schlemmer and, through her, to Tom and the Nine. Neither the film nor the first contact panned out although the script was written.

Film or no film, landing or no landing, Roddenberry conversed with Tom through Schlemmer. It was Roddenberry, for example who got the entity to affirm that some of us are "of Altean blood" and possess Altean "genetic features . . . mixed with our basic Earth features." Human-alien hybrids again.[12]

Thus, overall, we find that Judeo-Christians demonology has correctly identified "aliens" as being the very same being who in previous times and in various places have pretended to be gods, fairies, gnomes, elves, etc., etc., etc. and are today most popularly pretending to be extra-terrestrial aliens.

> *Satan disguises himself as an angel of light.*
> —2 Corinthians 11:14

Likenesses Between Spirit Channeler Mediums and Alien Contactees/Experiencers

Of the very many likenesses between spirit channeler mediums and alien contactees/experiencers there are a few noteworthy ones.

Succinctly stated, spirit channeler mediums and alien contactees/experiencers come in a variety of forms; both denote humans who claim to be in contact with otherworldly beings.

Spirit channeler mediums claim that the otherworldly beings are deceased humans and ascended masters and alien contactees/experiencers claim that they are extra-terrestrial aliens from other planets, other galaxies or even other universes.

Both spirit channeler mediums and alien contactees/experiencers are likely to have had a background of involvement in occult practices—by any other name. These may be generalized as practices that open one up. For example, emptying one's mind of one's own thoughts and thus allowing something else's thoughts to enter. Or, via chanting or pulsating repetitive motions or drumming, short circuiting the mind so that it blanks out and, again, allows something else to take over.

In fact, the most well-known psychics (who are essentially spirit channeler mediums) have a background of Catholicism (find evidence of this in *Appendix B:*

Catholicism and the Psychic/Medium Connection within my book *In Consideration of Catholic Doctrines, Traditions and Dogmas*. This is significant because Catholics are taught that communicating with the dead (necromancy, which the Bible forbids) is perfectly acceptable and holy. Thus, they pray to Mary, saints, etc. and it is merely one baby step away from communicating with any and all sorts of otherworldly beings.

Moreover, the point is that being a practicing spirit channeler medium is, itself, an occult practice. Being an alien contactee/experiencer is as well but some claim that they do not ask for it nor want it; however, there are those who do ask for it and want it.

Spirit channeling mediums and alien contactees/experiencers also report the appearance of spheres or globes of light; from large ones in their sky to small ones in their homes. Likewise, they both report electromagnetic disturbances.

Both spirit channeler mediums and alien contactees/experiencers claim to receive messages from otherworldly beings via telepathy; meaning that there is no need to be physically present with the otherworldly beings.

In the case of deceased humans, it would technically not be possible as they are no longer physical. In the other case, we run into the difference between extra-terrestrial alien *abductees*, on the one hand, and *contactees* and/or *experiencers* on the other. Abductees have the experience of being taken aboard spaceships, being experimented upon and also receiving messages but contactees/experiencers need never even have as much as seen a UFO off in the distant sky.

Both spirit channeler mediums and alien contactees/experiencers involve the same practices two of which are: 1) some claim to receive the messages in their minds and simply retell them and 2) some claim to be "walk-ins" which denotes when a being takes over their bodies and speak through the directly (usually with very poor British accents).

Beyond the reception of the messages themselves, there is also something similar about the actual messages:
1) Concern about our destructive systems of governance.
2) Concern about our destruction of the environment.
3) Assurance that the afterlife is a wonderful place wherein everyone and everything is wonderful (sure, you may have to pay back some karma or whatever but then; you're good to go).
4) They promulgate a theology according to which there is no personal God but an impersonal force (energy, qi, ki, chi, Prana, Vril, the Force, etc.) into which anyone can tap and manipulate via their wills.
5) The messages are 99.9% anti-Christian and .1% anti any other faith.

It is true that we have destructive systems of governance and have negative impacts on the environment. However, the spirit channeler mediums and alien contactees/experiencers answer, the how to, is always the same; forming a one world government and a one world religion—a new world order.

Time Traveling Aliens?

There is a fascinating correlation between the views regarding life's origins as held by Francis Crick, et al., and attempts to identify "extra-terrestrial aliens."

Some, such as Crick, saw and very clearly understood that DNA is a designed, information containing, information duplicating and information correcting system. Yet, Crick was an Atheist whose mind was enslaved to a materialistic worldview which restricts free thought. Thus, he chose to affirm design but to assign the design to extra-terrestrial aliens as per a view called "directed panspermia" which refers to the purposeful "seeding" of life on Earth.

This correlated with issues variously termed *UFOs, aliens, contactees, abductees, experiencers*, etc. in the following manner.

Some conclude from a myriad of claims—regardless of chronology, geography or theology (or, lack thereof)—that there are some or another (or, various) forms of flying vehicles which largely go unidentified (the literal meaning of UFO).

From this, they conclude advanced intelligence due to the claims that these vehicles can perform maneuvers and travel at speeds that are impossible with our current technology (keeping in mind that the general public actually does not know our level of technology as it is kept from us).

Some conclude that these phenomenon are the doings of, at one level, government secret black project experiments and, at another level, the manifestations of demonic beings.

It is largely agreed upon that long—and we are talking about extremely long—distance travel across space is impossible. Thus, the concept of actual extra-terrestrials from vast distances is generally rejected and often rejected for the accurate view that they are not "extra-terrestrial" but, rather, "extra-dimensional" (not E.T. but E.D.).

And yet, the phenomenon persists.

We have stated the above as preliminary to making this point: there are those who, by "faith," deny the existence of the supernatural and also deny the possibility of vast distance extra-terrestrials travel. So, what do they employ as an *explanation*?

One view that is growing in popularity holds that the aliens (or, *visitors*) are not extra-terrestrials and are not demonic but are human beings who have traveled back from the future.

The view holds that human technology advances to the point that we can time travel and we come back in order to well, do whatever: help ourselves evolve spiritually (keeping in mind that one can be an Atheist and be spiritual—just ask Sam Harris, the mystic, Buddhist, Atheist), to get us to clean up the environment so that it is not utterly wrecked for the future, etc.

As an example, here are five people who hold to this view (granting variations).

Paul Davies claims, "We in fact create reality." He claims that the reason that the universe is intelligently designed is that we humans traveled back in time and created it as such.

Davies is a physicist, cosmologist, and astrobiologist working at Arizona State University

Jeffrey Kripal, "human beings...are gods in disguise...the angels and aliens, gods and demons are us."
Kripal holds the J. Newton Rayzor Chair in Philosophy and Religious Thought at Rice University, where he is also the Chair of the Department of Religious Studies and he is self-admittedly "possessed."

Whitley Strieber is known as the poster-child for the alien/UFO phenomenon and yet, he has never claimed that his dealings were with extra-terrestrial aliens but with "visitors"; human ones from the future.
Strieber is an author, movie producer, lecturer and extremely well known within the UFO/Alien/abductee/contactee/experiencer communities.

Douglas Dietrich holds that so called "aliens" are, in reality, "our decedents from the future." His spin is not just that we travel back in time from a future Earth to a past Earth but that humanity will advance to the point that we colonize other planets. We then travel back in time in order to interact with our past.
Dietrich worked for the Department of Defense as a Research Librarian at the Presidio Military Base of San Francisco.

Barbara Marciniak claims that the Pleiadians with whom she is in touch "claim that they are kin to us, and that they have come back in time from their future to our present time...they've returned...to help us more clearly see our choices and possibly create an alternative probability based on personal empowerment and our connection to nature."[13]
Marciniak is an author, speaker, medium/spirit channeler

(in the guise of someone who receives messages from extra-terrestrial aliens from the Pleiades).

Perhaps we ought to throw in another interesting statement that whilst not as specific as the others, makes a similar point nevertheless.

Paul Levinson states that through technology we will "embody and extend our ideas, inject our minds into the world and disperse our theories to the far corners of the universe, and therein begin to mold the universe to human designs."[14]
Levinson is the Professor and Chair of Communication & Media Studies at Fordham University in New York City and the editor of the Journal of Social and Evolutionary Systems.

Of course, as ought to be readily discernible this view(s) explain precisely nothing at all. There is no evidence or proof of this and it is an attempt to explain an admittedly complex and difficult issue by appealing to an unknown time and place wherein those who hold to it can construct that which they will.

Nevertheless, a very, very (very) troubling aspect of this view is the fact that the appearance of these beings, especially to contactees, abductees and experiencers is that in the future humans became time traveling metaphysical, extra-dimensional, super-terrestrial, para-quantum, supra-vibratory torturing rapists who are integrally linked to occult practices.

The How, What and How of Alien Messages

*...there are beings of intelligence and power of a far
higher quality than anything we can conceive of as human;
that they are not necessarily based on the cerebral and
nervous structures that we know, and that the one and
only chance for mankind to advance as a whole is for
individuals to make contact with such Beings*
—Aleister Crowley

The title's reference to extra-terrestrial alien messages
"what" and "how" refers both to *what* their messages are
and the two *hows*: 1) how the messages are received and 2)
how their messages are to be turned into plans that are
subsequently to be carried out, put into place.

This will be a succinct and generally generic review of the
main points so that you may discern them when you
encounter them.

Extra-Terrestrial Aliens

There are very many forms of, supposed alleged, extra-
terrestrial aliens ranging from big headed, big eyed and
small bodied grays/greys (some of which are said to be just
as skinny but quite tall) to Nordics who are human in form,
having blue eyes and blond hair and from short hooded
gorilla-like faced beings to reptilians and many more.

How?, 1

As to *how* the messages are received; it varies quite a bit.
Nordics, for example, simply land their spacecraft, come
across someone and speak to them vocally. Others, such as

grays/greys communicate *telepathically* and this seems to be the preferred method for most extra-terrestrial aliens.

This, of course, is very convenient because it means that they can communicate to, and through, humans even from vast distances (and other points in chronology, see chapter *Time Traveling Aliens?*) and thus, without the necessity of being physically present before us. Also, this does not require them to travel and so we end up with the difference between *contactees, abductees, experiencers,* (also *channelers*) etc. In other words, one need not see or board a spacecraft nor see an extra-terrestrial alien in order to communicate with them.

This leads to the odd correlation between spirit channeling mediums and extra-terrestrial alien channelers; those who claim to channel the spirits of the deceased and those who claim to channel extra-terrestrial aliens do the very same things (and involvement in the occult is step one[15]). They both *open themselves up* to receive whatever happens to be out there and there are certainly beings *floating around* out there looking for those neon signs on people's heads that say "Come in, we're open."

What?

When it comes down to it, regardless of the variation in terminology and details, the message is the same whether it comes from New Agers, magickians, mystery schools, secret societies, extra-terrestrial aliens, etc.

The message is that we humans are destroying the Earth and ourselves. As we are part of some great cosmic community, our actions affect beings who are not earth-dwellers. And often it is said that we negatively affect the Earth itself with the view of the Earth as a living entity (*Gaia*, etc.).

The follow up from the observation that humans are causing such great harm is that we must come together and thus unite so as to achieve global change. We must set aside our outdated and destructive theologies, we must set aside our set aside our outdated and destructive governments, we must set aside our outdated and destructive social mores, etc.

How?, 2

The second *how* is (having set such outdated and destructive beliefs and practices aside) how such entities propose that we accomplish such changes. Again, regardless of terminology or details, it all leads to the same place; a new world order.

This is because the ultimate answer, the *how*, is for us to adopt a one world religion consisting of alien theology—which is always impersonal "pantheism," meaning that there is no personal God but only what is variously known as energy, prana, qi, ki, chi, vril, the force, etc. The how is that we must adopt a new governmental system, a one world government. And we must also adopt a new *morality* as traditional family units (and by extension clans, tribes, nations, etc.) only cause division and hoarding of goods.

Along with this—and again this is the same whether it comes from the happy faced New Age or the frowny faced Nazis—comes the concept that human population size must be drastically reduced and that vast numbers of people will be done away with. The Nazis had a very physical and hands on approach while the New Age conceptualizes it as people being taken off the Earth by some UFO related or metaphysical (or, both) event.

In short, always read between the lines because there is a reason that, on the ground level, New Agers, Nazis, Transhumanist, magickians, mystery religions, secret societies and many, many more agree. They all seek to establish a new world order—by any other name.

Are There UFOs and Extra-Terrestrial Aliens in the Bible?

While much could be and has been written on this subject, that which follows will consider three main topics: 1) Extra-Terrestrial Hybridization, 2) Zechariah's Flying Scroll and 3) Ezekiel's Vision Wheels.

It is always advisable to define terminology before offering an answer to a question. In this case, we are asking, "Are there extra-terrestrial aliens & UFOs in the Bible?"

Extra-terrestrial merely means non, not from or from beyond the Earth (terra).

Aliens can mean strange, unusual (or, illegal migrant human personages) but in this context is indicative of sentient, intelligent, volitional beings from elsewhere in the universe (or other universes as per the multiverse theory).

UFO simply means **U**nidentified **F**lying **O**bject and so could, literally, be anything from an airplane to a bird and from a satellite to swamp-gas reflecting off of Venus—or, something (just a little *Men In Black* movie reference). However, in common pop-occultural parlance, it is used to refer to extra-terrestrial alien spacecraft.

It is important to be aware that one can conclude that there are extra-terrestrial aliens and UFOs in the Bible by making eisegetical arguments. This means that one comes to the text with a preconceived notion that one reads into the text.

In other words, one forces the text to say that which one wants to hear, that which one already presupposes.

One popular tactic or approach is claiming that people of days gone by would have lacked the ability to adequately, at least to our modern sensibilities, describe extra-terrestrial aliens and UFOs. Thus, when they saw a UFO/spaceship they would have described it as a fiery chariot, said that God was causing thunderous sounds and shaking the ground, etc.
Moreover, they would have described actually extra-terrestrial aliens as angles (even though angels do not have wings and just look like humans: see my book *What Does the Bible Say About Angels? A Styled Angelology*), God, other gods, etc.

Perhaps the biggest problem with this, most popular, approach is that it is an argument from silence that merely overlays a preconception upon texts. In other words, it is merely picking and choosing that which one thinks one can apply to one's preferred views. It is to not explain anything but only to impose a *modern* day concept to an ancient text. However, the question is what is wrong with that; perhaps we are able to finally discern that which the text was actually stating.

Well, the problem is that it is merely un-contextual (disregards historical, cultural and grammatical context) speculation; it does not explain but only explains away. It does not consider that which the text is actually stating within the immediate and greater context.

For example, anywhere that something in the Bible is flying, makes loud sounds, or involves fire, a UFO misinterpretation is applied to bits and pieces of texts.

Following, we will get into specific texts and see how bits and pieces are accepted as extra-terrestrial aliens and UFO related while the point of the text, that which actually gives it meaning, is disregarded.

Extra-Terrestrial Hybridization

We must note the fact that, in fact, it is a fact that the Bible does, indeed, refer to extra-terrestrials descending to Earth, mating with humans and producing hybrid (half human, half extra-terrestrial) offspring.

Genesis 6:1-5 states:

> Now it came about, when men began to multiply on the face of the land, and daughters were born to them, that the sons of God saw that the daughters of men were beautiful; and they took wives for themselves, whomever they chose. Then the Lord said, "My Spirit shall not strive with man forever, because he also is flesh; nevertheless his days shall be one hundred and twenty years."
> The Nephilim were on the earth in those days, and also afterward, when the sons of God came in to the daughters of men, and they bore children to them. Those were the mighty men who were of old, men of renown.
> Then the Lord saw that the wickedness of man was great on the earth, and that every intent of the thoughts of his heart was only evil continually.

Keep in mind that as we noted above, "*Extra-terrestrial* merely means non, not from or from beyond the Earth (terra)." It does not necessarily refer to beings that travel to Earth in spaceships from other planets.

The term "sons of God" derives from the Hebrew *benei 'elohim* or *bene 'elim*. Within the (Hebrew) context of the Old Testament this term is sometimes applied to beings that come before God, sometimes along with whom comes Satan: "Now there was a day when the sons of God came to present themselves before the LORD, and Satan came also among them" (Job 1:6).

The sons of God are generally defined as being angels. Keep in mind that angels do not have wings and look just like human males. On the other hand, Satan is not an angel (is not a fallen angel) but is a cherub (Ezekiel 28:14). The cherubim are not a kind of angel but are another category of being (as are the seraphim, who have six wings). Cherubim, as per a text from Ezekiel that we will review below, have four faces and four wings, "Their legs were straight and their feet were like a calf's hoof, and they gleamed like burnished bronze. Under their wings on their four sides were human hands (Ezekiel 1:7-8).

The faces are described as one of *'adam* which means man or human, *'ariy* which is a lion, *nesher* which is an eagle, vulture (or, more specifically, a griffon-vulture) and *showr* which is a bull or ox. That is as per Ezekiel 1:10 while Ezekiel 10:14 lists the faces as being of an *'adam*, *'ariy*, *nesher* and not a *showr* but a *keruwb* which is cherub in Hebrew. Well, what does it mean that one of the cherub's face is the face of a cherub?

This may very well simply be a case of copying error. The scribe/copyist may have committed what is known in the business as a "parablepsis owing to homoioteleuton or homoiarkton." These technical terms refer to a copying error that occurs when one is reading a word in the original text, looks away to write it down and then looks back but accidentally ends up in a slightly different place in the manuscript. In Ezekiel chapter 10 the word cherub appears 21 times and so a scribe/copyist could have simply written down the word cherub twice whilst missing the word *showr*.

This is all just for the sake of descriptive details. In any regard, are the sons of God angels or are they angels, cherubim, seraphim, et al (these are all different *categories* of beings)? Well, Satan (the cherub) is not necessarily identified as being a son of God but as tagging along, as it were, with them yet, perhaps some will argue that all who came to God were sons of God and Satan just happens to be mentioned by name.

Considering that angles look like human males it is most likely that it is they who are described as sons of God as it is they who came to Earth, married and copulated with human women (in other words, they have the necessary, shall we say, *equipment*—capiche?).

So, indeed, within the Bible extra-terrestrials did descend to Earth, interacted with humans, taught humans occult (literally, at least as per apocryphal claims, *secret* or *hidden*) concepts and created a hybrid form of being. These beings are referred to in the Genesis text as "mighty men" which is translated as such from the actual repetition of a Hebrew word so that the Hebrew text reads, "gibbowr gibbowr" and thus, they are known as the *Gibbowrim* or simply *Giborim* (*im* is simply the Hebrew manner whereby to denote masculine plural—*ot* is feminine plural).

The name/title of these hybrids is Nephilim and they were giborim. Tracking down what they were and what they did would take us well beyond the context of this section as it would take us into further linguistics pertaining to the term Nephilim and just what made them mighty.

The take away lesson is that it was due to this hybridization event that, apparently, Nephilim DNA kept being spread by their, in turn, copulating with humans to the point that, "Then the Lord saw that the wickedness of man was great on the earth and that every intent of the thoughts of his heart was only evil continually." Thus, the great deluge, the worldwide flood, came about due to having to do away with the massive genetic corruption that had occurred (for more on this, see chapter *Was Noah Genetically "perfect in his generation"?* of my book *What Does the Bible Say About Giants and Nephilim? A Styled Giantology and Nephilology*).

Zechariah's Flying Scroll

The issue with the Zechariah text, chapter 5, is that it is claimed that he witnessed what has come to be termed *cigar* shape, thus cylindrical, UFOs or even what are known as *rods* (although, rods are thought to be circa 4-5 feet long or smaller).

Here is the relevant text, "I lifted up my eyes again and looked, and behold, there was a flying scroll." So, there you have it a scroll is a rolled up manuscript which looks cylindrical when it is thus rolled and it was flying. But, actually, a scroll is a long flat series of papyrus (or other materials) sheets that are interconnected (think of a long rectangle). It is rolled up to be stored and when it is read, the relevant portion is unfurled whilst the two ends remain rolled.

Note how the text continues, "And he said to me, 'What do you see?' And I answered, 'I see a flying scroll; its length is twenty cubits and its width ten cubits'" (circa 30x15 feet). The fact that he could discern its size means that it was not rolled up or, it unfurled as it approached him (although, the text does not envisage this) so either way, there is no reason to misidentify it as a cylindrical cigar shaped UFO.

Note how the text follows, "Then he said to me, 'This is the curse that is going forth over the face of the whole land; surely everyone who steals will be purged away according to the writing on one side, and everyone who swears will be purged away according to the writing on the other side.'" Thus, this scrolls was, as it were, an indictment and Zechariah could read the front and back of it.

Ah, but that is not the end of it as the text continues:
> "I will make it go forth," declares the LORD of hosts, "and it will enter the house of the thief and the house of the one who swears falsely by My name; and it will spend the night within that house and consume it with its timber and stones."
> Then the angel who was speaking with me went out and said to me, "Lift up now your eyes and see what this is going forth." I said, "What is it?" And he said, "This is the ephah going forth." Again he said, "This is their appearance in all the land (and behold, a lead cover was lifted up); and this is a woman sitting inside the ephah."

So forget the scroll as now you really have something with which to work: a "woman" is flying around a spaceship called an "ephah" which even had a metallic cockpit lid.

However, the text continues, "Then he said, 'This is

Wickedness!' And he threw her down into the middle of the ephah and cast the lead weight on its opening." So, it is not a spaceship but a symbolic representation of wickedness (the woman) that has been weighed (as in "weighed and found wanting") via the ephah and lead weight (a standard of measure). FYI: an ephah is "a dry measure of quantity...the receptacle for measuring or holding that amount."

But wait, there's more:

> Then I lifted up my eyes and looked, and there two women were coming out with the wind in their wings; and they had wings like the wings of a stork, and they lifted up the ephah between the earth and the heavens.
> I said to the angel who was speaking with me, "Where are they taking the ephah?"
> Then he said to me, "To build a temple for her in the land of Shinar; and when it is prepared, she will be set there on her own pedestal."

In short, this entire episode appears to be some form of vision wherein an actual situation is represented symbolically with a flying indictment representing swift judgment, a woman representing wickedness, an ephah and lead representing being weighed, women being those who carry out the judgment, stock wings representing the swift execution of judgment, that they are taking the ephah and woman to build a temple in Shinar for some future event as it will be her own pedestal.

But why would wickedness be given a temple wherein she sits on a pedestal? It appears to be in preparation for the future ultimate rebellion; Armageddon.

Women have long been connected to the occult and this is likely because when the sons of God married the daughters of men (angels and humans who produced hybrids, see my book *On the Genesis 6 Affair's Sons of God: Angels or Not?*) they did not have TV so they actually talked— shocking! Well, angels revealed heavenly occult teachings to them (with *occult* literally meaning secret, hidden, etc.— again, at least as per apocrypha, for what it is worth).

Yet, this is one woman in particular and while she may be symbolic the symbol may be more real than we imagine. Note that Revelation 17:3-5 notes of John that he:

> ...saw a woman sitting on a scarlet beast, full of blasphemous names, having seven heads and ten horns. And the woman was clothed in purple and scarlet, and adorned with gold and precious stones and pearls, having in her hand a gold cup full of abominations and of the unclean things of her immorality, and upon her forehead a name was written, a mystery, "Babylon the Great, the Mother of Harlots and of the Abominations of the Earth."

Noah had a wicked son named Ham who had a wicked son named Cush who had a son named Nimrod. Nimrod is said to have been a *gibbowr gibbowr* which is variously translated as that he "became a mighty one" (*chalal hayah gibbowr gibbowr*).
Succinctly stated, Nimrod became the head of the first attempt at a one world order (which the New World Order seeks to emulate); one language, one civilization, one religion and one monument-tower to bind them all as they sought to reach the heavens.

Genesis 10:10 notes, "The beginning of his kingdom was

Babel and Erech and Accad and Calneh, in the land of Shinar." So, we have his kingdom beginning at Babel after which the Tower of Babel was named and after which Babylon came to be named. His one world order kingdom began in the land of (geographical location) Shinar.

As for the tower, Genesis 11:4 notes that the people said:
> Come, let us build for ourselves a city, and a
> tower whose top will reach into heaven, and
> let us make for ourselves a name, otherwise
> we will be scattered abroad over the face of
> the whole earth.

They sought to build a centralized world headquarters, a city, and a tower. Some have noted that since they built this tower in a plain or level valley (*biq'ah*) they did not think to literally construct a tower tall enough to reach heaven (whoever tall that would have had to have been) but that via the tower they sought to make a name for themselves (some sort of commemorative monument relating information), they sought such unity so that they would not be "scattered abroad over the face of the whole earth," however, they were and yet, their monument remained—at least for some time.

Moreover, or however, note that the term "will reach" as in the tower into heaven is not in the Hebrew and so the text actually states that they built it so that its top/head heavens (*ro'sh shamayim*). They may mean that it was built to the heavens as in a styled temple/structure/monument in reverence, in the worship of, the heavens (planets, Zodiac, etc.).

All this to detail that the woman seems to be being set upon the stage of the final events, the last days, the end times.

Ezekiel's Vision Wheels

We now turn to the claim that the vision pertaining to wheels within wheels, etc. was a primitive depiction of an ancient alien/ancient astronaut UFO.

There is much to consider so let us review the bulk of the relevant text of Ezekiel chapter 1, to begin with. Note that Ezekiel saw vision(s) (*mar'ah*) whilst "among the exiles" in Babylon, "the land of the Chaldeans," which will become a very important detail:

> ...As I looked, behold, a storm wind was coming from the north, a great cloud with fire flashing forth continually and a bright light around it, and in its midst something like glowing metal in the midst of the fire. Within it there were figures resembling four living beings.
>
> And this was their appearance: they had human form. Each of them had four faces and four wings. Their legs were straight and their feet were like a calf's hoof, and they gleamed like burnished bronze. Under their wings on their four sides were human hands. As for the faces and wings of the four of them, their wings touched one another; their faces did not turn when they moved, each went straight forward. As for the form of their faces, each had the face of a man; all four had the face of a lion on the right and the face of a bull on the left, and all four had the face of an eagle. Such were their faces.
>
> Their wings were spread out above; each had two touching another being, and two covering their bodies. And each went

straight forward; wherever the spirit was about to go, they would go, without turning as they went. In the midst of the living beings there was something that looked like burning coals of fire, like torches darting back and forth among the living beings. The fire was bright, and lightning was flashing from the fire. And the living beings ran to and fro like bolts of lightning.

Now as I looked at the living beings, behold, there was one wheel on the earth beside the living beings, for each of the four of them. The appearance of the wheels and their workmanship was like sparkling beryl, and all four of them had the same form, their appearance and workmanship being as if one wheel were within another. Whenever they moved, they moved in any of their four directions without turning as they moved.

As for their rims they were lofty and awesome, and the rims of all four of them were full of eyes round about. Whenever the living beings moved, the wheels moved with them. And whenever the living beings rose from the earth, the wheels rose also. Wherever the spirit was about to go, they would go in that direction. And the wheels rose close beside them; for the spirit of the living beings was in the wheels. Whenever those went, these went; and whenever those stood still, these stood still. And whenever those rose from the earth, the wheels rose close beside them; for the spirit of the living beings was in the wheels.

Now over the heads of the living beings there was something like an expanse, like the awesome gleam of crystal, spread out over their heads. Under the expanse their wings were stretched out straight, one toward the other; each one also had two wings covering its body on the one side and on the other. I also heard the sound of their wings like the sound of abundant waters as they went, like the voice of the Almighty, a sound of tumult like the sound of an army camp; whenever they stood still, they dropped their wings. And there came a voice from above the expanse that was over their heads; whenever they stood still, they dropped their wings.

Now above the expanse that was over their heads there was something resembling a throne, like lapis lazuli in appearance; and on that which resembled a throne, high up, was a figure with the appearance of a man. Then I noticed from the appearance of His loins and upward something like glowing metal that looked like fire all around within it, and from the appearance of His loins and downward I saw something like fire; and there was a radiance around Him. As the appearance of the rainbow in the clouds on a rainy day, so was the appearance of the surrounding radiance. Such was the appearance of the likeness of the glory of the Lord. And when I saw it, I fell on my face and heard a voice speaking.

If that was not enough, consider Ezekiel 10:8-22 this time:

>…The cherubim appeared to have the form
>of a man's hand under their wings. Then I
>looked, and behold, four wheels beside the
>cherubim, one wheel beside each cherub;
>and the appearance of the wheels was like
>the gleam of a Tarshish stone. As for their
>appearance, all four of them had the same
>likeness, as if one wheel were within another
>wheel. When they moved, they went in any
>of their four directions without turning as
>they went; but they followed in the direction
>which they faced, without turning as they
>went.
>
>Their whole body, their backs, their hands,
>their wings and the wheels were full of eyes
>all around, the wheels belonging to all four
>of them. The wheels were called in my
>hearing, the whirling wheels. And each one
>had four faces. The first face was the face of
>a cherub, the second face was the face of a
>man, the third the face of a lion, and the
>fourth the face of an eagle.
>
>Then the cherubim rose up. They are the
>living beings that I saw by the river Chebar.
>Now when the cherubim moved, the wheels
>would go beside them; also when the
>cherubim lifted up their wings to rise from
>the ground, the wheels would not turn from
>beside them. When the cherubim stood still,
>the wheels would stand still; and when they
>rose up, the wheels would rise with them,
>for the spirit of the living beings was in
>them.

Then the glory of the Lord departed from the
threshold of the temple and stood over the
cherubim. When the cherubim departed,
they lifted their wings and rose up from the
earth in my sight with the wheels beside
them; and they stood still at the entrance of
the east gate of the Lord's house, and the
glory of the God of Israel hovered over
them. These are the living beings that I saw
beneath the God of Israel by the river
Chebar; so I knew that they were cherubim.
Each one had four faces and each one four
wings, and beneath their wings was the form
of human hands. As for the likeness of their
faces, they were the same faces whose
appearance I had seen by the river Chebar.
Each one went straight ahead.

Firstly, note something very telling: the cherubim are very
stiff and it is very interesting that he saw "figures
resembling four **living** beings." It may be nothing but
perhaps this is tantamount of that which we also know of as
figures that resemble living beings: statues, mannequins,
etc. (and now even computer animation—recall that this
was a vision). So perhaps they were not actually living
things but looked like living things; although later, in this
vision, they become animated and perform various tasks.

As an example of the stiffness, here are some relevant
portions of the texts above:

Their legs were straight…their wings
touched one another; their faces did not turn
when they moved, each went straight
forward…Their wings…touching another
being…each went straight forward…without

turning as they went…Whenever they moved, they moved in any of their four directions without turning as they moved [the cherubim and the wheels]…Whenever the living beings moved, the wheels moved with them…Wherever the spirit was about to go, they would go in that direction…When they moved, they went in any of their four directions without turning as they went; but they followed in the direction which they faced, without turning as they went…Each one went straight ahead.

By definition, by its very nature and character, the *vision* is *animated*. Thus, we see that whatever these various things are—the beings, the wheels, the seat, the structure itself, etc.—they are being animated (made to perform tasks, move about, burn, shine, etc.).

The bottom line is that beyond all of the details upon which one can focus: in exile in Babylon, is being shown, in an animated vision, a Babylonian throne upon which is not Marduk but the one true God, YHVH. YHVH is expressing to His people, via His prophet Ezekiel, that even then, even in Babylon, He is ultimately in charge, He is enthroned, He is upon the throne; He is the King of kings and Lord of lords.

This is evident from what is known as *Ancient Near East* (ANE) *throne iconography*. Via the various illustrations of ancient, historically contextual, thrones; you can see how the stiffness of the cherubim denoted the nature of a throne as it is made of wood, stone, metal, etc.

On the *Fifty Shade of Gray Aliens* Template and Images

Recall that within chapter *Time Traveling Aliens?*, various people of various fields were quoted and cited who conclude that *aliens* (by any other name) are highly evolved human beings visiting us from the future. This is not a recent conclusion but appears to be the original concept, the original identification of what the aliens are. Of the various forms of reported alien species, we are interested, specifically, on *Fifty Shades of Gray Aliens*; that is to say, the gray aliens.

One view could be that it is an original conclusion and another is that it was an original premise. That is to say that when you consider various images of grey aliens; it all began with thinkers and authors pondering what future humans may look like.

The concept was that greater intelligence was correlated with larger brains and thus, larger heads. Such as in the case of H.G. Wells concept of the "Man of the year million" which gains sustenance from dipping in fluids which would cause smaller jaws, mouth, lips, etc.
Eyes might grow along with the upper portion of the head whilst the nose is reduced along with lower portion.
Bodies would diminish in size along with their utility as various high tech machines would take over physical labor.

The step from future humans to future, or current, aliens was, thus, a small one; aliens being viewed as being far advanced; they would have already gone through such changes.

There are many today who see aliens as future humans time traveling from the future to visit the humans of the past; we current humans.

Yet, perhaps the earliest specific reference to and/or speculation regarding the diminutive bodies of aliens comes from Greek biographer Plutarch (46-120 AD) who in *De Facie Quae In Orbe Lunae Apparet* noted:

> When Theon had so spoken, I said...if the moon is not inhabited by men, it is not necessary that she have come to be in vain and to no purpose, for we see that this earth of ours is not productive and inhabited throughout its whole extent either but only a small part of it is fruitful of animals and plants on the peaks, as it were, and peninsulas rising out of the deep, while of the rest some parts are desert and fruitless with winter-storms and summer-droughts and the most are sunk in the great sea...[16]

He then states that the moon is "destitute of living beings" and yet that "nothing that has been said proves impossible the alleged inhabitation of the moon."

The discussion then gets pretty esoteric as Plutarch states that when Theon appeals to the "words of Alcman's, <Such as> are nourished by Dew, daughter <of Zeus> and of <divine> Selene."[17]

Plutarch continues:

> They err then who believe the moon to be a fiery and glowing body; and those who demand that living beings there be equipped

just as those here are for generation,
nourishment, and livelihood seem blind to
the diversities of nature, among which one
can discover more and greater differences
and dissimilarities between living beings
than between them and inanimate objects.[18]

Let there not be mouthless men nourished
by odours who <Megasthenes> thinks <do
exist>[19]; yet the Hungerbane,[20] the virtue of
which he was himself trying to explain to us,
Hesiod hinted at when he said
> Nor what great profit mallow has and
> squill[21]

and Epimenides made manifest in fact when
he showed that with a very little fuel nature
kindles and sustains the living creature,
which needs no further nourishment if it gets
as much as the size of an olive.[22]
It is plausible that the men on the moon, if
they do exist, are slight of body and capable
of being nourished by whatever comes their
way[23]…We have no comprehension of these
beings, however…

As noted, these may very well be the original views come
full circle.
Now, this does not mean that aliens are, actually, time
traveling humans. It may very well mean that, at one level,
aliens are a well formulated thought experiment gone bad.
That is to say that once fiction, fantasy, and philosophic
thinkers hit upon the archetypical grey aliens; the image
was used to fuel pop-occulture and, some may say, black
government ops and projects of all sorts.

Now, with regards to Plutarch I referenced *specific reference to and/or speculation* because some claim that ancient cave paintings and sculptures depict aliens. However, such claims are highly speculative on our part as it requires much specified anthropology to ensure that such is what those ancient cultures were depicting.

And this assumes that those artifacts, which are generally quite out of reach or direct observation of the average internet *researcher*, are actually authentic, have not been tampered with in modern times, are not photo-shopped, etc.

Here is one such example from Puma Punku in Bolivia.

Firstly, we are to think that at least one of these depicts an alien because someone asserted that at least one of these depicts an alien and it went viral.

Secondly, it is pretty clear that at least one of these is a later addition: the fact that it does not even fit the wall is a huge red flag—does not fit it stylistically nor structurally.

I would hate to think that we believe aliens were in Bolivia just because some ancient sculptures were just not very talented and/or some modern ones are likewise deficient in artistic abilities.

The Sixth Finger

Herein, is an elucidating example of the *template* via the *Outer Limits* episode "The Sixth Finger" (Season 1, Episode 5, originally aired October 14, 1963 AD).

The show's premise is augmented evolution or, conscious, intelligent manipulation of already existing bio-organisms. We find that a scientist is experimenting on how to make an ape more intelligent by speeding up evolution.

An unlearned young man, frustrated with the drudgery of his coal mining job, volunteers to be a human test subject. He is placed into a device and the first, physical, change that he experiences is that his forehead enlarges (causing a receding hairline).

We next see him with a much larger head, pointy ears (and a dying mullet as he is completely bald except for hair that is a few inches long towards the back and bottom of his head).

Finally, he appears with a very large head and while his eyes are not bigger, the sockets are. Oh, and grows a sixth finger on each hand.
In the meantime, he develops mind reading and telekinesis, etc.

Thus, with no alien/extra-terrestrial context, whatsoever, we end up with a future human looking much like a typical grey alien.

Here is a more detailed description:
> A scientist develops the means to advance the evolution of man by 20,000 years, and then continues beyond his control. The man who is evolving encounters police officers

and says to them: "Your ignorance makes me ill and angry"…

Set in a remote Welsh mining town, the story is about a rogue London scientist, Professor Mathers, who - feeling guilty about helping to develop a super-destructive atomic bomb - discovers a process that affects the speed of evolutionary mutation, for the purpose of bettering the human race.

A disgruntled miner, Gwyllm Griffiths, volunteers for the experiment, enabling the professor to create a being with enhanced mental capabilities.

As a man sent forward equal to 20,000 years of evolution, Gwyllm soon begins growing an overdeveloped cortex and a sixth finger on each hand. When the mutation process begins to operate independently of the professor's influence, Gwyllm takes control of the experiment.

Now equal to 1 million years of evolution, and equipped with superior intelligence and powers of thought that are capable of great destruction such as telekinesis, Gwyllm seeks vengeance on the mining town he loathes.

Later, however, he ends up evolving beyond concepts such as love, hate, and the desire for power, and instead intends to turn himself into a vortex of pure intellect with the help of his girlfriend, Cathy Evans.

Out of love for him, however, Cathy
reverses the process at the last second,
bringing Gwyllm back to his former self.

But, the out-of-control reversal is too much
for Gwyllm, and he slowly succumbs to the
adverse effects while Cathy comforts him.[24]

The opening and closing narration goes thusly:
Where are we going? Life, the timeless,
mysterious gift, is still evolving. What
wonders, or terrors, does evolution hold in
store for us in the next ten thousand years?

In a million? In six million? Perhaps the
answer lies in this old house in this old and
misty valley....

An experiment too soon, too swift. And yet
may we not still hope to discover a method
by which within one generation, the whole
human race could be rendered intelligent,
beyond hatred, or revenge, or the desire for
power?

Is that not, after all, the ultimate goal of
evolution?

The Images

The following images seek to illustrate the above-
referenced *template* and the concept behind it. Some of the
images portray future humans, some aliens and some
humans transforming into aliens.

The images are these are taken, mostly, from sci fi/fantasy

books, comics, and movies which subsequently inform pop-occulture which is why I also included some drawing of actual beings claimed to have been encountered.

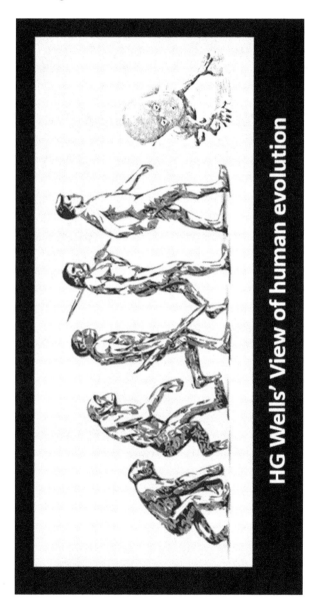

HG Wells' View of human evolution

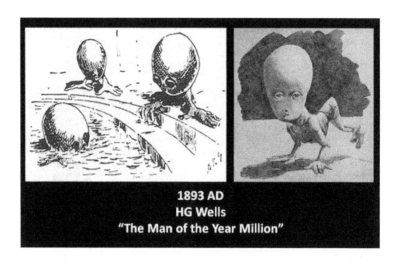

1893 AD
HG Wells
"The Man of the Year Million"

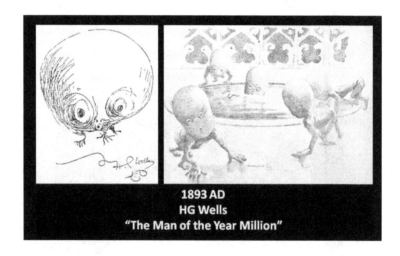

1893 AD
HG Wells
"The Man of the Year Million"

Description of an inner Earth dweller from *Etidorhpa*:
...less than five feet in height...skin, the
color of light blue putty...His forehead
extended in an unbroken plane from crown
to check bone, and the chubby tip of an
abortive nose without nostrils formed a short
projection...There was no semblance of an
eye, for there were no sockets.

1895 AD
John Uri Lloyd book "Etidorhpa"
(*Aphrodite* backwards)

1901 AD
HG Wells
"The First Men on the Moon"

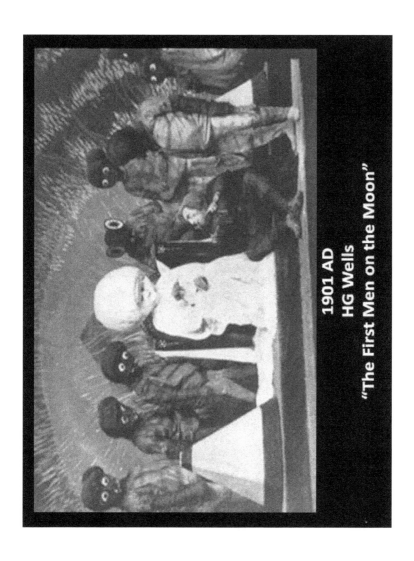

1901 AD
HG Wells
"The First Men on the Moon"

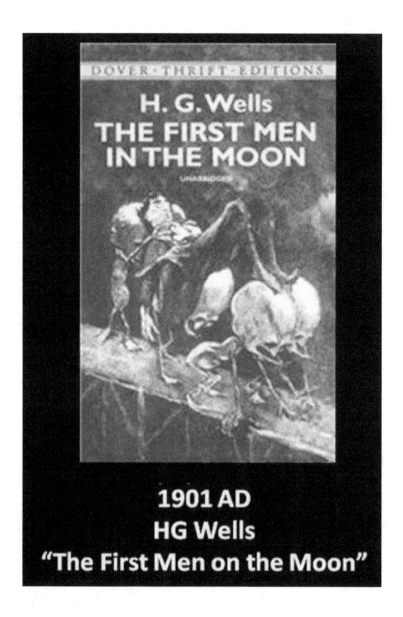

**1901 AD
HG Wells
"The First Men on the Moon"**

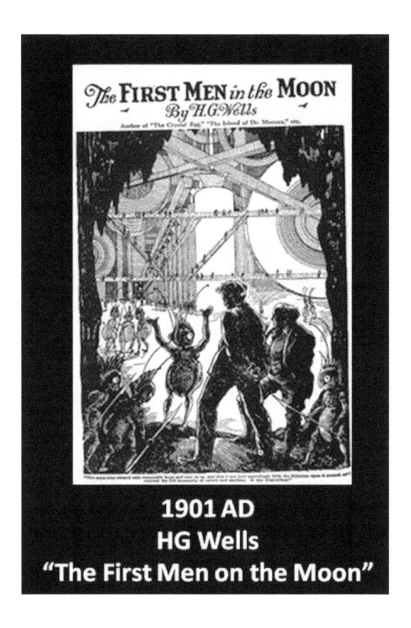

1901 AD
HG Wells
"The First Men on the Moon"

**1915 AD
"the dread spirit Astaroth"
Der Golem movie**

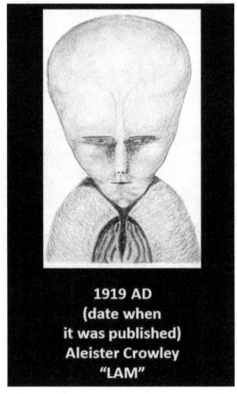

**1919 AD
(date when
it was published)
Aleister Crowley
"LAM"**

1926 AD
G. Peyton Wertenbaker
"The Coming of the Ice"

1926 AD
The Gernsback Awards, Vol 1

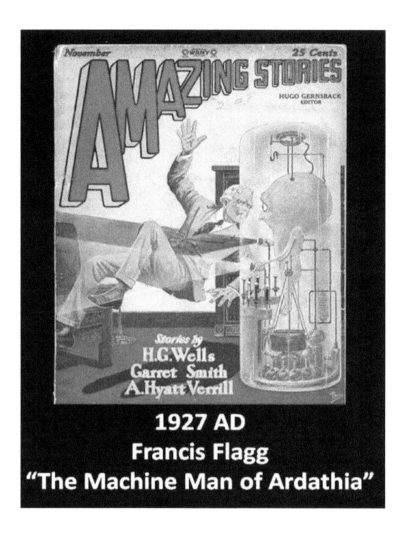

1927 AD
Francis Flagg
"The Machine Man of Ardathia"

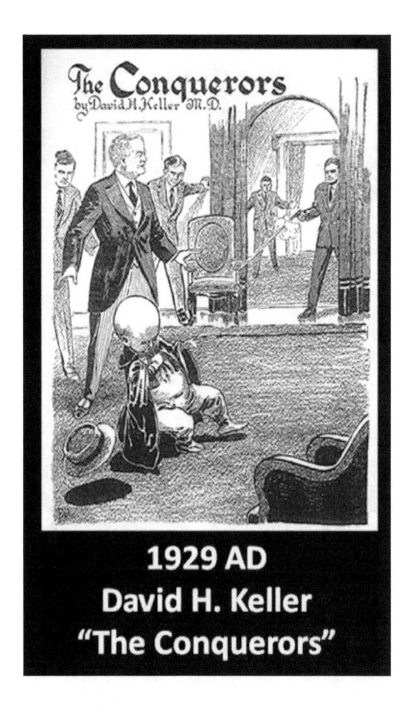

1929 AD
David H. Keller
"The Conquerors"

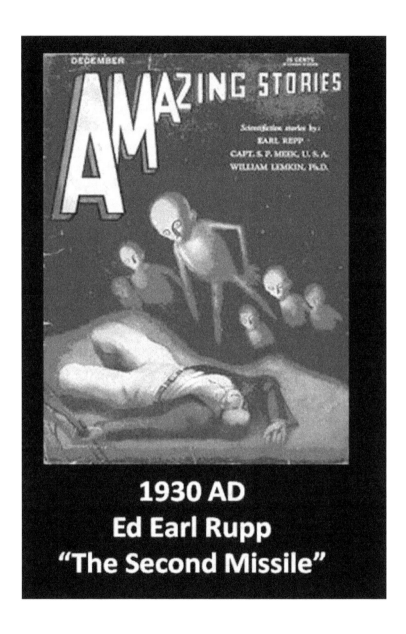

**1930 AD
Ed Earl Rupp
"The Second Missile"**

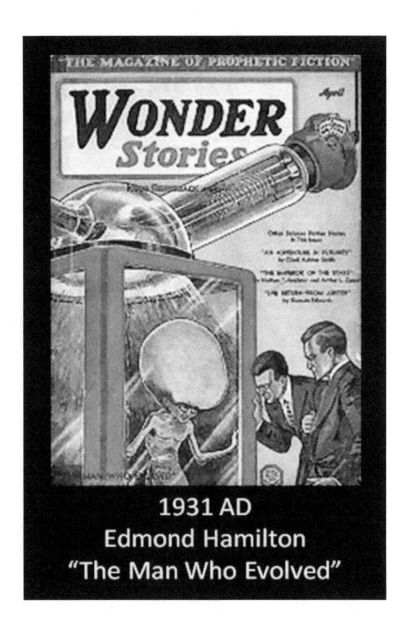

1931 AD
Edmond Hamilton
"The Man Who Evolved"

1933 AD
Gustav Sandgren aka Gabriel Linde
"Den okända faran: en framtidssyn"

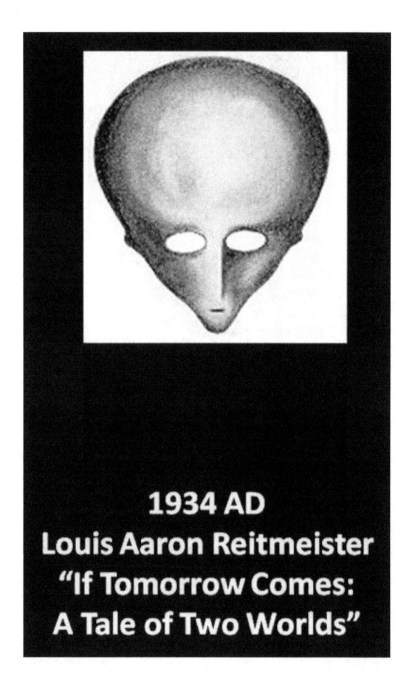

**1934 AD
Louis Aaron Reitmeister
"If Tomorrow Comes:
A Tale of Two Worlds"**

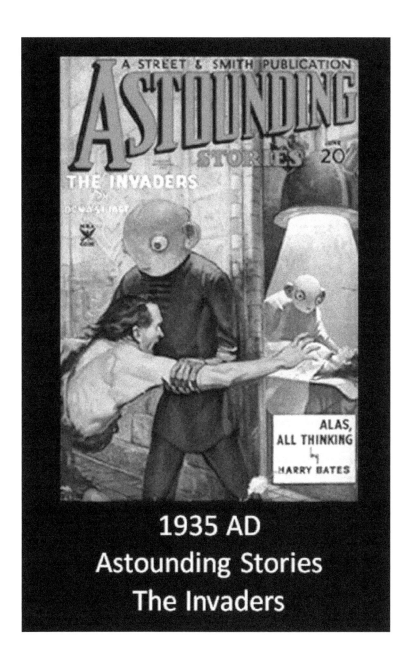

1935 AD
Astounding Stories
The Invaders

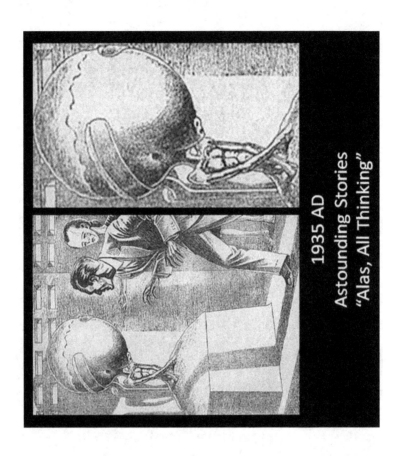

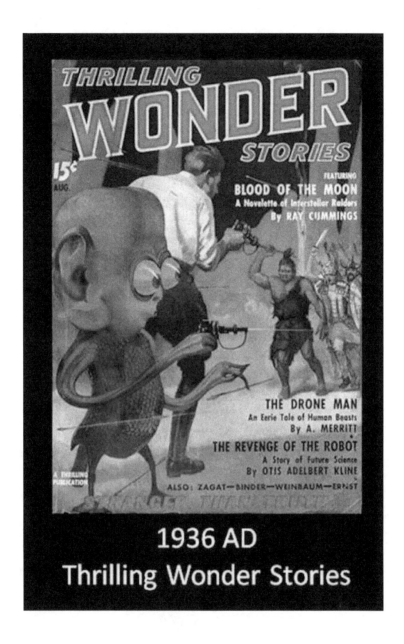

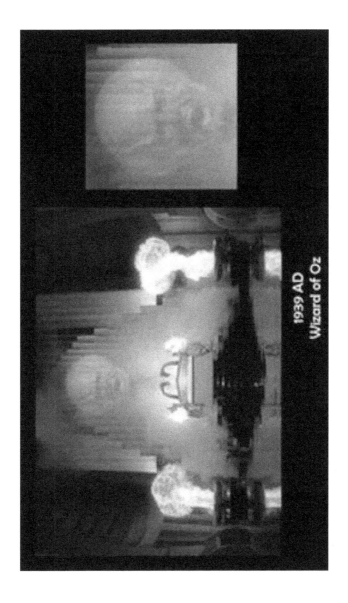

1940 AD
Starling Stories

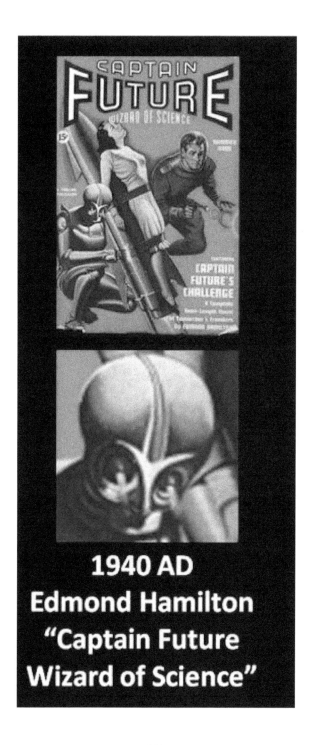

1940 AD
Edmond Hamilton
"Captain Future
Wizard of Science"

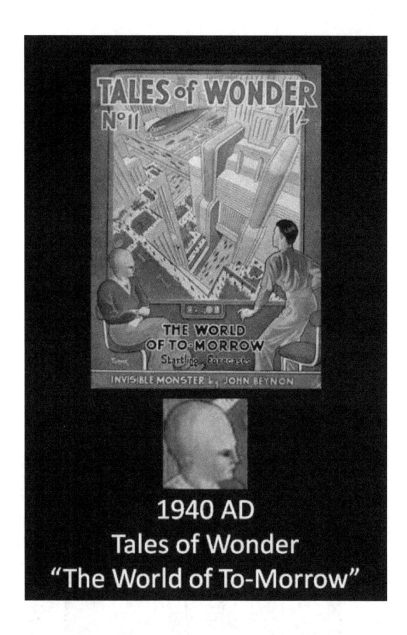

1940 AD
Tales of Wonder
"The World of To-Morrow"

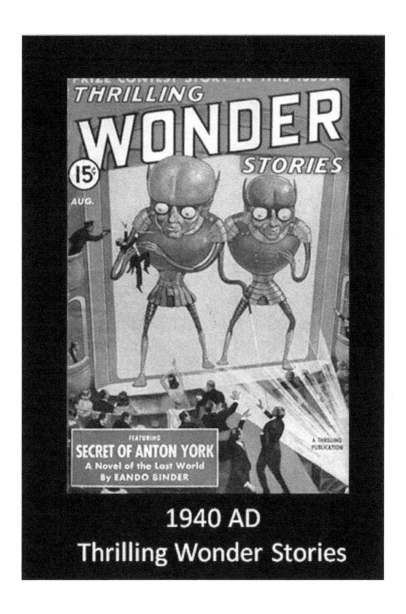

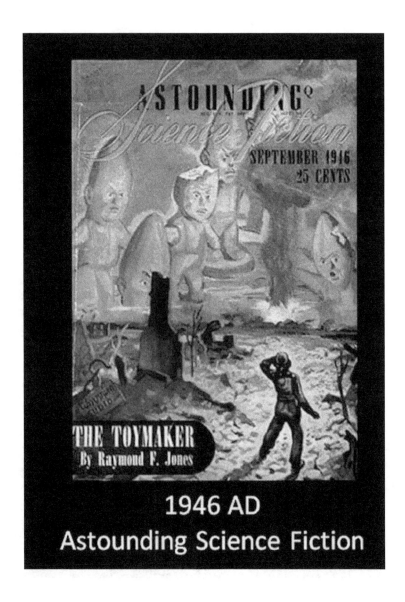

1946 AD
Astounding Science Fiction

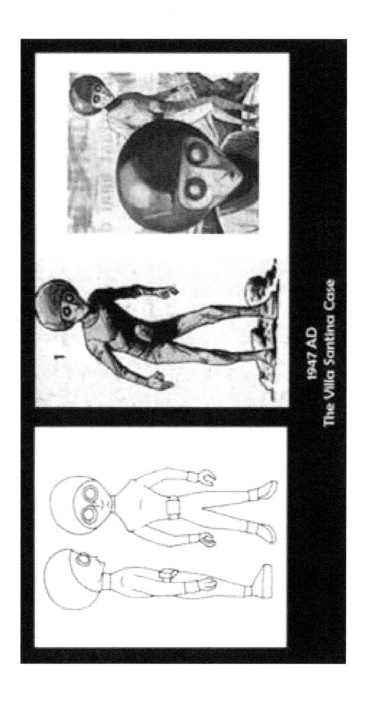

1950 AD
Weird Science
No. 15

1950 AD
Photo from the German newspaper Wiesbadener Tageblatt.
Editor Wilhelm Sprunkle and photographer Hans Scheffler
took a photograph of a 5 year old boy and painted over him.

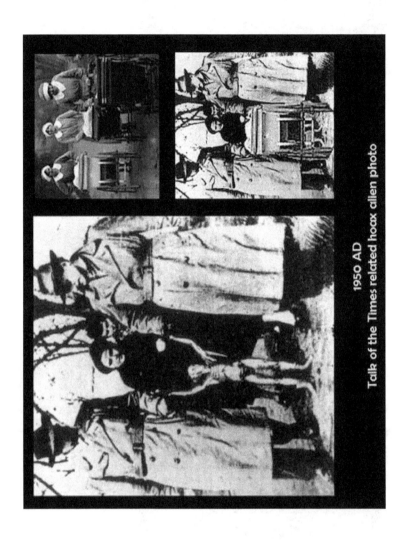

1950 AD
Talk of the Times related hoax alien photo

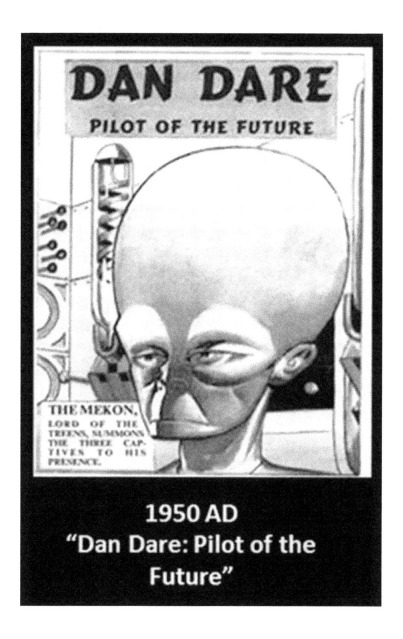

1950 AD
"Dan Dare: Pilot of the
Future"

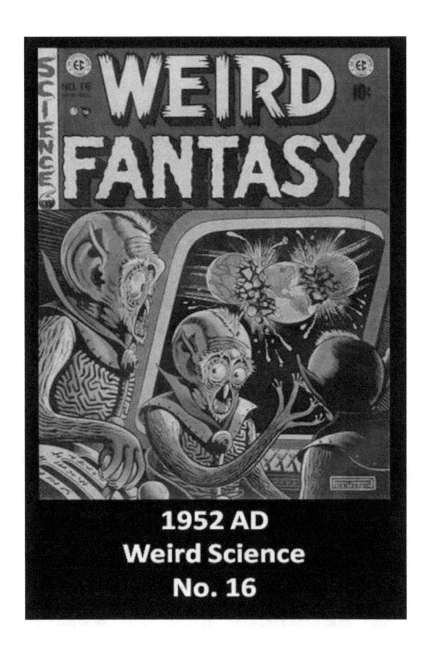

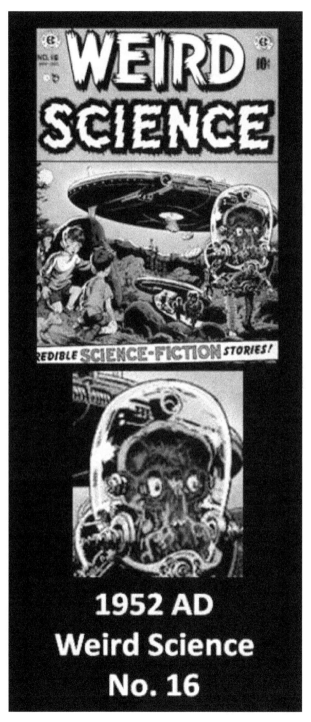

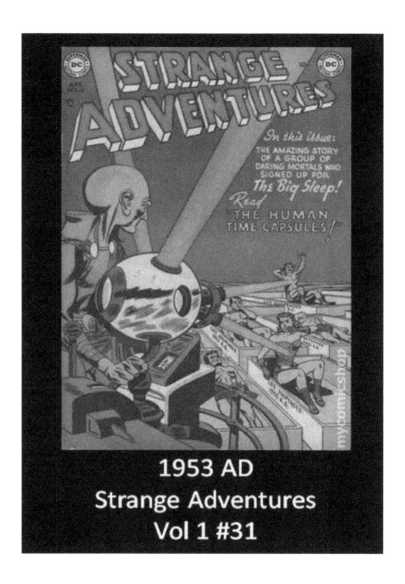

1953 AD
Strange Adventures
Vol 1 #31

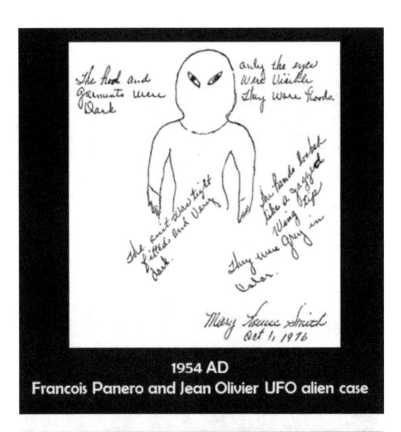

The hood and garments were Dark

only the eyes were visible they were Hoods.

the suit was tight fitted and very dark.

the hands looked like a jagged wing tip

They were grey in color.

Mary Louise Smith
Oct 1, 1976

1954 AD
Francois Panero and Jean Olivier UFO alien case

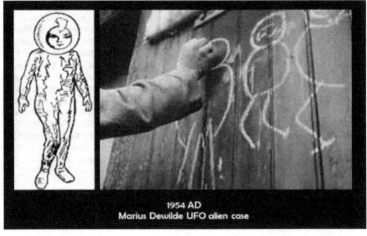

1954 AD
Marius Dewilde UFO alien case

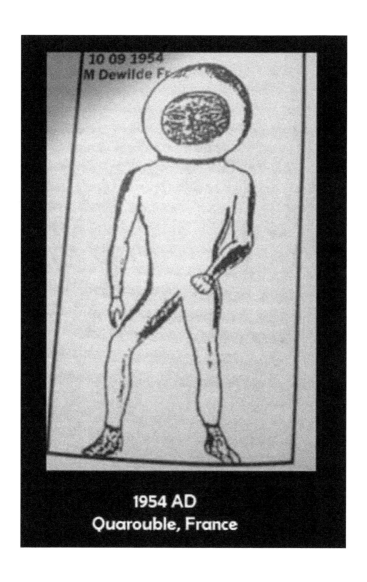

1954 AD
Quarouble, France

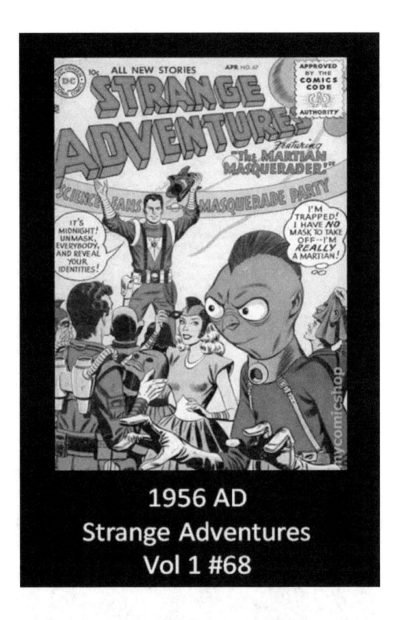

1956 AD
Strange Adventures
Vol 1 #68

1957 AD
"Invasion of the
Saucer-Men"

1957 AD
"The Brain From
The Planet Arous"

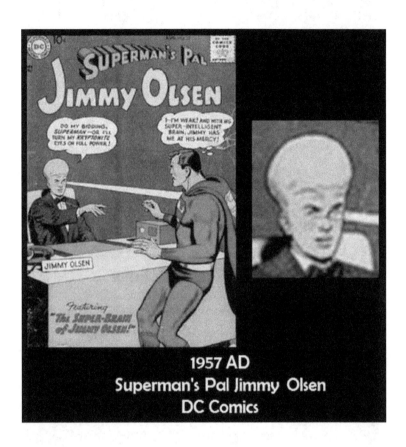

1957 AD
Superman's Pal Jimmy Olsen
DC Comics

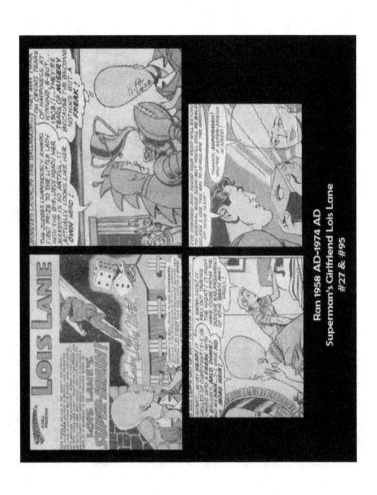

1958 AD
Strange Adventures
Vol 1 #90

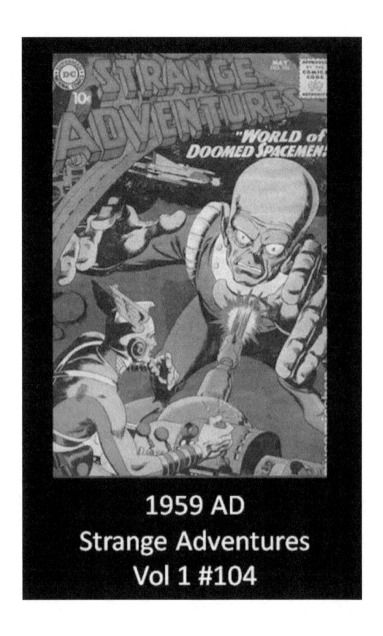

1959 AD
Strange Adventures
Vol 1 #104

1959 AD
Strange Adventures
Vol 1 #106

1959 AD
"Superman of the Future"
Action Comics #256

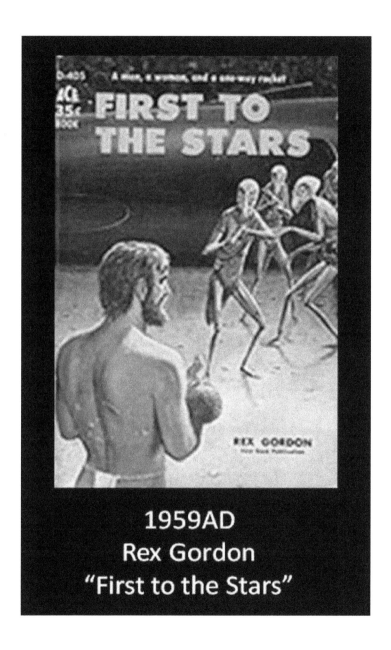

1959AD
Rex Gordon
"First to the Stars"

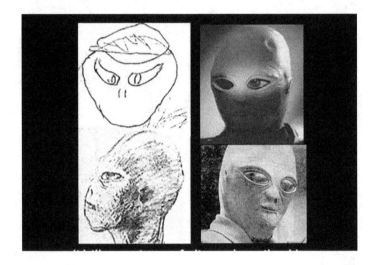

1961 AD
(L) Illustration of aliens described by
Barney and Betty Hill
1975 AD
(R) How the aliens were depicted in a movie about
the Hill case, "The UFO Incident"

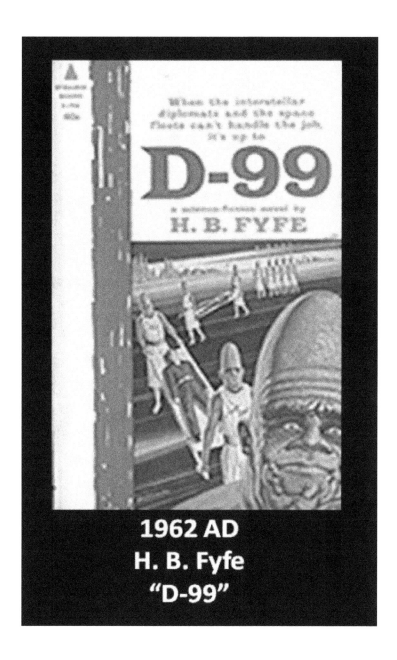

**1962 AD
H. B. Fyfe
"D-99"**

1962 AD
The Twilight Zone
Hocus-Pocus and Frisby

1963 AD
Strange Adventures
Vol 1 #154

1963 AD
David Grinell
"Messaggio per Plutone"
("Message for Pluto")

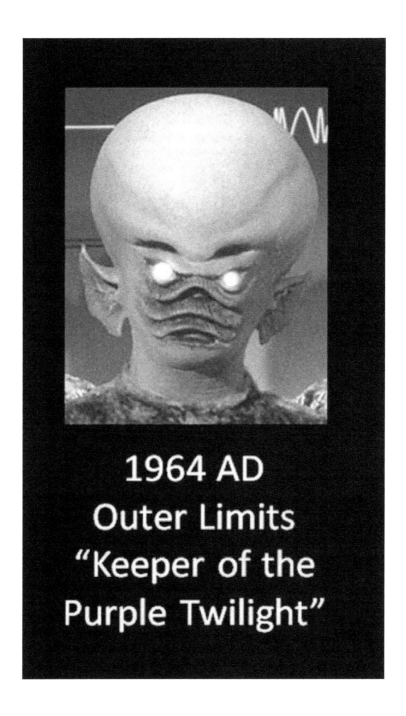

1964 AD
Outer Limits
"Keeper of the
Purple Twilight"

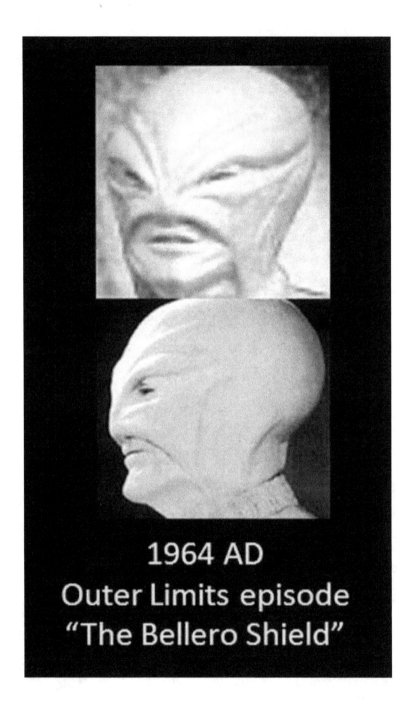

1964 AD
Outer Limits episode
"The Bellero Shield"

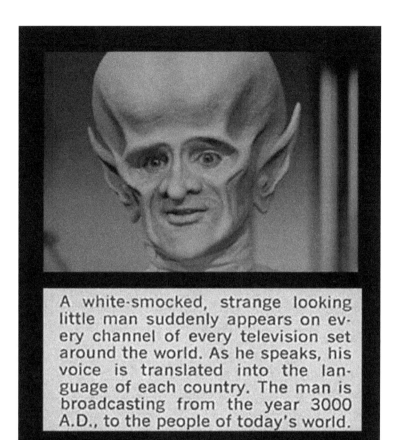

A white-smocked, strange looking little man suddenly appears on every channel of every television set around the world. As he speaks, his voice is translated into the language of each country. The man is broadcasting from the year 3000 A.D., to the people of today's world.

**1964 AD
The Outer Limits
"Visit from the Future"**

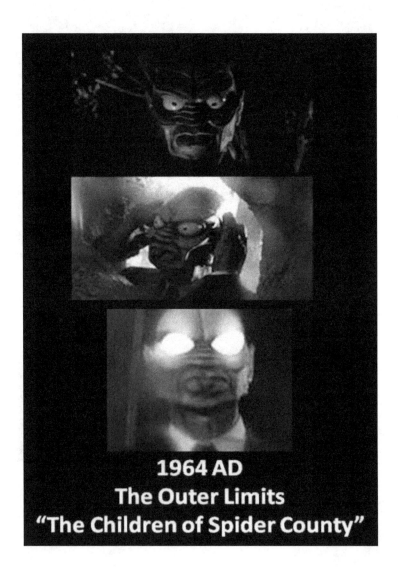

1965 AD
"Evil Brian from Outer Space"

1967 AD
Flying Saucers Comics, #2

1967 AD
Dell's *Flying Saucers*

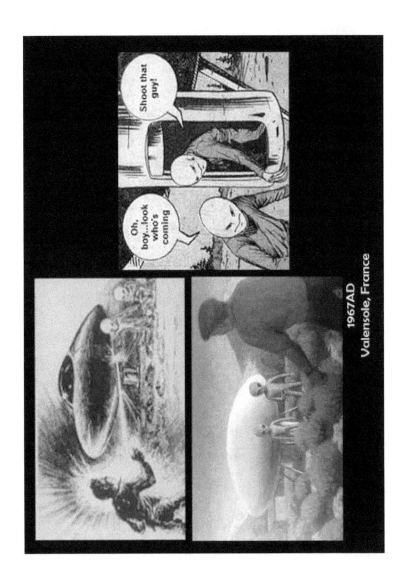

1968 AD
UFO Flying Saucers, #11

1968 AD
2001: A Space Odyssey
"Star Child"

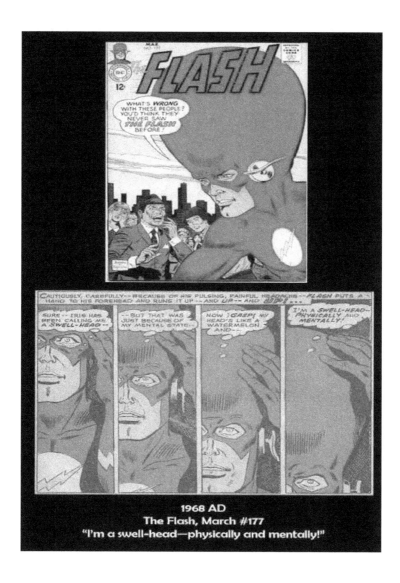

1968 AD
UFO Flying Saucers, #12

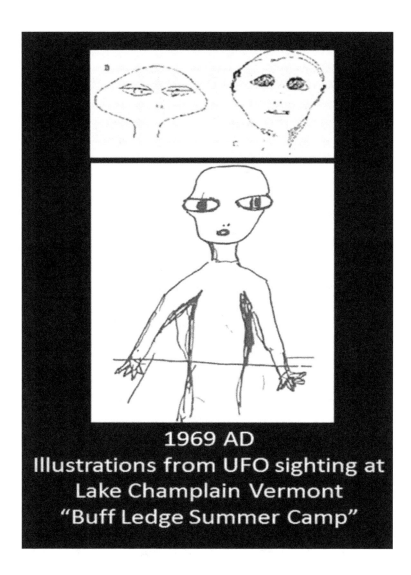

1969 AD
Illustrations from UFO sighting at
Lake Champlain Vermont
"Buff Ledge Summer Camp"

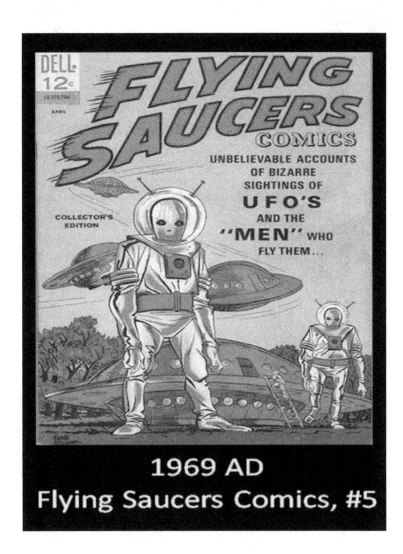

1969 AD
Flying Saucers Comics, #5

Fig. 15
Rendering of Steven Kilburn's abductors from his hypnotically retrieved recollections. Illustration courtesy Ted Seth Jacobs. Photograph by Geoffrey Clements.

1970s AD
Description by Steven Kilburn
Published in Budd Hopkins' book "Missing Time"

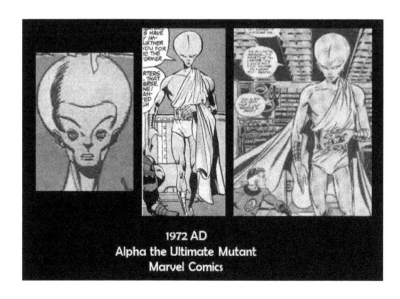

1972 AD
Alpha the Ultimate Mutant
Marvel Comics

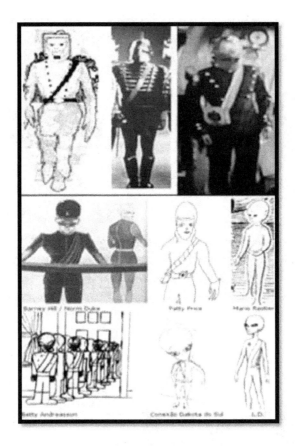

(Top L) 1974 AD: Description of alien seen at Warneton (France-Belgian border)
(Top R) 1940 AD: Flash Gordon "Space Soldiers Conquer the Universe" episode 11
(Middle L to R) Norm Duke's depiction of the Barney and Betty Hill case aliens (even though they did not report this particular look in 1961 AD), Patty Price 1973 AD, Mario Restier 1976 AD
(Bottom L to R) Betty Andreasson 1979 AD, Conexão Dakota do Sul (South Dakota Connection) 1983 AD, L.D. 1990 AD

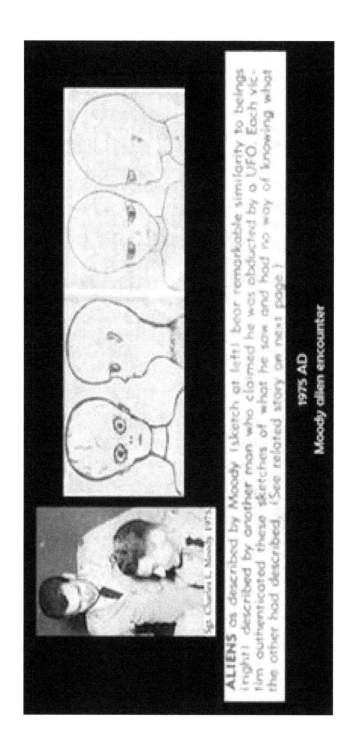

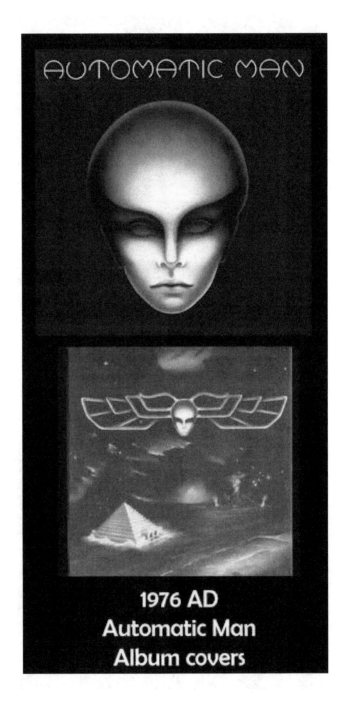

1976 AD
Automatic Man
Album covers

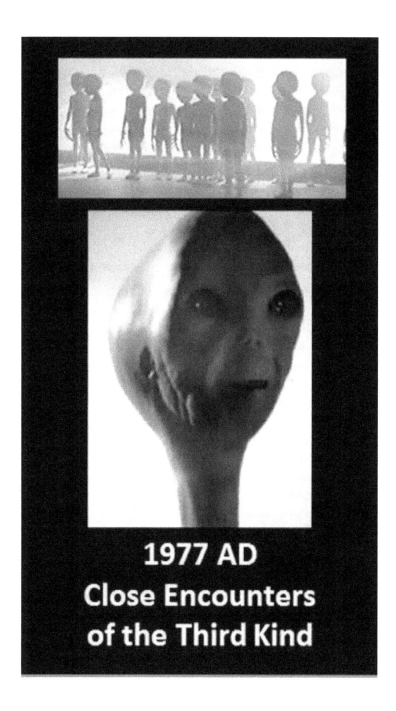

**1977 AD
Close Encounters
of the Third Kind**

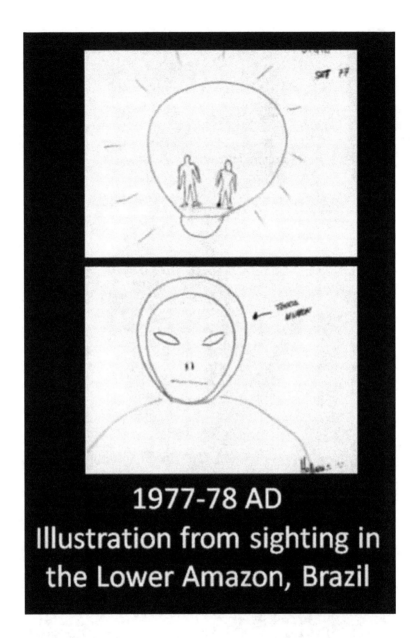

1977-78 AD
Illustration from sighting in
the Lower Amazon, Brazil

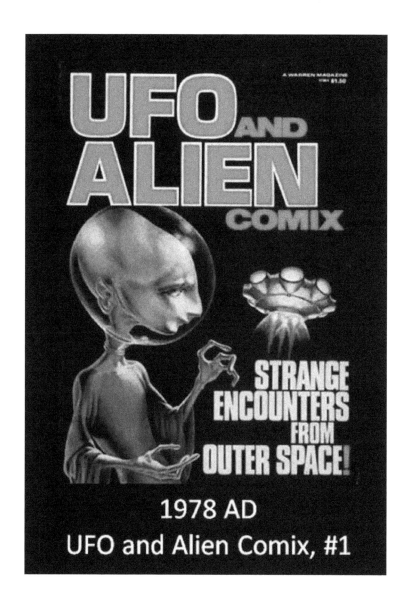

1978 AD
UFO and Alien Comix, #1

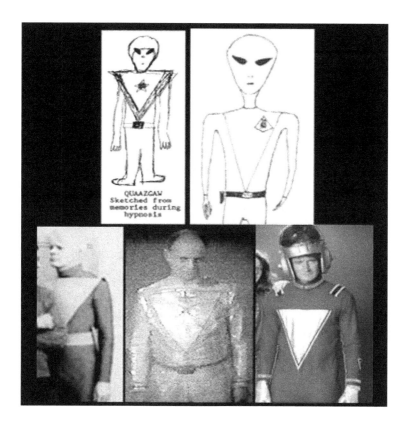

(Top L) 1981 AD *Quaazgaw* "Sketched from memories during hypnosis" from Barbara Schutte's article relating her alien encounters, "The UFO Connection, How Many Investigators Have It?"
(Top R) 1993 AD drawking by Bill Hamilton.
(Bottom L to R) "Starship Invaders" movie alien 1977 AD, Don Rickles playing the part of a Martian and Robin Williams in "Mork and Mndy"

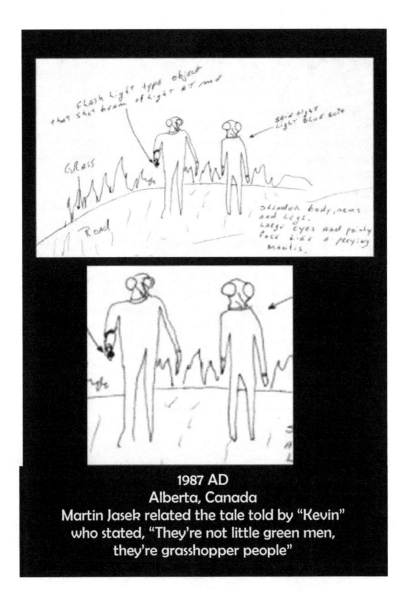

1987 AD
Alberta, Canada
Martin Jasek related the tale told by "Kevin"
who stated, "They're not little green men,
they're grasshopper people"

1987 AD
Toronto, Ontario, Canada, *Sun.* alien

1954 AD Quarouble, France

1988 AD
Budd Hopkins
"Missing Time"

Spider-Man (L) and
Venom (R) first meeting

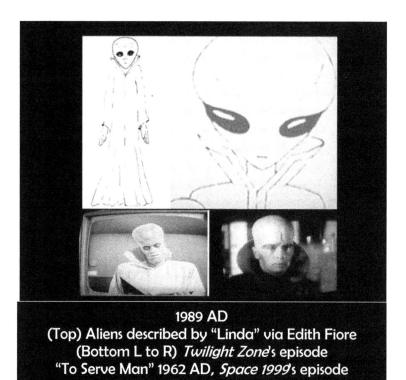

1989 AD
(Top) Aliens described by "Linda" via Edith Fiore
(Bottom L to R) *Twilight Zone*'s episode
"To Serve Man" 1962 AD, *Space 1999*'s episode
"War Games" 1975 AD

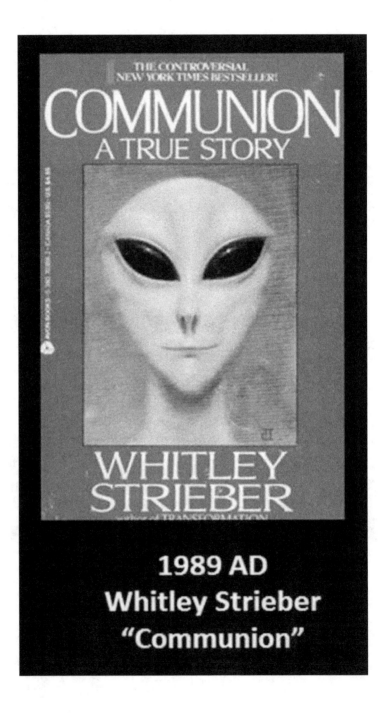

1989 AD
Whitley Strieber
"Communion"

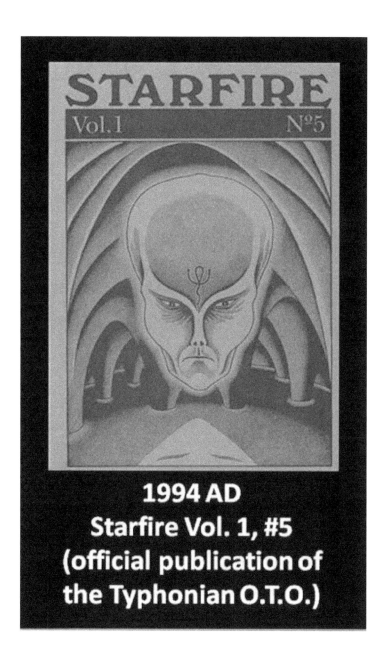

**1994 AD
Starfire Vol. 1, #5
(official publication of
the Typhonian O.T.O.)**

1996 AD
Michael Wolf
"The Catchers of Heaven: A Trilogy"

1997 AD
"The Roswell Files"
Time magazine

Claude Vorilhon aka Raël
"The True Face of God"
1998 AD

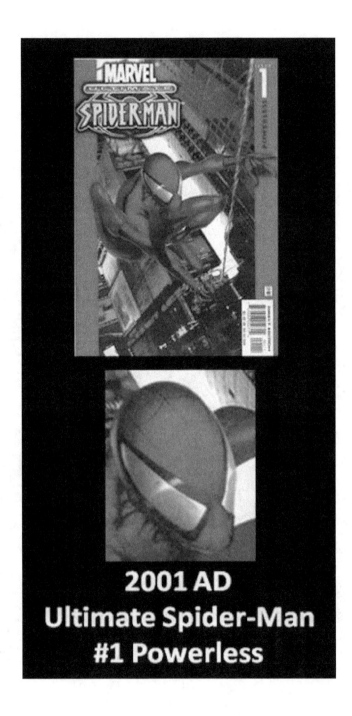

**2001 AD
Ultimate Spider-Man
#1 Powerless**

2001 AD
"A. I." movie
Some call these "aliens" but, as per Steven
Spielberg and Stanley Kubrick, they are
silicon based artificially intelligent robots.

Source and date unknown

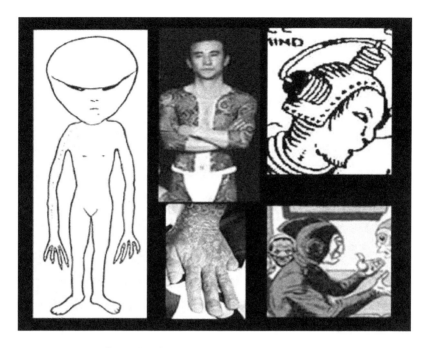

As per Douglas Dietrich's theory: "alien" compared to small bodied Japanese Yakuza members who would have been piloting dirigibles over the USA, such as over Roswell, having heads shaved to reduce electrical conductivity.

Compare with comic book alien villains such as from *Buck Rogers* and *Mystery in Space*.

The gray alien description could be a simplification and exaggeration of Asian features; small stature, slant or almond eyes, etc. such as four fingers in the case of the Yakuza (for whom it is common to have one finger chopped off).

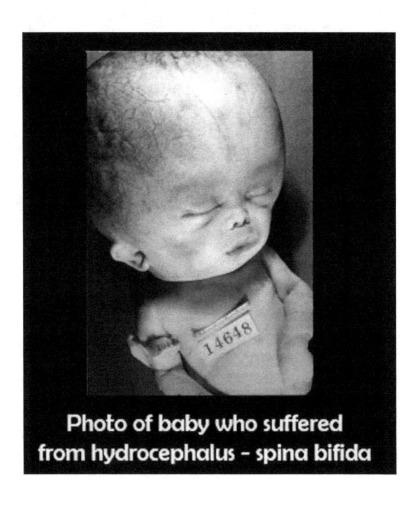

Photo of baby who suffered
from hydrocephalus - spina bifida

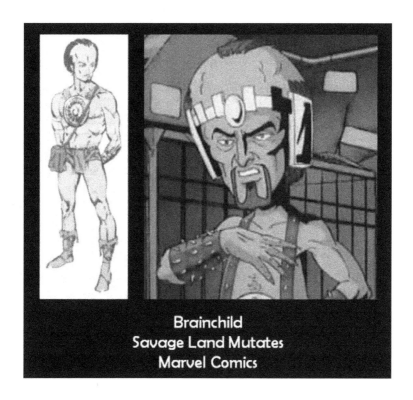

Brainchild
Savage Land Mutates
Marvel Comics

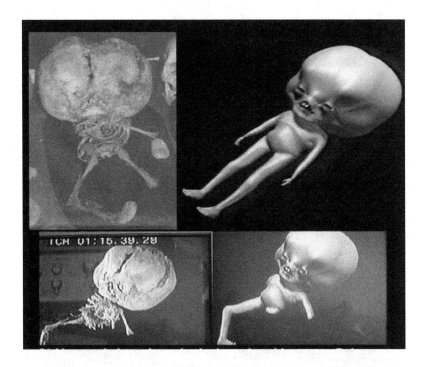

(L) Human skeleton from the Anthropology Museum in Bahia, Brazil of a child who suffered from hydrocephalus, palatine fissure, leporine labia and curved feet.
(R) Biased reconstruction of an "alien" skeleton by a Japanese TV show: how, for example, could they know from a skeleton that the skin was blue?

Green Lantern villain Hector Hammond

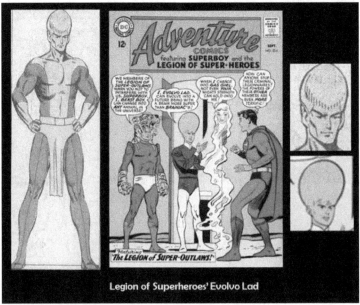

Legion of Superheroes' Evolvo Lad

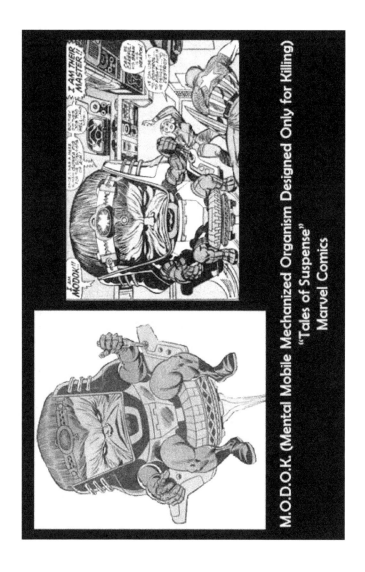

M.O.D.O.K. (Mental Mobile Mechanized Organism Designed Only for Killing)
"Tales of Suspense"
Marvel Comics

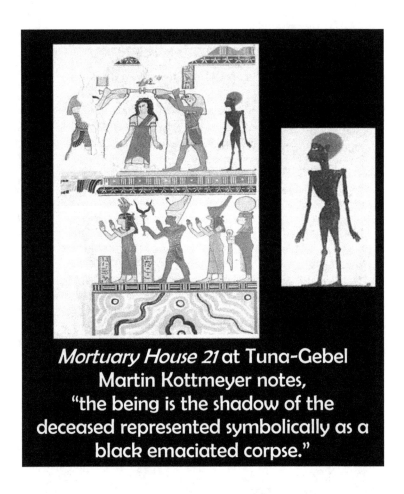

Mortuary House 21 at Tuna-Gebel
Martin Kottmeyer notes,
"the being is the shadow of the
deceased represented symbolically as a
black emaciated corpse."

The Leader from The Hulk comics

Sean Stone's Spirit Aliens

Sean Stone, son of famous director Oliver, serves as a great, and troubling, example of the tangled wed that is weaved at the intersection of occultism and UFOs and aliens.

Stone became part of the team on Jesse Ventura's show *Conspiracy Theory*. In the episode *Skinwalker Ranch* (S03E05) the issue is UFOs and aliens, "extra terrestrial contact," etc. *Skinwalker Ranch* is an aka for *Sherman Ranch* which is owned by Robert Bigelow.

Stone has stated that he did not *convert* to Islam but that he "accepted" Islam meaning that he accepts Muhammad as a prophet within his own concept of progressive revelation (he is actually not very well verse on such theological issues, by the way). My point in bringing this up is that he seems to have gotten involved in some sort of Islamic mythicism and this seems to play a part in the show in question.

The team sought to investigate the ranch and as they approach they claim to be receiving messages from alien on their car's radio. We are told "something has taken over the car radio" and in a very cheesy robotic voice, the aliens say "Get off," "True evil!," "Evil!" and "So evil!" Now, I am quoting directly from the show's very own subtitle transcriptions since, as these things tend to go: the producers know that it is very difficult to actually hear those words or hear them in a clear and obvious way so someone transcribed what they heard.

In any case, either the show's producers, or someone hoaxing the producers, or aliens though to say such things—for whatever reasons.

In one scene, they are in the dark of night somewhere within range of the ranch and someone says, "Hold on a second, you alright Sean?" who is standing quietly with his left hand raised, hand opened and palm facing away from him. He is asked, "What you got Sean? What're you doing?" And within a segment of a show about UFOs and aliens, he states, "Inviting the spirits to come out"—not, "Inviting the aliens to come out" but "the spirits."
The narrator states, "Sean's **ritual** pays off" and well, we are shown a black screen with a little tiny dot on it which are apparently the manifestation of well, whatever, in the night sky and the narrator informs us that "It's a UFO."

Damien Echols Might Be An Alien

Damien Echols is famous and infamous for being an occult practitioner and for having been convicted multiple times of murdering three eight year old boys: Steve Branch, Christopher Byers, and James Michael Moore (he was eventually released under an Alford Plea)—this was the *West Memphis Three* case.

Considering the correlations that have been drawn between demonism and "extra-terrestrial alien" abduction experiences, it is fascinating that Damien Echols at one point wrote, "I thought maybe I was an alien" and went on to recall experiences which may be categorized as "sleep paralysis" which is applicable to, both, demonism and "alien" abduction:

> …when I was very young one night I woke up and there was someone in my bed. It scared me so bad I couldn't even move…
>
> I can remember one night when I was a little older and I woke up to see a man standing in my room. It paralyzed me. I wouldn't even blink because I knew as soon as I opened my eyes he would be right in my face…
>
> These things always happened at night…one night when there was an old man in my room. I thought if I just ignored him he would go away.
> But when I looked again he was right in front of me. He licked my hand and said "Does that feel like a dream to you?" He

talked for awhile of things that arn't
important yet. [sic.]

This is actually one mere step in what appears to be Echols
admitting that he became, purposefully, more and more
possessed as I elucidate in my book *The Necronomiconjob,
Liber I.*

Pop-Celebs and Aliens

Lady Gaga, Rhianna, Will.I.Am and Katy Perry – In Space!

For whatever reason, pop-occulture-stars have taken to the stars. Along with constantly displaying symbolism and terminology indicative of secret societies, mystery religions, witchcraft, in short, the occult by any other name; they have taken to an interest in UFOs and aliens.

Of course, the two have always been tied together, the occult and aliens, as occultists see them as ascended masters, higher selves, space brothers, etc. and alien messages 99% condemn Christianity (see chapter the "The How, What and How of Alien Messages.").

Rihanna

Taking a typical stance, in two ways, the UK's *Daily Star*'s writer Ed Dyson wrote an article titled "Rihanna gets 24-hour Alien updates," (September 3, 2013 AD) and subtitled, "HERBAL princess Rihanna must be puffing on some seriously strong stuff these days."

Firstly, this continues a long history of instantly dismissing people who believe in aliens/UFOs are nuts.

Secondly, this missed the point about the occult nature of Rihanna's actions, videos, lyrics and worldview; she may believe that aliens are beings from another planet but she may believe that they are…something else, something extra-dimensional.

Rihanna, the drug using self-professed "Illuminati Princess" is "paying a UFO watcher in the Mojave desert for round-the-clock updates on extraterrestrial activity. The *UFO watcher* calls himself a "sky scanner" and "keeps in touch with her from the Little A'Le'Inn – a motel which hosts UFO hunters." The motel is near Area 51 in Rachel, Nevada (get it? *Little Alien*).

For whatever it is worth, the UK's *Daily Star* claims that "A source in the stargazer's camp told us: 'Rihanna has always been convinced aliens will land on Earth in her lifetime.'"
Rihanna's brother Rorrey "also confirmed that obsessing over little green men was a childhood hobby in the Fenty household." He noted, "She really believes there are UFOs. No-one knows for sure, but Ri[hanna] and I definitely think they're out there. It kept us occupied as kids."
Rihanna herself has stated, "My dad used to make me sit outside on the steps all night long in Barbados looking for UFOs flying by. I had to do that for years. I didn't see any, but I saw a falling star once and I was like: 'Yes, Dad! Come and see!'"

<u>Katy Perry</u>
Something is certainly afoot betwixt the top pop-occulture stars and "aliens." As considered below, Katy Perry's song and video for "E.T." mixes aliens with the devil; beings with different "DNA." Perry, who has stated "I sold my soul to the devil," sings, "Could you be the devil? Could you be an angel? They say, be afraid…futuristic lover, different DNA, they don't understand you. You're from a whole 'nother world, a different dimension, you open my eyes, and I'm ready to go, lead me into the light. Kiss me, kiss me, infect me with your love and, fill me with your poison. Take me, take me, wanna be a victim, ready for abduction. Boy, you're an alien…it's supernatural, extraterrestrial."

This is saturated with occult references. Perry has her fans, who are mostly prepubescent, going around speaking into the ether (speaking to those malevolent being who inhabit the ether) "infect me…fill me with your poison…wanna be a victim, ready for abduction"; the nature of demonism is litigious and this is an invitation to come on in.

Lady Gaga

Ann Oldenburg repots "Lady Gaga to sing in space" (*USA Today*, November 7, 2013 AD):

> The plan is for Gaga to sing at Zero G Colony, a three-day high-tech music festival at Spaceport America in New Mexico, the world's first commercial spaceport. On the third day of the event, Gaga will take off on board a Virgin Galactic spaceship…
> Zero G Colony is a three-day hi-tech festival set to take place at Spaceport America in New Mexico that features world-class entertainment and cutting-edge technology. Gaga's performance in space is planned to take place on the third day at dawn, which is approximately six months after the first Virgin Galactic commercial flight.

Zero G Colony sounds like a transhumanism conference. Is anyone getting this? She will be within the virgin (as in Jesus and Mary) and perform on the third day at dawn (as in when Jesus resurrected).

Nicole Eggenberger and Ian Drew wrote the article "Lady Gaga to Sing in Space in 2015" (*US Magazine*, November 6, 2013 AD). Gaga, "has to do a month of vocal training because of the atmosphere."

Before you say, "What, like, ever, and stuff" note that one of Gaga's many alter egos/pseudonyms is Mother Monster who's aforementioned "Manifesto of Mother Monster" contextually noted, "a Government Owned Alien Territory in space."

She once spent a specific 72 hours within an egg in order to be reborn. The number 72 is important in occultism as it denotes the 72 demons that rule the world according to the *Goetia* which is the first book of the *Lemegeton/The Lesser Key of Solomon* which is a 17th century AD grimoire/occult text.

At the 2009 AD annual White House Correspondents' Association dinner, Barack Obama said:

> I would like to talk about what my administration plans to achieve in the next 100 days…During the second 100 days, we will design, build and open a library dedicated to my first 100 days…I believe that my next 100 days will be so successful, I will be able to complete them in **72** days – and on the 73rd day I will rest.

Here are some lyrics from her most recent album *Artpop* which contains song titled such as "Aura," "Venus," "Do What U Want" (which is Aleister Crowley's motto "Do what thou wilt", etc.:

> I can't help the way I'm feeling / Goddess of love, please take me to your leader.
> Jupiter/Mercury, Venus – uh ha! / Uranus / Don't you know my a** is famous?
> Touch me in the dark / Put your hands all over my body parts / Throw me on the bed…
> You're just a pig inside a human body.

The album is largely extremely perverse and will encourage her, prepubescent fans, whom she calls, "Little Monsters," to do what they will. Sandro Botticelli's painting *The Birth of Venus* was used as part of the collage which makes up the *Artpop* album cover which is very perverse; showing Lady Gaga naked, covering her breasts with her hands and having a blue sphere (egg?) covering her nether region as her legs are spread.

Will.I.Am

In my article "Illuminati occult fashion model photo shoots"[25] I noted that the author of a very occult-laced article accompanying an even more occult photo shoot of Kate Moss was written by "Will Self." Well, guaranteed that his parents did not name him that, unless they are in on it, as "Will Self" is a very occult name which expresses the reliance upon self to exercise the will, which is *Occultism 101*.

In fact, you can hear another "Will" expressing this very thing. Will Smith actually believes that when he sets his mind, his will, towards a goal; the universe bends to his will.

Well, *Black Eyed Peas* member William Adams goes by the name "Will.I.Am" or "will.i.am" which expresses the same concept: will and self. In this case, he takes upon himself the titled "I AM" which was expressed to Moses by YHVH when asked what His name was at the burning bush discussion of Exodus chapter 3.

Will.I.Am is a well-known transhumanist, amongst other things, and saturates his pop-occultural work with references to occultism and the New World Order.

As *CNN* reported in "Will.i.am premieres song – from Mars" (Faith Karimi, August 29, 2012) Will.I.Am premiered a song from Mars:

> The Black Eyed Peas singer wrote the song, "Reaching for the Stars," to mark the successful landing of NASA's Curiosity

rover on the Red Planet…it features a 40-piece orchestra set to a futuristic beat. The song is set to transcend time and cultures, he said.

"Mars has always fascinated us, and the things Curiosity tells us about it will help us learn about whether or not life was possible there," said Charles Bolden, the NASA administrator. "And what future human explorers can expect, will.i.am has provided the first song on our playlist of Mars exploration."

Some of the lyrics to the song read, "Told your people that we don't mess around…Please don't turn this down…Louder than it was before, like the lion at the jungle, you can hear us roar, when I lie hear, it's like a sonic blaster, flying just like NASA, out of space master…Hands up, if you really feel alive, live it up, live it up."
NASA, which times its mission to occult calendars and gives its missions occult names (those of false gods, etc.) correlated with the roaring of the lion is quite enough to raise the red flags to discerning listeners as 1 Peter 5:8 states that satan roams the Earth as a lion, seeking whom he may devour.

The tune…completed a trip of more than 300 million miles from Earth to Mars and back, according to NASA…"This is about inspiring young people to lead a life without limits placed on their potential and to pursue **collaboration between humanity and technology**," will.i.am said. [Emphasis added for transhuman emphasis]

NASA also sent *The Beatles'* song "Across the Universe" into space on February 4, 2008 AD, a date which "marked the anniversary of the day The Beatles recorded the song and the 50th year of NASA's founding." Some of the lyrics, written by John Lennon and Paul McCartney go:

> Pools of sorrow waves of joy, are drifting through my open mind...Jai Guru Deva, om...Images of broken light, which dance before me like a million eyes, they call me on and on across the universe...Inciting and inviting me...shines around me like a million suns...Nothing's gonna change my world.

"Jai Guru Deva, om" means *in praise / honor of the teacher / master goddess.*
McCartney stated, "Amazing! Well done, NASA!... Send my love to the aliens."

Something is afoot and everyone from pop-occulture's stars to the Vatican are looking towards the heavens; may they look past the heavens and find the one within the heaven of heavens; the Messiah Jesus.

Is Gaga's "Venus" a Sequel to Katy Perry's "E.T."?

Katy Perry's song, lyrics and video for "E.T." gained great popularity for various reasons. The one reason we are interested in is the occult signification.

Here are some of the lyrics written by Katy Perry, Max Martin, Lukasz Gottwald and Joshua Emanuel Coleman (we will consider these again as we progress):

> You're so hypnotizing / Could you be the devil? Could you be an angel? / Your touch

magnetizing / Feels like I am floating, leaves my body glowing

They say be afraid / You're not like the others, futuristic lover / Different DNA / They don't understand you

You're from a whole other world / A different dimension / You open my eyes / And I'm ready to go, lead me into the light

…Infect me with your love and / Fill me with your poison…Take me…Wanna be a victim / Ready for abduction

Boy, you're an alien / Your touch so foreign / It's supernatural / Extraterrestrial

…Every move is magic…This is transcendental…I wanna walk on your wavelength / And be there when you vibrate / For you I'll risk it all

Understood for that which it is, this song is a virtual invitation for possession. Katy Perry, who has stated, "I sold my soul to the devil," has her, mostly prepubescent fans, going around repeating, "Infect me with your love and / Fill me with your poison…Take me…Wanna be a victim / Ready for abduction." Considering the litigious nature of demonism, this is quite concerning.

As noted, Gaga's *Artpop* is saturated with encouragement to perform perverse sexual acts. Some of the song titles are Aura, Sexxx Dreams, Jewels N' Drugs, Dope, Applause (how pathetic to have to beg your fans to applaud you), as well as "Do What U Want."

Her song "Venus" picks up where Katy Perry's "E.T." left off. Here are some of the lyrics which were written by Paul Blair, Herman Poole Blount, Hugo Pierre Leclercq, Nick Monson, Stefani Germanotta and Dino Zisis (it is amazing how many people it takes to write pop trash):

> Rocket #9 take off to the planet (to the planet) Venus
>
> Aphrodite lady seashell bikini (garden panty) Venus / Let's blast off to a new dimension (in your bedroom) Venus...
>
> I can't help the way I'm feeling / Goddess of love, please take me to your leader / I can't help, I keep on dancing / Goddess of love, goddess of love
>
> ...When you touch me, I die / Just a little inside / I wonder if this could be love / This could be love / 'Cause you're out of this world / Galaxy, space, and time / I wonder if this could be love (Venus)
>
> Have an oyster, baby, it's Aphrod-isy / Act sleazy Venus / Worship to the land a girl from the planet (to the planet) / To the planet
>
> ...Neptune, go / Now serve Pluto / Saturn, Jupiter / Mercury, Venus, uh ha! / Uranus! / Don't you know my *** is famous? / Mars, now serve for the gods / Earth, serve for the stars!

Note that nine, as in *Rocket #9*, is the number of the beast as per occult numerological reduction as 6+6+6=18 and 1+8=9 thus, 666=9. So, the song remains the same; songs blurring the lines between the demonic and alien (which are one in the same in such cases) and urge the worshipful sexual union between humans and…something else.

Is "Part of Me" an Alien, an Angel or the Devil?

Katy Perry stated, "I sold my soul to the devil." In light (pun intended) of this it is interesting to read her lyrics and see if she is attempting to send a dual message.

For example, her song "E.T." appears to be about well, what most pop songs appear to be about, sexual perversion. However, once you view the video to this song, you may want to re-read the lyrics and then plug in a little basic understanding of story lines and symbolism.

First, let us see the lyrics as is:
>You're so hypnotizing / Could you be the devil? Could you be an angel?
>Your touch magnetizing / Feels like I am floating / Leaves my body glowing
>They say, be afraid / You're not like the others / Futuristic lover / Different DNA / They don't understand you
>[Pre-Chorus] You're from a whole 'nother world / A different dimension / You open my eyes / And I'm ready to go / Lead me into the light
>[Chorus] Kiss me, kiss me / Infect me with your love and / Fill me with your poison
>Take me, take me / Wanna be a victim / Ready for abduction

Boy, you're an alien / Your touch so foreign
/ It's supernatural / Extraterrestrial
You're so supersonic / Wanna feel your
powers / Stun me with your lasers / Your
kiss is cosmic / Every move is magic
[Pre-Chorus] [Chorus]
Take me, ta-ta-take me / Wanna be a victim
/ Ready for abduction
Boy, you're an alien / Your touch so
foreign/ It's supernatural / Extraterrestrial
[Bridge] This is transcendental / On another
level / Boy, you're my lucky star
I wanna walk on your wave length / And be
there when you vibrate / For you I'll risk it
all / All
[Chorus and repeat]

Even at pure face value this is pretty bizarre stuff. At one
level it is about infatuation with a guy, at another
infatuation with an alien and yet, at another level, the actual
level suggested by the video, it is about infatuation with the
being to whom she admitted having sold her soul: the devil.

One oddity is that the lyrics seem to be about her
expressing infatuation for whomever. Yet, in the video she
is the alien/devil.

But we are getting ahead of ourselves. In short and
generically, the video depicts a futuristic world in ruin. A
man within a robotic body is lying on a ruined desolate
garbage dump of a world. An alien which turns into a
human, Perry's character, descends from space/the heavens
to the robot/man and powers him up, as it were. She frees
him from the robotic body and they walk off into the
sunset, a scene which reveals that the Perry, supposedly
human, character actually has goat/faun/deer-like, legs.

Ultimately, the video seems to depict a neo-Genesis, a new beginning which is much like the original beginning and the same old tempter.

Let us now go step by step and describe the video in light (or darkness) of the lyrics.

The video opens to a scene of a wasteland, a styled garbage dump of a world, whereupon lays a mechanical robot with a tear drop shaped form on its chest which is flickering.

Since the video is in collaboration with Kanye West (who also states that he sold his soul to the devil—and the crowd love it), he appears within a spaceship (which looks like an eyeball of sorts) and sings the following:

> I got a dirty mind / I got filthy ways / I'm
> tryna Bathe my Ape in your Milky Way
> I'm a legend, I'm irreverent / I be reverend /
> I be so fa-a-ar up, we don't give a ****
> Welcome to the danger zone / Step into the
> fantasy / You are not invited to the other
> side of sanity
> They calling me an alien / A big headed
> astronaut / Maybe it's because your boy
> Yeezy get *** a lot

And after the [Chorus and repeat] part he comes back to sing:

> I know a bar out in Mars / Where they
> driving spaceships instead of cars / Cop a
> Prada spacesuit about the stars
> Getting stupid *** straight out the jar /
> Pockets on Shrek, Rockets on deck / Tell me
> what's next, alien sex
> I'm a disrobe you, than I'm a probe you /

See I abducted you, so I tell ya what to do / I
tell ya what to do, what to do, what to do

Doesn't that just want to make you buy all of the Katy
Perry and Kanye West albums for your little kiddies?
As Kanye's ship flies off screen swirling silky materials are
seen gyrating in space and we see that they are the clothing
of an alien which looks like a grey (the well-known alien
with a large head and large eyes). This happens at the
moment when Perry sings "You're so hypnotizing / Could
you be the devil? Could you be an angel?"

Well, which is it angel or devil? Strange question as it is
neither, it is an alien. Well, of course, that only begs the
question.

The alien is seen singing the first few lyrics such as
Different DNA which may be in reference to the concept of
directed panspermia: the view that aliens purposefully
seeded life on Earth. There are many such concepts such as
that they came to Earth after random chance evolution
resulted in humanity and the aliens manipulated our DNA,
etc. It could also be in reference to that to which we shall
come below which is the plans, by some, to genetically
modify human DNA.

Next, the alien being's cloths turn shades of red and we see
that the alien has turned into a human (at least in form) who
is the Perry character. Images are flashed which appear to
depict life and death: the decaying corpse of a fox, a plant
sprouting, etc.

Between the question of angel or devil reference is made to
"It's supernatural / Extraterrestrial." The question of angel
of devil is almost a false dichotomy as Biblically the devil
and demons are fallen angels. In this light, they are both

supernatural and also, literally, extra-terrestrial and they are not of, nor from, the terra, the Earth.

The silky cloths, now more of a flowing dress/gown is now white with styled angel's wings. Perry's eyes are seen to be not human but what some, particularly within the alien context, would call reptilian. This has various connotations such as that the devil is described in Genesis in reptilian serpentine terms, as a snake (due to his wiles, craftiness, etc.). Also, the character was initially a grey alien which are stereotypically depicted with solid black eyes but the Perry character has reptilian eyes. Also, something which is difficult to identify is seen reflected in the eyes during an extreme close up of them.

When she sings "You're from a whole 'nother world / A different dimension / You open my eyes / And I'm ready to go / Lead me into the light" fast images are cut which are violent scenes of a nuclear blast, a cheetah catching a gazelle by the neck, etc.

Whether the Perry character is alien, angel or devil is now made quite clear as we find that she has been falling to Earth. The Bible states:

> How art thou fallen from heaven, O Lucifer,
> son of the morning! how art thou cut down
> to the ground (Isaiah 14:12).
> [Jesus said] I saw Satan fall like lightning
> from heaven (Luke 10:18).

But this could be about an alien landing on Earth, why bring the devil/satan into it? Context, context, context, as the further context of the video makes this connection. Perry/devil finds the robot laying in the heaps of refuse with its little tinge of life (some little spark of energy). She, now wearing a more form fitting golden outfit, wipes the dust from the robot's head (glass domed on the front) and it is revealed that inside is a man (who looks to be of African descent but with white skin). She then touches the robot/man's tear shaped chest piece and it lights up as Kanye West comes back within the space ship to sing the second verse we read above.

The robot/man gets up and when West sings "Tell me what's next, alien sex / I'm 'a disrobe you, than I'm a probe you / See I abducted you" fast cut images are shown of animals having sex. This may be a reference to the theory that aliens/demons had sex with humans which some assert, gave rise to giants, etc. Some read this into Genesis 6:1-2 & 4:

> And it came to pass, when men began to multiply on the face of the earth, and daughters were born unto them, that the sons of God saw the daughters of men that they [were] fair; and they took them wives of all which they chose…
> There were giants [nephiyl] in the earth in those days; and also after that, when the sons of God came in unto the daughters of men, and they bare [children] to them, the same [became] mighty men which [were] of old, men of renown.

See my book *On the Genesis 6 Affair's Sons of God: Angels or Not?*

At this point the Perry character kisses the robot/man through the glass domed head and a very bright light engulfs them. When the light dims we see that the robot body is now gone and the black/white man is left behind.

216

There may be three meanings—or more ;o)—to this:
1) Firstly, the robot man concoction may refer to what used to be known as biomechanoids and is now known as transhumanism. That is, the attempt by some to meld human biology and technology so as to artificially evolve humanity.

2) The black and white (that he is a "black man" whose skin is white—not cream skin color but actual white) may be in reference to the black and white checkerboard floor design which is found in Masonic structured.

3) The black/white man may also represent the concept of one people which follows form the desire by some for a one world government, one world religion, one new world order, etc.

The Perry character is displaying eye makeup very much in the Isis Egyptian style or, rather, the eye of Horus (a Masonic / Illuminati symbols—perhaps why the spaceship looks like an eye). On the ground we see glass canisters one of which contains the long dead remains of a bird labeled, "pi-ge on : A common bird went extinct 2030." Another canister contains sunglasses labeled, "Human sunglasses Circa 2011" which are picked up and worn by Perry (such encased extinct animals are also displayed in an über weird Denver National Airport mural).

A classic metaphor for "worldview," a way to define, describe and understand what is meant by the term, is the example of putting on of glasses, sunglasses with lenses of whatever color. This is because once we put them on we see everything differently as everything is viewed through the lenses, the new perspective. The lenses re-interpret everything in accordance to our view, our color, our lenses, our glasses.

Next, the bottom of her dress is blown by the wind and reveals that she has the legs of a goat/faun/deer. This is widely used to represent various half human/gods half animals such as the devil, the Greek god Pan, the Roman god Faunus, satyrs which were companions of Pan and Dionysus, etc.

So, what does this all mean? Who knows? Well someone knows because someone wrote the song lyrics, the script to the video, etc. But we do not know what they meant by it and can only discern the obvious and hidden symbolism. It appears to be a tale of a human race which has been melded with technology so as to make them into automatons, robotic creatures who have all but become extinct.

Understand that luciferians (aka rightly or wrongly as Satanists, devil worshippers, etc.) still consider lucifer as being that which he actually was before his rebellion against YHVH when he became satan. Note that lucifer was the faithful servant of YHVH, the light bearer but then became satan the faithless oppose of YHVH, the adversary.

They view the story of Genesis as lucifer brining revelation to humanity, the knowledge of good and evil, freedom from YHVH's restraints, etc. This seems to be what the video portrays as the fallen devil is involved in a neo Genesis as it approaches the (apparently) only human on Earth, brings light to humanity, appeals to humanity, gains humanity's trust and love and walks away leading humanity. Recall that this creature is a deceiver as it was appeared as an alien, a human, a human reptilian, a half human half animal, etc.

The Bible notes that satan transforms/disguises (Strong's #G3345 *metaschematizo*) into an angel of light.

To reiterate, someone meant the lyrics and video to mean something and such somethings are constantly being put forth into our culture of a reason(s).

Be vigilant, "Test everything. Hold on to the good" (1st Thessalonians 5:21).

Byron LeBeau on UFOs and Aliens in Brad Steiger's "The Fellowship"

The late *Christian UFOlogist* Byron LeBeau wrote an article titled, "Semjase as Pleiadian Queen of New Age Rabbit Holes" which is "A mini-review (with observations) of certain portions of Brad Steiger's **THE FELLOWSHIP** - published by Doubleday, New York, 1988."

The focus is the anti-Christian sentiments which seem to creek into most alien messages to humans (see above for chapter *The How, What and How of Alien Messages*) and LeBeau notes that claims such as that "Jesus is not the only Christ, nor God" that "God is impersonal" that "Man is God" that "Man gets his instruction from the spirit world" that "All religions are good" that "Ancient wisdom comes from Babylon, Egypt & Greece, and replaces the Bible as truth" and that "Good & evil do not exist, but only peace & love" are basic claims made via alien messages and that these "have also crept into the aforementioned Brad Steiger's book, with an emphasis on a 'woman' by the name of Semjase" about whom we will learn more below. This is the same Semjase who was a key player with the Billy Meier alien UFO contract case and who "goes about communicating with people like Fred Bell, the 'contactee' who is one of the focus people in this book."

LeBeau emphasizes that "The tragedy of Brad Steiger's book, he seems oblivious to the spiritual danger in promoting this NEW AGE 'gospel' as if it were – perhaps – an 'upgrade' of the spiritual message given by Jesus Christ about two thousand years ago."

Steiger's *The Fellowship* chap 1 refers to "UFO contactees" as neo-apostles of a sort as they represent the "future evangelism" of a "New Age religion, a blending of technology and traditional religious concepts" which are the forerunners of a "new consciousness": a trans-alien-humanism of sorts.

For his part, Steiger is very upfront about his mission:
> Whoever or whatever the Space Beings may be – whether cosmic missionaries or projections of the Higher Self – the channeled material contained in this book may be the scriptures and theological treatises of the New Age.

In other words, exactly as I noted about Barbara Marciniak in chapter *What Whitley Strieber and Barbara Marciniak Do Not Know*, personages such as Steiger, Marciniak, et al. have no idea with whom they are dealing but still decide to devote their lives to relating messages which, Steiger takes as far as referring to as "scriptures and theological treatises."

And yet, note his false dichotomy as these beings are either "cosmic missionaries" or "projections of the Higher Self" and he appears to consider no other option. Another option may be, for example, Whitely Strieber's original identification of his "visitors" as being demons—as we will see within the chapter on Strieber. Also, note that these messages were "channeled" which means that, quite conveniently, no UFOs or aliens need be present (although they may have been claimed to be present) since channeling denotes a person opening themselves up to receive messages from beings unknown via telepathic like methods.

Within this context, channeler Aleuti Francesca relayed a

message from an alien named "Orlon" which stated, "I'm afraid that we Space Brothers of the Confederation (Federation of Planets) must step in before it is too late."

As variously transliterated, Semjase is the name of a fallen angel as per the apocryphal Book of Enoch aka Ethiopic Enoch aka 1 Enoch—this will be a key portion of the chapter on Billy Meier.

Steiger does not mention this fact, "even though Brad is conversant with 'The Book of Enoch,' and even quotes from it."

"What he does do" notes Byron LeBeau "is introduce one, Dr. Fred Bell, who happens to have a love affair with this same mysterious 'woman'…Bell is pictured as a type of 'Renaissance Man' while he discusses the home of Semjase: the Pleiades."

The *Rays of Truth* web site, which is really just a platform from which to sell products, wrote the following with regards to Fred Bell's *Firestarr Orb* device which is said to have been demonstrated at the Pyramid Peak in the Blue-Bell Mountains, Colorado in 1982 AD and, from what we are told, "a UFO came into the beam." It was then again demonstrated in Marnau, Germany, Bavarian Alps in 1988 AD.

The device is said to function on the "principal of subtle vibration called etheric transmission…it sends a beacon-like signal deep into space where it can be received by and homed in on by alien space travelers and guides." And the key reason for mentioning this is the Bell connection to Steiger and the Bell connection to Semjase as we are told that "This communication technology was [related to Bell by] a Pleiadean woman named Semjase…In the Pleiades communication is done via scalar waves because they are instantaneous in nature."

Moreover, we are told:

> The Pleiadeans use auric amplifiers or signature devices for telepathic transmission. The device is tuned to the users chakras/ endocrine glands via gemstones and crystals and amplifies the human aura, becoming a transmitting and receiving scalar wave antenna.

What is of real interest is not the claims about Pleiadean high tech but that according to Billy Meier, anyone claiming that Semjase is a Pleiadean is a fraud and not really in contact with her/because, well, that is an interesting story.

Meier originally claimed that Semjase was Pleiadean but, oops, as scientific data accumulated with regards to life, as we know it, being impossible in the Pleiades, Meier received a convenient alien message update to the effect that Semajse is not Pleiadean but is *Plejaren*.

Thus, in order to solidify his, supposedly, unique ambassador status, Billy Meier asserted that we can identify a fraud by noting those who claim that Semjase is Pleiadian rather than Plejaren.

Another side note comes forth from a certain Den Rad who wrote an article titled, "Small History of Dr. Fred Bell Discoveries and Instructions Given to Him by Semjase Herself!" in which case he relates his building of a gold and diamond blinged out "Holographic Projector" which "was designed specifically to alter ones consciousness to work on a higher plain of existence."

As it turns out, or so we are told, Fred Bell was allowed "to copy and create a similar receptor, much more powerful then yesteryears Nuclear Receptor" by the *Andromendan Galatic* [sic.] *Federation Council* and that this "ANK" device, the aka Holographic Projector, is to be "Worn along side [sic.] of the Holographic Projector" as "they truly complement each other but they do opposite operations in the wearers sphere of influence."

Also, "Semjase gave Dr. Bell at the temple of Hathor in Egypt the directions where to find special things (treasures) within the temple." Thus, we have a supposed alien connection with ancient, Pagan, Egypt. This offers us the context of understanding that the above noted *ANK* is in reference to the Egyptian *Ankh* aka "breath of life" aka "key of the Nile" aka "crux ansata" which is Latin for "cross with a handle." This T with a circle or upside down tear drop shape above it represented the hieroglyphic character for life or, rather, eternal life.

Den Rad also asserts that the Nazi "Gestapo's job was to collect all over the world anything that has significance that come from the Pleadian galaxy." In fact, the article we have been considering contains the following references to that which Meier would say makes Fred Bell, Den Rad, Barbara Marciniak, et al. frauds:

> Pleiadian instruments along with the Andromeden instrumentations…Andromaden and Pleiadian technologies…Pleiadian ship…the Holographic Projector designed by the Andromedan's not the Pleiadians…Pleiadians instruments…

As LeBeau, et al., have noted, many supposed aliens share namesakes with ancient gods, angels, demons, etc. Thus, let us take another side trail to the *Sphere Alliance*'s alien message #62 wherein we are given a window into just who and/or what is this being called Semjase, at least from the perspective of some of her devotees:

> SEMJASE is a construct by many energies to make contact with your MEIER…WE say to you that this vessel/construct/body/vehicle called SEMJASE was not a complete biological interface. THERE was MUCH MORE TECHNOLOGY than DNA OPERATING in HER/IT. NO NOT A ROBOT…

> A CONSTRUCT is a vessel that is predetermined to withstand the different air qualities/air pressures/gravities/and oxygen levels required for long visits. IT is not a SPACE SUIT. IT is biological/technology hybrid of sorts, operated by ETERNAL ESSENCE strings, with other operational help/assistance from aboard ships. A Singular EVENT in MOST CASES.

> TRANSPLANTs AFTER SEMJASE were more attuned BIOLOGICALLY for the "environment". NOW we speak from our PERSPECTIVE of the ASHTAR COMMAND. MANY other CONSTRUCTS/TRANPLANTS were used by many other civilizations/cultures for purposes of interface/visitation. END

Thus, we also run across another ancient name as "Ashtar" is obviously a transliteration of "Ishtar" who is "the East Semitic Akkadian, Assyrian and Babylonian goddess of fertility, love, war, and sex. She is the counterpart to the

Sumerian Inanna, and is the cognate for the Northwest Semitic Aramean goddess Astarte." And/or Ashtar could refer to "Ashtoreth" (aka "Ashteroth" or "Ashtaroth") which, not surprisingly, refer to *a star* and is:

> ...the principal female divinity of the Phoenicians, called Ishtar by the Assyrians and Astarte by the Greeks and Romans. She was by some ancient writers identified with the moon.

But on the other hand, the Assyrian Ishtar was not the moon-goddess, but the planet Venus; and Astarte was by many identified with the goddess Venus (or Aphrodite), as well as with the plant of that name.

It is certain that the worship of Astarte became identified with that of Venus, and that this worship was connected with the most impure rites is apparent from the close connection of this goddess with ASHERAH. (1 Kings 11:5, 33; 2 Kings 23:13)

George Van Tassel claimed that he was told by his alien contact *Ashtar* that aliens seek to save humankind from itself. New Ager, Ruth Montgomery, claims that "the guides" stated (*Aliens Among Us*, p. 44):

> ...She would be wise not to infuse so much biblical religion into her messages, as the Ashtar Command is nondenominational and, like all space beings, worships the one Creator of us all. She is not hearing from the ones you mention, but is feeling what they might have conveyed. We don't like to see the issue unduly tied in with biblical stories.

The "She" with which the statement commences, LeBeau and the context inform us, someone who was "mixing in

too much Bible with her psychic revelations" and "the ones you mention" refers to Jesus, Mary, and other saints.

Now, back to LeBeau's article wherein he notes, "What is **not even offered as a possibility**" as per my reference to Steiger's false dichotomy, "is that she may well be a devil (fallen angel) yet *disguised as an angel of light*, so much so ~ that the likes of Fred Bell cannot see through her clever disguise" (emphasis in original).

LeBeau quotes a statement by Semjase from Brad Steiger's p. 37:

> Whether we work for God or against God, it matters not, for we are all of God – and our forms preserve our Karmic quest in search of the unmanifest.

Just think about what this does for ethics since for or against does not matter since we are all god.

From God to angels as Brad Steiger wrote that "There seems little question that the Space Beings function as the angels once did. They are concerned about Earth. They seem to be actively trying to protect it.

They are powerful…yet they are benevolent." Well, one must ask to what angels he is referring as, for example, biblical angels are not New Age Earth Day Gaia worshipers of any sort and are not seen being "concerned about Earth" so as to "protect it."
Rather, they are God's messengers to humans.

French journalist Claude Vorilhon claims to have boarded an alien spacecraft on October 7, 1975 AD which was piloted by the *Elohim* who regaled him with tales of how they are the ones who created humanity. These aliens decided to rename Vorilhon as "Rael" meaning "the man who brings light."

Rael went on to found the UFO cult *Raelians* who some years ago perpetrated a fraudulent hoax to the effect they had cloned a human. They appear to be not much more than a nudist, "free love" (sex) cult who built a mockup of UFO.

Manly P. Hall: UFOs, Flying Saucers, Space Ships, Aliens and Gov. Black Ops

It is always curious to ponder how much of that which Manly P. Hall expounded to the uninitiated is factual. After all, Hall was a 33 degree Freemason and thus, sworn to secrecy and deception. Of course, all one can do it take that which he stated and dissect it. In this case, we are focusing on a lecture of his dated to 1950 AD titled, "The Case of the Flying Saucers."

The *Manly P. Hall* website which reproduced the lecture notes introduces it by stating, "of great value in an historical sense and may or may not reflect either the **genuine views or tactical obfuscations** of such secretive fraternal organizations as the Scottish Rite or the Dark Brotherhood of the Langley Lodge" (emphasis added, point made!).

One complexity pertaining to the issue of aliens, UFO, flying saucers, etc. is that there are a lot of concepts and experiences that are lumped together. These include literal *UFOs* (simply an object that is flying but is not identified which could be anything at all) and *spaceships/spacecraft* which may be termed *flying saucers* (if they are in a saucer-like shape).

Moreover, there are *contactees, experiencers, abductees,* etc. An abduction by "aliens" may not have anything to do with spaceships as finding oneself in an operation-like room may or may not be in a craft. Also, people who have contact and experiences with "aliens" may or may not have seen or have been taken aboard a craft.

In any regard, to survey that with which Hall dealt in his lecture, consider his following statements.
He notes that "some of these accounts, including the flying cucumber, and the report of a great space ship that took fifteen minutes to float across the horizon…huge disks, some being two hundred and fifty feet in diameter…some of them are comparatively small."

He also mentions "floating cigars" (likely the same as the "flying cucumber"—what, no pickles!). He also notes that "There is the report that some are luminous, according to others, they appear to be either a silver light or white disk."

Overall, he sets the premise of the lecture as "our purpose is to analyze certain aspects of the human mind in connection with the mysterious case of the Flying Saucers." Since his premise is "certain aspects of the human mind" he tells of the doings of a stage magician, an illusionist, and refers to "the disorientation of [the audience's] judgment" and the possible correlation to the UFO phenomenon via "the delusion of masses."

On this issue of the mind, he notes:
> Once a story starts it is almost impossible to determine how far it will go and how many variations it will assume before the journey is ended. Like interesting fragments of gossip it develops jet propulsion and also passes through innumerable transformations, so the final account has little resemblance to the original story.
> Knowing these tendencies of the human mind, these tendencies that are present in

perfectly honest and honorable people, we
have to approach all remarkable accounts,
not in an effort to demonstrate how
remarkable they are, but to discover, if
possible some simple, natural, normal
explanation, clinging to that until that
explanation itself obviously falls.
There are always levels of explanations
ascending from the simple to the complex.
We should carefully wear out every level,
exhausting its most reasonable probabilities
before we ascend to more rarefied strata of
opinions.

Interestingly, he notes that one reason that the impressive
magical illusions failed to capture the audience is that
"folks of our generation are insulted rather than amused
when they are fooled." We have reached a point when folks
of our generation expect to be fooled (by the media,
government, etc.) and often do not bother going beyond to
find the facts behind the acts.

One may expect that a personage so learned in the
occult/esoteric as Hall would delve into metaphysics,
mystical mystery religions in order to seek to understand
the "mysterious case of the Flying Saucers." Yet, from that
perspective, just about the only thing he states is, "I do not
believe the next Avatar will arrive on a flying saucer."

In fact, as noted above, the complexity of the subject also
includes that UFOs, here meaning objects that are flying
and thought to be alien in nature, can be actually real
material 3D vehicles but can also be spheres of light, etc.

It appears that Hall restricted his lecture, perhaps on
purpose, to actual vehicles and thus, keeps the focus on

secret government projects and human technologies
(which, he assures us time and time again, are best kept
secret and thus, from the public so as to ensure national
security).

For these reasons, he concludes, "the space ship as a
solution to the present dilemma should be held, it seems to
me, as a last recourse to be considered only when every
other explanation fails." He concludes that they are not
alien space ships but human craft of whatever sorts.
He does, it seems rightly, note that we should, "bear in
mind also the association between the concept of the flying
saucer and the rapidly intensifying scientific-fiction
literature which is getting more and more attention in the
popular mind each year."
He also notes that "we can only assume that the space ship
theory is interesting people who are interested in the
scientific-fiction approach to life, but not those deeply
concerned with the salvation of the planet."

Here he is referring to nuts and bolts vehicles and thus the
scientific interest. Had he gone the other way, the
metaphysical mystical route he would have seen that "those
deeply concerned with the salvation of the planet" are very
much interested in UFOs of that sort. This is because
"aliens" are constantly urging humanity to come together in
order to save the Earth and this inevitably leads to the, shall
we say interesting, conclusion that humans must for a one
world government, one world religion, etc.; a *New Age
Alien World Order*.

He retells of his own, literal, UFO experience and what /
how he thought about it:
        Out on a ranch there of several thousand
        acres, and standing on the side of a hill with
        the view extending from ten, twenty or thirty

miles, I noticed one afternoon an extraordinary roar. It was far stronger and more powerful than the sound of any ordinary airplane motor, even a large transport or passenger plane. Suddenly without any warning whatever, this roaring took on the proportions of a definite vibration and something moved at an incredible rate passing almost directly over the place where I was standing.

That it was moving very close to the ground was evidenced from the fact that pinion trees not more than ten feet high were bent half way to the ground. The thing passed in a fraction of a second, but I saw absolutely nothing although there was ample visibility for miles in the direction in which the sound seemed to fade out. What it was I have not the slightest idea…

The thought that came to mind was that it was a jet-propelled instrument of some kind, moving more rapidly than the human perception could follow, and by the time I could organize myself to look for it, it was gone. That almost certainly was the answer. It is also quite possible that the sound of the instrument, or whatever it was, was such that it actually was moving in the opposite direction from that which the sound seemed to be traveling, and in looking in one direction I failed to see it because it moved in the opposite direction.

Anyway, nothing was visible, it left no track

of any kind, no smoke or gas, there was a terrific roar as it moved over the ground, bending the trees and it was gone. Well, at that time what was going on in these research laboratories was not known to us, but it seemed almost certain that it was a high powered, possibly jet-propelled plane.

I thought no more of it and said nothing about it until it came to my mind in connection with the project saucer. Almost certainly these things have an explanation in terms of the incredible advancements that have been made in scientific research in recent years.

With regards to "the possibility that the so-called flying saucers were a guided or propelled weapon, and that they were the result of experimental research in military armament" he stated, "I imagine that if at any time since the flurry began Mr. Gallup had conducted a poll on public opinion, he would have found the idea that they were experimental research in arms was held by the majority of people."

Well, the fact is that Gallup had already taken a poll August, 1947 AD which concluded that out of ten people, nine had heard of the "shining discs" reported as "flying saucers" cited by Kenneth Arnold in June 1947 AD near Mount Rainier in Western Washington (which were most likely WWII style "flying wing" airplanes). As it turns out by that year's end circa 850 UFO sightings were reported in the USA alone.

But having heard about it is one thing and speculating

about what they are is another. The poll asked "What do you think these saucers are?" and the results are as follows:

No answer, don't know: 33%

Imagination, optical illusions, mirages, etc.: 29%

US secret weapon, part of atomic bomb, etc.: 15%

Other explanations: 9%

Hoax: 10%

Weather forecasting devices: 3%

Searchlights on airplanes: 2%

Russian secret weapon: 1%

The percentages add up to 102 because some gave more than one answer.

More specifically, "Guesses ranged all the way from practical to miraculous….a sign of the world's end….radio waves from the Bikini atomic bomb explosion…a new product being put out by the 'DuPont people'…a publicity or advertising stunt…some kind of meteor or comet."

Hall notes that "Winchell mentioned the flying saucers in his column, telling the people not to worry, it was a government secret." This would date to 1949 AD but no further citation is offered. This is, essentially, Hall's own view:

We know that on various continents in secluded areas very elaborate experimental laboratories have been functioning for a number of years…There seems to be very good grounds for believing flying saucers are an experimental project…are the products of our own research equipment, that the flying saucer is some type of research device, an experimental device for either defensive or offensive armament. It is the only practical explanation that exists.

This explanation violates none of the
essential facts of the matter.

On the question of extra-terrestrial aliens, he concludes:
There seems to be no reason for the
assumption, and no actual-proof, that these
mysterious flying saucers and their retinues
of other factors have to be explained as
belonging to some other universe, or coming
to us from out of space...where it means
fifteen, twenty or twenty-five years of travel
through space at an incredible speed, with
fuel problems almost beyond estimation,
traveling at a speed almost as great as that of
light, we might be wise and look for
something simpler, and only depend upon
such a concept in an emergency. Where
everything else fails we are forced to fall
back on the miraculous as an explanation of
the problem we face.

Lastly, note that he notes:
It would be impossible to assume that we
would have the present sense of
complacency in the matter if we really
believed that these ships navigated by
intelligent creatures capable of building
them were approaching and sailing around
in good military formation, not alone
entirely, but in bunches and clusters, without
a definite reaction from the only group that
could really estimate what it means, and that
is, your scientific body.

Well, considering the "Arizona lights" and other cases,
perhaps they have come "in good military formation...in

bunches and clusters." But then again, would not the secret gov. ops human military fly "in good military formation…in bunches and clusters"?

In fact, we identify "good military formation…bunches and clusters" in relation to "good military formation…bunches and clusters" by being previously aware of "good military formation…bunches and clusters" via experience with "good military formation…bunches and clusters."

In other words, this point seems to be neither here nor there.

> *…the prince of the power of the air, of the spirit that is now working in the sons of disobedience…*
> —Ephesians 2:2

Allen H. Greenfield's Occult UFOnauts and Men in Black

When there are no words to literally
describe what one knows, one speaks
in the language of mythos. So have I done.

Secret Cipher of the UFOnauts

The claims made for Allen H. Greenfield's 1994 AD book *Secret Cipher of the UFOnauts* are, with a statement from Amazon as an example, that "For decades, rumors have circulated that the UFO phenomenon is somehow directly linked to Occultism. Now, veteran UFOlogist Allen Greenfield" who is also an occultist himself, goes "beyond speculation" via "the discovery of a hidden Secret Cipher used by UFOnauts, Contactees, Occult Adepts and their Secret Chiefs."

In short, Greenfield concocted a numerological system whereby to allegedly break down the names of "aliens" the names of their planets, etc. into numbers and then these numbers are interpreted so as to derive some sort of meaning.

I am going to quote extensively so as to relate how he views the relationship between UFOs and aliens with occultism. Note that most of that which he has to say is very esoteric so take from it that which you can discern.

Au fond, his premise is:

> To those few of us trained in both occultism
> and UFO lore over many years, the parallels

are remarkable. If nothing else, we deal here
with similarly constituted mythologies.

Greenfield notes the subjective nature of his cipher in, for
example, asking a question based on some results he got

Does this mean that ORTHON is JESUS, or
LAM is GOD?
Hardly. The cipher, as becomes apparent to
the diligent researcher, only uses the name
or key-word for those in the know to
examine and find a curious correspondence,
pointing the way to whatever the essence of
the encounter is.

In the intro Jonathan Sellers writes:

I had come to some conclusions of my own,
as a result of study and practice of the body
of works that have been written by and
about Aleister Crowley, The Book of the
Law, Thelema, and other related paradigms.
These conclusions had a lot to do with the
idea of contact — or — rather —
communication: not only with the very same
types of Entities encountered by Crowley
and others, but Contact with what I came to
regard as "The Authentic Tradition."

He is referring to the attempts to trace the lineage of
magick to its original source. He continues:

The idea that there is an Authentic Tradition,
whose Initiates (and Custodians) contact
each other using these ancient tools, and
whose Contact and Communication extends
to those in the world of the Profanes is not
an idea that is new or shocking, certainly, to
those of us who have experienced such

Contacts and/or researched and studied the histories of THOSE WHO HAVE…It is interesting to see what society regards as "real" research, "real" scholarship, and so forth: anything that further divorces us from our roots in the Authentic Tradition is considered a good thing.

The term "the world of the Profanes" refers to the magickian's view of the world which they dichotomize between they, those in the (magickal) know, and the rest of humanity. Little children were taught this "us versus them" worldview via the Harry Potter stories and many others— within the Potter mythos non-magickians are "Muggle" or "No-Maj."

We are told of:

Aleister Crowley, who contacted "præterhuman intelligences"—such as "LAM," or Aiwass - an early prototype of the now familiar Grey Alien or E. T.

In the next book of Greenfield's that I will quote, he added:

Crowley's rather well-known sketch of the being Lam resembles anticipates, in fact - the large headed beings described in many more recent UFO Abduction Cases.

As I elucidated within my book *Aleister Crowley in Pop-Occulture*: as per Crowley, LAM is the being who dictated a very Satanically blasphemous text, *The Book of the Law* the infamous motto of which is "Do what thou wilt shall be the whole of the law.

In any case, that is why Aiwass is noted as being a gray alien prototype.

In the next book noted Greenfield adds, "AIWAZ, the original name for what Crowley called, 'mine own guardian angel.'"

Quoting Crowley's *Magick in Theory and Practice* (p. 131), William Ramsey points out:
> THE BEAST 666 (Crowley) has preferred to let names stand as they are, and to proclaim simply that AIWAZ — the solar-phallic-hermetic "Lucifer" is His own Holy Guardian Angel, and "The Devil" SATAN or HADIT of our particular unit of the Starry Universe.[26]

Greenfield notes:
> IN 1944, near the end of his life, Aleister Crowley wrote one of his students in California:
>> "My observation of the Universe convinces me that there are beings of intelligence and power of a far higher quality than anything we can conceive of as human ... the one and only chance for mankind to advance as a whole is for individuals to make contact with such beings."

We are also told of the "Greatly Honored Brother P-Achad-O" who is also specified as having been "Crowley's 'magical son'" and who:
> ...in The British Journal of Ceremonial Magick. He went on to say,
>> "The law of Thelema is the green shoot of spring opening up amongst the death and decay of a defunct Aeon. It is hardly visible, yet it will

grow to produce an as-yet unknown
species of Mankind.
A Mankind who will look back on
these centuries as the truly dark ages
of instinctual man: when men killed
each other for illusory gain based
upon the idea that it is possible to gain
anything in a world in which we have
no permanent home. It is as
impossible to imagine Thelemic man
as it would be impossible for an ape to
imagine he could be us."
("Thelemic" being from the Greek word for
Will, thelema—that is, a humanity governed
by Pure Will rather than idle whim.)

We are beginning to see a claimed correlation between
occultism, aliens and human evolution.

Greenfield continues:
It was widely assumed that the Men in Black
were either government agents or
extraterrestrials, but as researchers Wilgus
and Keel have shown, the eye in the triangle
was sometimes their only insignia, while my
own research showed startling parallels to
certain black magick rituals in medieval
times which provoked visitations by what
was often called "the Man in Black" —
widely understood to be the Devil himself.
Even [UFOlogist Gray] Barker noted that
Albert K. Bender's experiments were more
like a magical conjuration than an attempt at
extraterrestrial communication. Any
initiated magician reading Bender's

accounts would recognize the elements of magical conjuration immediately.

As for "the eye in the triangle," it had previously been noted:

> Crowley encountered "the one eye" or "Achad Ayin" in Bou-Saada, near Max Theon's home, on December 4, 1909, while scrying the 13th Enochian Aethyr.

In essence, "Christian Gnosticism" is a contradiction in terms as it denotes taking that which is stated by the Bible and turning it upside down, inside out and backward. On this view, God is evil and the serpent/Satan is the savior. Greenfield notes:

> ...confusions of a deliberate nature exist; the ancient Gnostics uncovered a cipher which clearly indicates that the story of the Garden of Eden in its conventional form is turned on its head. The Serpent is clearly the symbol of Knowledge, Wisdom, the Kundalini Yogic force, the Will-current—that is, it is the symbol of Liberation and Self-Mastery. The jealous "gods," as read in the original manuscripts, are clearly the forces of blockage, self-denial and repression—which is to say, the Intelligences governing the Black Lodge. This Knowledge of Good and Evil and Life and Death has been the Terrible Secret of Initiates throughout history, recorded in ciphers and myths, and passed on through ritual.

He touches upon this again in the book from which I will quote below:

Perhaps the early Gnostics had it right in turning the Genesis story on its head. In the Gnostic Version, as in the ancient Hypostasis of the Archons ("the reality of the rulers") we find that the Serpent of Wisdom is the defender of humanity (in Hebrew Cipher "serpent" and "messiah" have the same numerical value), offering us the Tree of Wisdom and the Tree of Immortality, in opposition to The Authorities, or Celestial Rulers, who wish to keep us in ignorance and in the shadow of death.

The Serpent or Dragon is a close relative (mythically speaking) to our presumed benefactor, the Oannes, Prometheus, Odin and the other celestial Titans who, at great cost to themselves, steal for us the fire of heaven.

But, as the Yada di' Shi'ite, Aiwass, G.I. Gurdjiefi, Phil Dick or Frederich Nietsche would tell us, we are our own salvation or damnation.

Some side notes:
Yada di' Shi'ite refers to an *ascended master* style being who lived on Earth circa 500,000 years ago in the Himalayas.

We were already told of the stereotypical alien gray Aiwass.

I mention the mystic G.I. Gurdjiefi within the chapter on Whitley Strieber.

Phil Dick was an author and appears to have been possessed as you can hear him described it in his own words in a video I posted.[27]

Frederich Nietsche (actually Friedrich Nietzsche) was an Atheist philosopher. Interestingly, recall the reference to a future "as-yet unknown species of Mankind" well, Nietzsche spoke of such as being the *Übermensch*, the supermen, the overmen.

Well, Greenfield notes, "This Unmanifest cannot be understood in the external sense, but can be Known in the Gnostic sense by the initiate or perfected sentient being, the Ubermensch" and:

> It would seem that the immediate goal of the Black Brothers is to delay the Manifestation of the New Aeon, the birth of the magical child and the realization of the ubermensch through diversion of the Will-current into less than useless power plays, demoralizing materialist and superstitious delusions, New Age jargon, etc.
> The classic example in the Twentieth Century was the Nazi appropriation, under Black Lodge influence, of the very concept of the ubermensch, and sidetracking it into a pathetic racialist caricature of Nietzsche's super being.

In the next referenced book he writes, "What is sometimes called 'the Black Lodge,' which we may associate with the Gnostic Demiurge."

A relevant connection to this is that which Greenfield explains as "The story of our interaction with the UFOnauts begins with the Qabalistic Tree of Life, and the Chakra system of the body." I take this to mean that, as was the case with Whitley Strieber, Barbara Marciniak, et al., when you open a door into your body there something will inevitably enter and take residence therein, "the unclean spirit…taketh with himself seven other spirits more wicked than himself, and they enter in and dwell there: and the last state of that man is worse than the first" (Matthew 12:45).

Within Greenfield's second appendix *Identifying Aliens*, he writes:

> …we have not been taken over, we are not property, not because aliens do not want our planet, nor because others have protected us, but because the dark forces from deep space are, quite simply, and for some mysterious reason, afraid of us Earthlings.

> They are, in fact, frightened to death of us.

> This shows up in some of the literature,
> • the jealousy of the gods of genesis that having gained wisdom from the Tree of Knowledge, we might eat of the Tree of Life and thus become gods ourselves
> • the story of the Titan Prometheus bringing fire from heaven to humanity, for which the gods punished him in unimaginable ways

Note that Greenfield referred to the serpent as being "the symbol of Knowledge, Wisdom…the Serpent of Wisdom" referred to "the Tree of Wisdom" and this is just about where every Gnostic-style reading of Genesis 3 ends: with generic knowledge and/or wisdom. Surprisingly, Greenfield more accurately references that it is, specifically the "Knowledge of Good and Evil" and adds "and Life and Death."

Of course, "good" had already been mentioned eight times before Genesis 2:9's mention of the tree of knowledge of good and evil. So, pray tell, what could possibly have been gained from the fruit of that tree? Evil (perhaps the dichotomy between good and evil).

In any case, Greenfield's presupposition has him reading Genesis 3 as being about "the jealousy of the gods of genesis" and their fear of Adam and Eve "having gained wisdom from, note the lack of specificity (since this fit his context at the time he stated it) "the Tree of Knowledge" period, and claims that ousting them from the garden was so as to keep them from becoming gods (which Greenfield applies to humanity as a whole).

Yet, Genesis 3:22 states, "And the LORD God said, Behold, the man is become as one of us, to know good and evil: and now, lest he put forth his hand, and take also of the tree of life, and eat, and live for ever." This seems to be about Adam and Eve having "become as one of us" only in the way of "know[ing] good and evil" and, I will add, having a propensity towards choosing evil and not just knowing about it, so that "lest he put forth his hand, and take also of the tree of life, and eat, and live for ever" so that God was gracefully preventing them from an eternal life of sin.

Greenfield continues:

> …secret chiefs or hidden masters may have good reason to mythologize themselves, and encourage those in direct contact with them to follow suit on the border where magical philosophy meets with its political implications, the need for secrecy assumes a more practical rationale. The Secret Chiefs

may be secret not because they are myths or immortals, but because they are neither.

He refers to "S.L. MacGregor Mathers' account of his relations with the Secret Chiefs":

>...there should be some eminent Member especially chosen to act as the link between the Secret Chiefs and the more external forms of the Order...such a member should be me who...in every sense to a blind and unreasoning obedience to those Secret Chiefs...I believe they are human beings living on this Earth, but possessed of terrible and super-human powers.

Aleister Crowley's Liber LXVI/Book 66, the "Book of the Bloody Star" may, Greenfield tells us, "be thought of as the Inner Order instruction in a kind of sexual magick designed to make the Adept superior to any 'mind control' available to the Gray Aliens or any such beings who use psychosexual and implant techniques during Abductions to control humans."

Secret Rituals of the Men in Black

In 2005 AD, Greenfield published a follow up book titled *Secret Rituals of the Men in Black* from which I will now quote:

>The reason for all these profoundly bizarre goings-on became apparent only when we "cracked" the key secret cipher used in such rituals and spontaneous encounters. Once realized, a bizarre design, previously suspected by only a few diverse researchers working in widely differing fields, was fully exposed. It revealed an intricate worldwide pattern of communication between

Ultraterrestrial Forces almost totally beyond
our comprehension and human adepts,
stretching from remote antiquity to the
present moment....

In distant times...there is a fairly consistent
account of God-like and perhaps amphibious
beings from the sky...They visited Earth,
establishing a nucleus of priest-kings and
scientists who have carried forth a secret
tradition of contact, communication and
Ultraterrestrial overlordship - and rebellion
against that overlordship. This tradition is
displayed in various rituals through myth
and cipher...

The entire literature of magical invocation
and evocation, seen in this light, is revealed
to be a disguised transmission of these
technologies...

Odin, or Wotan in Teutonic myth, is
identified with Hermes, Thoth and other sky
gods who, at great cost to themselves (in
some cases) come to Earth to teach
humanity the liberal arts and sciences.

Note that within different contexts, by "technologies" he is
either referring to actual nuts and bolt or to know how—or
both.

He also notes:
    ...the strange words and names that show up
    in Masonic Lodge settings are similar in
    form and purpose to those which show up in
    contact cases. They show up in modern

> cases of Angelic Visitation…They also
> show up in demonology…
>
> The occult literature has always considered
> ASHTAR, or Astaroth, a fallen angel, that
> is, a malevolent demon.

He also notes that "The pulp fiction magazines of the 1930s
and 40s were…full of occultists, future UFOlogists, and the
like." I will add that such magazines and comic books (and
the cartoons and movies which followed therefrom) were
created by people with mental disorders, drug addicts,
occultists—or were some combination of two or all three of
these.
For details on this see my articles on Jeffrey Kripal's book
Mutants and Mystics and on Christopher Knowles' book
Our Gods Wear Spandex.[28]

Greenfield deles into more esoterism by writing, "13th
Enochian Aethyr, called 'ZIM' transports the scryer
directly to the Sirius planetary system, where one can meet
the Oannes…under the name NEMO" and, just to put the
fun back in dis*fun*ction, I will note that *nemo* backwards is
omen.

Alec Hidell's *Chronicles of the Grey Lodge* is quoted
thusly:

> The research community has consistently
> failed to address the real issues posed by
> flying saucers, which relate not to
> propulsion systems, aerodynamics and the
> like, but to the human psyche and the
> magical currents that inform it.

Greenfield notes:

The highest-ranking public initiate-adept known by the present writer, Rev. Michael Bertiaux of Chicago, has long maintained that the (Egyptian) Rite of Memphis-Misraim was a "front" (in a sense) for Ultraterrestrial technology.

...the Knowledge of the Secret was, indeed, intentionally hidden in the symbolism and structure of "High Degree Freemasonry" including the Egyptian Rite of Memphis and Misraim, as Grand Master Michael Bertiaux has suggested.
"That rather lifeless system, which contained some rather interesting Egyptian roots," Bertiaux wrote, "was really quite remarkable. It was the design for the computer and energy system of what we might now be tempted to call something like a UFO object or projection from some empirical or chaotic [occult power zone]; but, which at that time, as strange as it might seem to the uninformed reader of these matters, was posing rather inconspicuously as an Egyptian Rite of Ancient Freemasonry with the name of 'Memphis-Misraim.'"

It is noted that "The Vesica" also know as *vesical piscis* "shows up again in the impression of the Right foot print of George Adamski's space contact ORTHON."

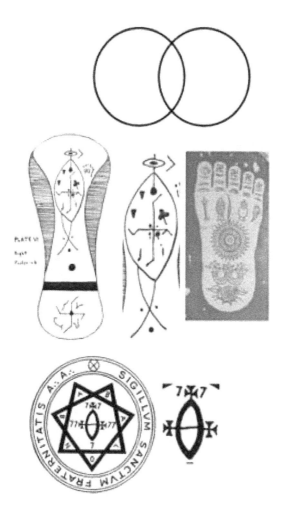

Here I am depicting a vesical, the Adamski related footprint and how Adamski seems to have stolen the concept from Buddhism's footprint of Buddha. Now, since Paganism, by any other occult name, is all about sex (and blood) they interpret the interlocking section of the vesical as representing a generative matrix: as in a woman's reproductive organ. Thus, the symbol is often simplified by removing the outer portions of the circles and only using the middle football-like shape as can be seen within Aleister Crowley's *Seal of Babalon* sigil.

Greenfield writes:
> ...a ritual last revised in English in the year 1911. The ritual goes on to inform the candidate that, "there are in heaven very many pleasant cities, and none without a divine garrison"...

> Those who survive, the candidate is told, shall be those that "neither the flood, nor the black conflagration" can harm, i.e. those who are space borne or amphibious in nature.

> The senior initiator, termed "The Highest" now explains the reason for this ritual mythological drama.

> "There are in it," he tells the candidate, "traces of the primeval creed which taught that humanity arose from a marriage of Heaven and Earth."

Within this context, it seems notable that in the previous book he had noted that as "Annemarie Schimmel explains it, 'the sacred marriage between macrocosm and microcosm'—which is the precise role of the medium and contactee as well."

L. Ron Hubbard and Scientology

Scientology is black magic that is just spread out over a long time period. To perform black magic generally takes a few hours or, at most, a few weeks. But in Scientology

it's stretched out over a lifetime, and so you don't see it.
—L. Ron Hubbard, Jr. aka Ron Wolf[29]

Speaking of vesical, Scientology's *Church of Spiritual Technology* wing has been using a version of it to mark some of their territory.

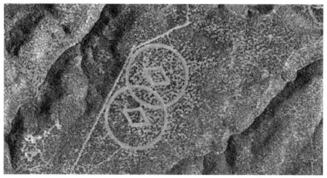

Greenfield writes the following of the founder of *Dianetics* and *Scientology*:

> Hubbard Sr. made clear he was talking about
> the sex magick central to the OTO system,
> but with a unique twist:

> "Sex by will, Love by will - no caring
> and no sharing - no feelings... Sex is
> the route to power. Scarlet women!
> They are the secret to the doorway.
> Use and consume. Feast. Drink the
> power through them. Waste and
> discard them."[30]

> ...with his "friend" Hubbard, then in the
> very process of making off with [Jack]
> Parsons' money and lover; a man who was
> to tell his son, Ron Jr., a few years later, to
> use and discard Scarlet Women. In what
> sense "scarlet?" the younger Hubbard
> asked...

> "Scarlet," the Scientology "Source" replied,
> "the blood of their bodies; the blood of their
> souls... bend their bodies; bend their minds;
> bend their wills; beat back the past."
> This is the grossest perversion of Crowley's
> teaching.

As an example of Greenfield's cipher, he writes, "'The
blood of their bodies, the blood of their souls,' as he put it.
It should therefore come as no surprise that L. RON
HUBBARD = 115 = BLOOD TO BLOOD in The Book of
Babalon." But, of course, Hubbard's name is not "L." but
"Lafayette" which would result in a different number which
would result in a different sentence, etc.

As for L. Ron Hubbard, Jr. aka Ron Wolf, see my article *L.
Ron Hubbard's son speaks out: Scientology or
Satanology.*[31]
But was Hubbard, Sr.'s the grossest perversion of
Crowley's teaching or is this Greenfield's perversion of

Crowley's teaching? After all, Crowley wrote "One can always replace a woman in a few days" (letter dated January 17, 1929 AD) and "Practically all women ought to be chloroformed at 35...they're all whores, anyhow" (diary entry, January 3 & 4, 1931 AD).

Crowley, under the pen name *Baphomet*, is quoted from his *De Arte Magica*:

> We do opine that it is better and easier that the other party should be in ignorance of the sacred character of the Office. It is enough if that assistant be formed by Nature signally for the physical task, robust, vigorous, eager, sensible, hot and healthy; flesh, nerve and blood being tense, quick, and lively, easily enflamed, and nigh inextinguishable.

Greenfield elucidates "Crowley is telling us that a partner in sexual magick should, ideally, in his opinion, be involved for the sake of sensual pleasure, pure and simple." Note that the band *Aerosmith*'s Steven Tyler admitted that he practiced Crowley's sex magick in his autobiography. He specifies that he is not claiming that "every girl I slept with" was consciously involved or that he "asked her to pray for the same thing I was praying for" but that he was consciously practicing ritualistic sex magick and having sex as a vehicle for prayer "namely that Aerosmith would become the greatest American band.'"[32] This is why I included Tyler in my book *Aleister Crowley's Influence on Pop-Occulture*.

Greenfield continues:

> Parsons and Hubbard were out in the Mojave Desert...and received a "communication" he referred to as Liber 49,

The Book of Babalon, which identifies its
source as Babalon Herself...
[Jack Parson's] Liber 49 asserts, among
other things...
> "Let me behold thee naked and lusting
> after me, calling upon my name... Let
> me receive all thy manhood within my
> Cup, climax upon climax, joy upon
> joy... Gather together in the covens as
> of old... Gather together in secret, be
> naked and shameless and rejoice in
> my name."

...a vision Hubbard had "of a savage and
beautiful woman riding naked on a great catlike beast."

Of course, the very concept of "Babalon" is that of Babylon
(with spelling changed so as to meet some occult
numerological agenda) and Hubbard's vision is reminiscent
of "a woman sit upon a scarlet coloured beast, full of names
of blasphemy...And upon her forehead was a name written,
Mystery, Babylon The Great, The Mother Of Harlots And
Abominations Of The Earth" (Revelation 17:3, 5).

Referring to the Mojave:
This is, of course, the same area that the
Adamski Orthon contact took place a few
years later, the area in which Dr. Wilhelm
Reich, M.D. conducted his experiments with
shooting down UFOs with Orgone Energy,
and various other UFO-related events.

Greenfield thinks that "the timing of the Babalon Working
and the arrival of the Post War Baby Boom is simultaneous

in an eerie sort of way" as much as he thinks that it ushered in the modern UFO era.

Recall the point about the authors of early sci-fi and comics well, we are told about Hubbard that:

> In pulp magazine circles, he had
> encountered any number of occultists and
> border occultists (Talbot Mundy, Col.
> Arthur Burks, Major Donald Keyhoe, Ray
> Palmer and Richard S. Shaver come to
> mind), and had already formulated the core
> of the "inner Scientology teaching" outlined
> above....

> He wished to bring this other world into
> Manifestation, but lacked the technical
> knowledge to do so. So, he came to the
> innocent sex magician Jack Parsons. In this
> version, the Babalon Working, guided by
> Hubbard, had little to do with "Babalon" and
> more to do with the hideous Old Ones of the
> H.P. Lovecraft Cthulhu Mythos.

> "A door opened; something came through"
> is the essence of this thesis, and the
> appearance of the first "flying saucer" case
> the following year is considered, in this
> outré rumor, not coincidental at all.

> The Babalon Working permanently
> alienated Parsons from Crowley, but the
> work of the ill-fated rocket scientist has
> more recently been reevaluated in a more
> favorable light by present day occultists and
> UFOlogists alike....

Hubbard...probably learned the [UFOnaut] cipher from his pulp magazine occultist connections....Ray Palmer and Richard Shaver were using the cipher, or something much like it, throughout the 1940s, in the pages of Amazing Stories and elsewhere...

Hubbard, we recall, according to biographer Bent Corydon, spoke to his son Ron, Jr. about the blood of the Scarlet Woman in terms of being the key to "real power."

Hubbard has a connection to the occult and to UFO alien speculation. In fact, he goes well beyond speculation and builds the core of his *therapy*, the very point of his *Church of Scientology* upon aliens.

OT III was once a top level secret of *Scientology*'s hierarchical mysteries. Warren McShane, president of the Scientology subsidiary *Religious Technology Center* claimed that OT III "are not trade secrets."[33]
Well, whatever that means, it is a fact that there was much—litigious—ado when that of which it consists was revealed. The, public, revelation occurred via a 1995 AD court case *Religious Technology Center v. F.A.C.T.Net, Inc., et al.*, via a Feb. 2011 AD *New Yorker* article, via the *Trapped in the Closet* episode of the satirical cartoon show *South Park* (which led to Scientologist Isaac Haze, who was the voice of one of the characters, to quite the show— apparently, besmirching everyone else was acceptable but not once it hits home) and subsequently in innumerable websites, etc.

OT III was conceptualized by L. Ron Hubbard circa 1967 AD and is a history of how psychological trauma came to be within humans—in a manner of speaking. The story goes that 75 million years ago Xenu (aka *Xemu*) was the head of the Galactic Confederation and faced the problem of overpopulation. His final solution was to load circa a billion alien beings into spaceships/UFOs, deposit them on Earth inside of volcanoes and drop hydrogen bombs on them.

So traumatizing was this that the souls, which Hubbard termed *thetans* (generally pronounced as *thee-tons* and somewhat like *satans*), of these alien beings fanned out into the Earth and possess, as it were, human beings. These are what Scientology claims to be able to dislodge via their styled form of exorcism.

Of interest may be the fact that they believe that traumatic past life memories can be triggered as to bring the thetans to the surface so as to do away with them. This is why, for example, the book cover of, and commercials for, *Dianetics* features an exploding volcano. It is not an erupting volcano but a volcano that is being exploded by bombs by Xenu.

Keep in mind that the bottom line is that alien beings came to Earth, died a traumatic enough death so that they became disembodied, that they sought to inhabit, or embody, humans and that Hubbard claims the most effective method for removing them. Finally, note that Xenu, the perpetrator, is said to have been imprisoned by his own lieutenants who mutinied and is said to still (75 million years later) be alive and incarcerated here on Earth "in an electronic mountain trap."

As per Greenfield's cipher "XENU = 78 = ALL POWER and FIRE and MAGICK and MY STAR and NUIT, the latter being the Egyptian (and Crowlean) Star Goddess."

Greenfield had noted:

> Hubbard almost certainly used his
> considerable charismatic and hypnotic

ability to implant Parsons with a bogus "4th Chapter of The Book of the Law" - but he could not resist leaving his signature all over it, in terms of his name, ideas and motives, encrypted in the UFOnaut Cipher. He probably learned the cipher from his pulp magazine occultist connections.

That Hubbard was into implanting ideas and doing so in the form of encryptions seems to be a major premise upon Scientology. This is because, for example, the cover of Dianetics is an image of a volcano but knowing the Xenu story we realize that it is not erupting but is being made to explode. In fact, the original cover of *Scientology: A New Slant on Life* is nothing but a dropping bomb: how do you like that for a therapy-style book? (later editions replaced the bomb with Jesus on the cross and later ones still have a colorful upon door within a black and white background).

In my book *Aleister Crowley's Influence on Pop-Occulture* I note how Scientology is now using a simplified Rosicrucian cross as their main symbol, he had a teaching called *The Golden Dawn*, etc.

The purpose of employing such symbols is to trigger past life memories of when humans were aliens so as to begin dealing with ridding oneself of the side effects of trauma.

Some more cipher examples are:
The nonsense name given to Earth by Hubbard in the Xenu legend, TEEGEEACK = 158 = BABALON TIME in The Book of Babalon, but also NINE MOONS , the gestation cycle of human beings. More ominously, as Xenu regarded Earth as a disposable backwater planet, TEEGEEACK

= 158 = AN APPENDIX…Most
significantly, defying all chance
expectations, TEEGEEACK = 158 =
PLANET EARTH!

Dozens of such Hubbard-specific phrases
exist in this Book [Liber 49], suggesting that
Parsons, in writing it, was responding to a
posthypnotic suggestion by Hubbard.
Parsons then apparently proceeded to "open
a door" and the era of flying saucers began.

The Stuff of Dreams

"The Stuff of Dreams" is the title of Greenfield's postscript
wherein he writes:

IN 1980 I ran into the dead end wall that
many UFOlogists have encountered in their
research.

The evidence I had accumulated suggested
to me that the UFO mystery was something
closely akin to an infinite series of nested
boxes, and that illusion after illusion after
illusion produced much speculation but little
useful information. My old friend Gene
Duplantier had once described UFOlogy as
"like a long walk down an endless tube,"
and many of the best, most thoughtful
students of the subject, on realizing this,
simply gave up.

Ten years were to pass before another break
came my way in the form of the Ultraterrestrial Cipher that provided the
breakthrough that explains, for me, not only
the UFOs, but many Masonic pass words,

ancient legends and occult secrets [just keep in mind the subjective nation of the cipher].

I stumbled upon the cipher; I did not invent it, owe no allegiance to it, make no claims for it other than that it "fits" easily the subject matter I have applied it to in this and my previous work, Secret Cipher of the UFOnauts. I regard it as experimental, but consider it a working solution to some of the most profound enigmas thoughtful people have dwelt upon over the last several centuries.

Two things to take note of: First, in discussing various Masonic degrees, words and "secrets" I have been at some pain to avoid violation of the ritual privacy of these societies...Such rituals are "Mystery Plays" and are fully understandable only in the doing, not merely in the telling.

Second, there is a sense in which the Oannes Mythos, the Mystery Plays and Rituals presented here, the very Ultraterrestrial Visitors themselves inherently overlap with the stuff of dreams.

They represent a Reality more profound than our own, and as such cannot be taken verbatim or too literally. In this volume I have pulled out the stops and taken a plunge beyond the Reality Barrier. What I have found is the core of the Ultraterrestrial Secret, too numinous to be other than ineffable...

"To puzzle out an imaginary meaning
for this 'nonsense' sets one thinking of
the Mysteries; one enters into deep
contemplation of holy things and God
Himself leads the soul to real
illumination."
A. Crowley, "An Interlude," Book Four

Terry R. Wriste on the Ultraterrestrials

This is from an appendix and is a discussion between
Greenfield and Wriste. We begin with Wriste telling
Greenfield:

Neither you nor I have ever assumed that
Ultraterrestrials are either benevolent or
truthful...

Though supposedly the dual nature of the
[Sirius] system has been known for only
about a century, a number of traditional
African tribal peoples have retained a
detailed knowledge in their initiatory rituals
of Sirius B. Most well known are the Dogon,
but other related peoples also are aware of
this...

Greenfield: I had sort of thought Robert
Temple had covered that so well in The
Sirius Mystery that I hesitated to repeat his
data. I wanted to concentrate on the survival
of the Oannes legend in Freemasonry,
through applying the Ultraterrestrial Cipher
contained in The Book of the Law.

Wriste: ...In essence, the Dogon and other
tribal peoples which had contact, through

trade routes and the migration of peoples in ancient times, with the Berber-Carthegenian-GrecoRoman world, have accurate information on the fifty year rotation of Sirius B, its incredible mass, knowledge of the stars and planets, the human circulatory system and other matters as astoundingly out of historical sequence as the old maps of a preglacial Antarctica which, they say, was brought to them by 'fish men' from Sirius called Nommo, paralleling exactly the Babylonian Oannes, the Phonecian Dagon, and so forth.

The name of the Dogon people is derived, almost certainly, from that of the fish-god Dagon. It also reminds me a bit of "NEMO" as Crowley described his encounter in the Enochian Aethyrs. Crowley scryed the 13th Aethyr, called "ZIM" on December 4th, 1909 in a river bed near Bou-Saada in North Africa. He meets a being called "Nemo".

As I elucidate with the chapter on Robert Temple, this is simply inaccurate and it denotes a fundamental wrench within their ciphering and deciphering systems as they are basing some puzzle pieces upon falsehoods.

Wriste continues:

It is of more than passing interest that Sirius, Procyon, The Pleiades and Orion are names which show up quite often in the lore of UFOlogy and contacteeism. The contact-source identified as "Semjase" from the

Pleiades in the cases of Fred Bell and Billy
Meier is an example.

In occult lore, "Semjaza" (or Semyaza,
Semiaza, Shemhazai, etc.) is the fallen angel
Azza, or Uzza, a seraph who was tempted by
Ishtar to reveal the Secret Explicit Name.

This relates to the Masonic Third Degree, in
which the Grand Master is slain for failure
to reveal the "Master's Word" to ruffians.
Semjaza is said to hover between heaven
and Earth with lowered head, in the
constellation Orion. According to The Book
of Jubilees, Semjaza is one of the Watchers
sent from Heaven to instruct humanity.

Semjaza taught humanity what might be
called "witchcraft" - herbalism,
enchantments, etc.

I deal with the Semjase issue within the chapter on Billy
Meier.

Wriste notes:

> …what is mythic in this mythos, and what is
> literally real….The strangest thing is in
> figuring out why the UFOnauts abduct
> people, and what stops them from doing so.
> Since magical ritual contacts them and
> banishes them, we know either that they are
> magical beings, or magick is a technology,
> or both. But when I started working with
> Reichian technologies the Knights of Malta
> would give their fortunes to have, I noticed

something most strange. UFOs can be disintegrated by Reichian energies.

Greenfield: Well, that's strange, but hardly new; Reich himself said he did that in the '50s.

Wriste: Right. But consider what Reich worked with. He called it "Orgone Energy" which was a direct outgrowth of his work with Freudian Psychotherapy. Up through a certain point, he was an orthodox Freudian, until he discovered that the very energies that Freud addressed in psychological terms were explainable as a Universal Energy or Current, a kind of 'orgasmic flux' inherent in the universe, which could be channeled, quantified and, apparently, used to shoot down flying saucers.

Orgone Energy, it seems to me, is identical to the Love/Will current of Aleister Crowley's Book of The Law.

Greenfield: Wait a minute. Are you telling me that the energy behind human libido destroys Ultraterrestrial craft?

Wriste: "They drink our fear, like hungry ghosts. To drink instead our love is death unto them and their kin."

Martin Cannon "The Controllers: A New Hypothesis of Alien Abductions"

Such is the title of a most fascinating book that was published in 1996 AD (and has all but disappeared from public view which is why I posted an e-book version on my site[34]); who can tell what an updated version would look like, one that reflected today's technologies?

Martin Cannon writes:

Some time ago, I began to research these claims, concentrating my studies on the social and political environment surrounding the events…

Among ufologists, the term "abduction" has come to refer to an infinitely-confounding experience, or matrix of experiences, shared by a dizzying number of individuals, who claim that travelers from the stars have scooped them out of their beds, or snatched them from their cars, and subjected them to interrogations, quasi-medical examinations, and "instruction" periods.

Usually, these sessions are said to occur within alien spacecraft; frequently, the stories include terrifying details reminiscent of the tortures inflicted in Germany's death camps. The abductees often (though not always) lose all memory of these events;

they find themselves back in their cars or beds, unable to account for hours of "missing time." Hypnosis, or some other trigger, can bring back these haunted hours in an explosion of recollection — and as the smoke clears, an abductee will often spot a trail of similar experiences, stretching all the way back to childhood.

Perhaps the oddest fact of these odd tales: Many abductees, for all their vividly-recollected agonies, claim to love their alien tormentors. That's the word I've heard repeatedly: love.

...abduction scenarios have elicited two basic reactions: that of the Believer and the Skeptic.

The Believers — and here we should note that "Believers" and "abductees" are two groups whose memberships overlap but are in no way congruent — accept such stories at face value. They accept, despite the seeming absurdity of these tales, the internal contradictions, the askew logic of narrative construction, the severe discontinuity of emotional response to the actions described. The Believers believe, despite reports that their beloved "space brothers" use vile and inhuman tactics of medical examination — senseless procedures most of us (and certainly the vanguard of an advanced race) would be ashamed to inflict on an animal. The Believers believe, despite the difficulty of reconciling these unsettling tales with their own deliriums of benevolent off-worlders.

Occasionally, the rough notes of a rationalization are offered: "The aliens don't know what they are doing," we hear; or "Some aliens are bad." Yet the Believers confound their own reasoning when they insist on ascribing the wisdom of the ages and the beneficence of the angels to their beloved visitors. The aliens allegedly know enough about our society to go about their business undetected by the local authorities and the general public; they communicate with the abductees in human tongue; they concern themselves with details of the percipients' innermost lives — yet they remain so ignorant of our culture as to be unaware of the basic moral precepts concerning the dignity of the individual and the right to self-determination. Such dichotomies don't bother Believers; they are the faithful, and faith is assumed to have its mysteries. *Sancta Simplicitas.*

Conversely, the Skeptics dismiss these stories out of hand. They dismiss, despite the intriguing confirmatory details: the multiple witness events, the physical traces left by the ufonauts, the scars and implants left on the abductees. The skeptics scoff, though the abductees tell stories similar in detail — even certain tiny details, not known to the general public...

They [UFOs and UFO abductions] may well
be separate issues. Or, rather, they are
connected only in this: The myth of the UFO
has provided an effective cover story for an
entirely different sort of mystery. Remove
yourself from the Believer/Skeptic dialectic,
and you will see the third alternative.
As we examine this alternative, we will, of
necessity, stray far from the saucers. We
must turn our face from the paranormal and
concentrate on the occult — if, by "occult,"
we mean secret.

I posit that the abductees have been
abducted. Yet they are also spewing fantasy
— or, more precisely, they have been given
a set of lies to repeat and believe. If my
hypothesis proves true, then we must accept
the following: The kidnapping is real. The
fear is real. The pain is real. The instruction
is real. But the little grey men from Zeti
Reticuli are not real; they are constructs,
Halloween masks meant to disguise the real
faces of the controllers. The abductors may
not be visitors from Beyond; rather, they
may be a symptom of the carcinoma which
blackens our body politic...

Substantial evidence exists linking members
of this country's intelligence community
(including the Central Intelligence Agency,
the Defense Advanced Research Projects
Agency, and the Office of Naval
Intelligence) with the esoteric technology of
mind control. For decades, "spy-chiatrists"
working behind the scenes — on college

campuses, in CIA-sponsored institutes, and (most heinously) in prisons have experimented with the erasure of memory, hypnotic resistance to torture, truth serums, post-hypnotic suggestion, rapid induction of hypnosis, electronic stimulation of the brain, non-ionizing radiation, microwave induction of intracerebral "voices," and a host of even more disturbing technologies.
Some of the projects exploring these areas were ARTICHOKE, BLUEBIRD, PANDORA, MKDELTA, MKSEARCH and the infamous MKULTRA...

As a result of this research, I have come to the following conclusions:
1. Although misleading (and occasionally perjured) testimony before Congress indicated that the CIA's "brainwashing" efforts met with little success,[35] striking advances were, in fact, made in this field. As CIA veteran Miles Copeland once admitted to a reporter, "The congressional subcommittee which went into this sort of thing got only the barest glimpse."[36]

2. Clandestine research into thought manipulation has not stopped, despite CIA protestations that it no longer sponsors such studies. Victor Marchetti, 14-year veteran of the CIA and author of the renown expose, *The CIA and the Cult of Intelligence,* confirmed in a 1977 interview that the mind control research continues, and that CIA claims to the contrary are a "cover story."[37]

3. The Central Intelligence Agency was not the only government agency involved in this research.[38] Indeed, many branches of our government took part in these studies — including NASA, the Atomic Energy Commission, as well as all branches of the Defense Department.

To these conclusions I would append the following — not as firmly-established historical fact, but as a working hypothesis and grounds for investigation:
4. The "UFO abduction" phenomenon might be a continuation of clandestine mind control operations.

I recognize the difficulties this thesis might present to those readers emotionally wedded to the extraterrestrial hypothesis, or to those whose political Weltanschauung disallows any such suspicions. Still, the open-minded student of abductions should consider the possibilities. Certainly, we are not being narrow-minded if we ask researchers to exhaust all terrestrial explanations before looking heavenward.

Granted, this particular explanation may, at first, seem as bizarre as the phenomenon itself. But I invite the skeptical reader to examine the work of George Estabrooks, a seminal theorist on the use of hypnosis in warfare, and a veteran of Project MKULTRA. Estabrooks once amused himself during a party by covertly hypnotizing two friends, who were led to believe that the Prime Minister of England had just arrived; Estabrooks' victims spent an hour conversing with, and even serving drinks to, the esteemed visitor.[39]

For ufologists, this incident raises an inescapable question: If the Mesmeric arts can successfully evoke a non-existent Prime Minister, why can't a representative from the Pleiades be similarly induced?

But there is much more to the present day technology of mind control than mere hypnosis — and many good reasons to suspect that UFO abduction accounts are an artifact of continuing brainwashing/behavior modification experiments.

Moreover, I intend to demonstrate that, by using UFO mythology as a cover story, the experimenters may have solved the major problem with the work conducted in the 1950s — "the disposal problem," i.e., the question of "What do we do with the victims?"

If, in these pages, I seem to stray from the subject of the saucers, I plead for patience. Before I attempt to link UFO abductions with mind control experiments, I must first show that this technology exists. Much of the forthcoming is an introduction to the topic of mind control — what it is, and how it works.

Thus, my reference to technology as Cannon's research links known tech (again, dating up until 1996 AD) directly with abduction phenomenon. In other words, his hypothesis is that with the utilization of such tech, government entities *could* endues abduction experiences.

Billy Meier and the Plejarens

The Many Faces of Billy Meier: Semjase and the Buddha

Meier's is one of the most long-term alien contact cases and I will consider it from various vantage points from the message he received from the Pleiadians/Plejarens to the issue of the photos he took of the spacecraft and the various version of just who is Meier.

In a manner of speaking; reading about Meier is, in many ways, like reading about the Buddha.

According to some accounts; Meier is merely a nearly illiterate good ol' farm boy suddenly found himself the conduit of a wealth of other worldly wisdom via unexpected contact with aliens.

According to some accounts; Meier is the current embodiment of a millions of years old soul/being who came to Earth in order to impart a wealth of other worldly wisdom. Moreover, he was a world traveler (circa 42 countries) who met with world leaders and held many, many different jobs such as sailor, soldier, security guard, detective, etc. He also lived in a New Delhi Ashram for some time. Prof. Jim Deardorff, a proponent for the *Talmud Jmmanuel* (to which we shall come), notes that Meier acquired "first-hand religious learning, particularly under a Hindu guru at the Ashoka ashram in Mehrauli, India."

Still, a third tale, or a combination of the first two, is that Meier is the ancient alien-man who also interacted with various aliens in order to, in a manner of speaking, get his current and ongoing marching orders.

Siddhartha Gautama (if any such person ever existed) is said to have become the (or, a) Buddha, at birth at which time he took a few steps and spoke; basically announcing his knowledge of the whole cycle of reincarnation and that he was at the tail end. The other tale is that that this enlightenment did not occur until much later in life whilst meditating under a tree.

In fact, Meier claims that he is an ancient spirit who is routinely incarnated on Earth. At a very young age, he was directed to observe a "pear shaped" UFO wherein a device was placed on his head which caused him to become aware of all of his past life memories. Thus, another specific likeness to Buddha is made.
Surely, Meier followers would be delighted at such synchronicity as within that realm (alien-UFO-New Age) such synchronicities only make sense.

On the side of the *millions of years old soul/being* tale, we note that Eduard Albert Meier aka *Billy* hailed, at least in his most recent Earthly incarnation, from near Hinwil which itself is near Zurich, Switzerland. Born in 1937 AD; his contact with aliens began at the age of 5. This was with a *Pleiadian* aka *Plejaren* named *Ptaah* or *Sfath* (Egypt's *Thoth*?) with whom he interacted for just over a decade.

Directly thereafter, and for just over another decade, he had contact with a woman from the *DAL Universe* (which is said to be a parallel/twin to our universe which is known as the *DERN Universe*) by the name *Asket*.

His next, and most famous, contact came in 1975 AD when contact resumed; this time with Sfath's granddaughter who is named Semjase. Thereafter, contact with others has been ongoing.

Who is Semjase?

It may be advisable to point out what may be a synchronicity. As far as transcription goes, spelling is that which it is; our attempt to glyph sounds. So the most famous Meier related alien is *Semjase*. Historically, we know of another being with the same name (or, one similar enough) who is named Semyaza (aka Semihazah, Shemyazaz, Shemyaza, Shemhazai, etc.). But, pray tell, who is this? The claim is that she is a Pleiadian/Plejaren who came to Earth for reasons that will become apparent. The Pleiadian/Plejaren live circa 1,000 years and Semjase was a youthful 300 years old at the time of contact with Meier. But, digging deeper, who is "Semjase"?

The Ethiopic *Book of Enoch* aka *1 Enoch* 6:1-7, 8:1-3, 10:11-14 notes (playing off of Genesis' chapter 6: for details see my book *In Consideration of the Book(s) of Enoch*) :

> In those days, when the children of man had multiplied, it happened that there were born unto them handsome and beautiful daughters. And the angels, the children of heaven, saw them and desired them; and they said to one another, "Come, let us choose wives for ourselves from among the daughters of man and beget us children." And Semyaza, being their leader, said unto them, "I fear that perhaps you will not consent that this deed should be done, and I alone will become (responsible) for this great sin." But they all responded to him, "Let us all swear an oath and bind everyone among us by a curse not to abandon this

suggestion but to do the deed." Then they all swore together and bound one another by (the curse)...

Semyaza taught enchantments, and root-cuttings...
And the Lord said unto Michael: "Go, bind Semyaza and his associates who have united themselves with women so as to have defiled themselves with them in all their uncleanness. And when their sons have slain one another, and they have seen the destruction of their beloved ones, bind them fast for seventy generations in the valleys of the earth, till the day of their judgment and of their consummation, till the judgment that is for ever and ever is consummated.

In those days they shall be led off to the abyss of fire: [and] to the torment and the prison in which they shall be confined forever. And whosoever shall be condemned and destroyed will from thenceforth be bound together with them to the end of all generations..."

Thus, Semyaza (aka Semjase?) is a fallen angel who *defiled themselves with all uncleanness*. Note that Semyaza taught enchantments and the cutting of roots contextually for the purposes of *pharmakeia* aka magickal occult workings. This is part of the many "secrets" that the fallen angels taught humanity as per the apocryphal text of Enoch.

In fact, Prof. Jim Deardorff, a proponent of the *Talmud Jmmanuel* (to which we shall yet come), notes that according to the *Talmud Jmmanuel* "Adam's father had been Semjasa, the leader of the celestial sons, who were El's or God's guardian angels, and who were 'distant travelers.'"

Jim Nichols on Billy Meier

In the article, "Those Mythical Pleiadians," Jim Nichols goes with the first version of the Meier tale (even though he is certainly aware of the other version as is clear from his other works). Note that Nichols states that the Meier case was "the prime catalyst for my own personal involvement in UFO research." Nichols has accepted the alien/UFO worldview hook, line and *stinker* and has concluded that as all alien/UFO inevitably conclude, "we are gods."

He notes that the 1975 AD event began with Meier "Responding to a compelling, 'pleasant' inner voice" which directed to travel to "remote pine-woods in the Swiss countryside" where he saw:

> ...a gleaming silver disc-craft, approximately 21 feet in diameter, descending from the clouds. The craft slowly hovered lower to the ground and finally landed on extended tripod legs. After a few moments, Meier could see what looked like a person approaching him from the craft. As this figure drew near, he could see what appeared to be a petite young woman. Her flowing hair was long and blonde and she was dressed in a close fitted, textured gray bodysuit.

As for the bodysuit; seems like a case of *Seinfeldian Futurism* (from the episode *The Jacket* of the TV show *Seinfeld*):

> I think eventually fashion won't even exist. It won't. I think eventually we'll all be

wearing the same thing. 'Cause anytime I
see a movie or a TV show where there's
people from the future of another planet,
they're all wearing the same thing.
Somehow they decided "This is going to be
our outfit. One-piece silver jumpsuit, V-
stripe, and boots. That's it."

We should come up for an outfit for earth.
An earth outfit. We should vote on it.
Candidates propose different outfits, no
speeches. They walk out, twirl, walk off. We
just sit in the audience and go, "That was
nice. I could wear that."

In any case, she "introduced herself as 'Semjase' and
explained that she was visiting the Earth from a distant star
system we know as the Pleiades."

It is specifically noted that "they strolled together to the
foot of a nearby tree, where they sat and talked for more
than an hour." More Buddha synchronicity as Meier
received his (most recent?) revelation under a tree.

The circa 130 meetings with Semjase resulted in hundreds
of photographs and circa 3,000 pages of notes written by
Meier.
Lt. Col. Wendelle Stevens (USAF ret. And UFO researcher
since 1947 AD) became the primary investigator of the
Meier case. Nichols notes that the notes were written by
Meier in German and that he "was eager to learn more of
Semjase's wisdom and always pressed Wendelle to
complete and publish an English version of the full
transcript." Eventually, Wendelle stated, "You know, some
of the material in those notes could be considered
seditious."

Sedition pertains to involving or encouraging rebellion against an authority. As it turns out, the Pleiadian/Plejaren messages were critical of human politics and religion. In fact, Wendelle Stevens' 4-volume text *Message From The Pleiades: the Contact Reports of Eduard Meier* (MFTP), is "an incomplete…edited and often incorrect English-language translation of the original German-language Contact Reports" (this is as per <u>Brinkster</u>) and "sections critical of religion & politics have often been expurgated" yet, "the CD-ROM reissues of MFTP1 & MFTP2 are unexpurgated but do not contain all the Stevens annotation material; also the photos are cropped differently with the edges containing more photo material than the print version."

Semjase and Meier's Message to Earth
What Semjase had to say initially is:

> For a long time we've had an urge to contact someone who sincerely wants to be helpful in our mission…we prepare them for the thought that they are not the only rational, thinking beings in the universe.

Key points: when you read anything about the case keep in mind the various versions of the Meier saga as much of it may make sense according to one version but not another. For example, what she had to say would, indeed, be news to Billy version one but old news to Billy version two (or, three).

Another key point is her key words; they are here to 1) make contact with a willing person "who sincerely **wants to** be helpful," 2) they are here on a "mission, and 3) they seek to "prepare them for" alternative "thought[s]."

A note to the point about the *revelation* that we humans "are not the only rational, thinking beings in the universe": speaking biblically, it is clear that we are not since the Bible reveals that there are non-human beings such as angels, Cherubim, Seraphim, demons, etc. They too are *extra-terrestrial*. But whether there are rational, thinking beings who were created to live on other planets (or universes) and who visit us is another issue.

In fact, the most likely scenario is that beings claiming to visit us from other planets/universes are demons in disguise. They put on a happy face and inevitably end up telling us that Judeo-Christianity is false (even if they employ biblical terms into which they pour their own redefinitions).

To the key point about the Pleiadian/Plejaren "mission" to prepare the willing for new thoughts:
> Meier insisted the primary intent of the Pleiadian visit was "not to harm us, not to make war, not to bring peace, just **to bring a teaching**…They see us here as their little brothers or something. And they want to bring **a real teaching** of the natural life, and of the spiritual belonging, **spiritual teaching**, spiritual life and all this."
> [Emphasis added for emphasis, ellipses in original]

Let us keep track of this; the Pleiadians/Plejarens have a "mission" to "bring a teaching…a real teaching" a "spiritual teaching."

We also learn of a summation of the "Pleiadian visitation" by Wendelle Stevens "After years of painstaking, meticulous research," part of which is that "only a **change** of mass **mind** on a **mass scale** can" keep us from destroying ourselves. A mass change of mind on a mass scale in acceptance of their worldview and theology. In fact, Nichols affirms that the Pleiadian/Plejaren missionary message "taught me how to look at my world from an extraterrestrial's point of view!" thus, his worldview has changed and accommodated theirs at the deepest most fundamental level as he believes that "we" humans "are gods."

In fact, Meier himself wrote that they have "come here again to teach the Earth people. That's the only reason they have" and that "we have to change everything."

Also, Semjase stated, "We are neither superior nor super-human, nor are we missionaries."

Note the importance of keeping up with the key claims as she previously stated that they came to Earth on a "mission" but now she states that they are not "missionaries" even though Meier related that they are here to bring a real spiritual teaching.
Moreover, "Meier claimed the Pleiadians sought only to impart fundamental metaphysical 'truths.'"

Semjase's Identity and Billy Meier's State of Mind and Occult Background

Nichols notes that researchers wondered whether Meier's experiences were "fanciful embellishments from his own imagination or a fascinating glimpse of an 'other worldly' culture." Well, in a biblical manner of speaking the truth lies between the two offered options; they were the fanciful embellishments from his own imagination which played off of, or upon, a fascinating glimpse of an other-demonic-worldly culture.

Remember that Meier once lived at a New Delhi Ashram and one does not do that just for kicks. He was involved in occult practices with the happy face of Eastern mysticism placed upon them. Prof. Jim Deardorff, a shill for the *Talmud Jmmanuel*, notes that Meier acquired "first-hand religious learning, particularly under a Hindu guru at the Ashoka ashram in Mehrauli, India."

It is also noted that "Psychological Stress Evaluation of Meier himself could not detect deception." Of course, this does not mean that he was expressing the real, actual, 3-D (as it were) truth but means that he believed what he was saying.

Consider, for example, that on a day time TV show a woman claimed to have been raped by her boyfriend and he denied it, claiming that it was consensual sex. Lie detector tests were administered to both and both tests resulted that they both told the truth. The issue is that in her mind she really was raped but in his mind it really was consensual. Thus, the test does not determine truth but only that which a person believes to be true.

Now, thus far we have referred to the Pleiadians/Plejarens as "aliens" since that is common parlance and they are extra-terrestrial and yet, they claim that we share a common ancestor with humans or that we came from them. As Semjase put it:

> We too are still far removed from perfection
> and have to evolve just like yourselves…we
> feel duty bound to the citizens of Earth,
> because our forebearers were their
> forebearers…our knowledge and our
> understanding exceeds yours considerably,
> especially in the technical field.

Moreover, "Meier claimed the Pleiadians sought only to impart fundamental metaphysical 'truths', such as these observations from 'Semjase'":

> Above everything stands one force alone.
> We call it the CREATION. It regulates the
> laws over all - the life and death of
> everything in the universe, because it is
> everything in the universe.
> Real spirituality comes from the
> understanding of the laws of nature - the
> natural working of cause and effect - each
> contributing to, and sharing with all. When
> you indulge in ritual and ceremony real
> spirit pines away until it is gone.
> A spiritually developed being, as a part of
> creation, acknowledges creation in all
> things, even the smallest microbe, and
> leading a creative life causes fears and
> doubts to vanish like rain before the
> sun…wisdom is the mark of a human who
> has recognized the existence of his spirit and
> works with it according to the Creational
> laws…By creative thinking man acquires
> knowledge and wisdom and a sense of
> unlimited strength, which unbinds him from
> the limitations of convention and dogma…
> One can never identify God separately from
> creation because God itself is a part of it.

So now, you are not a "spiritually developed being" if you do not agree with the Pleiadian/Plejaren dogma. Did you catch that? They speak out against dogma even whilst promulgating one of their own; let us review.

According to Semjase the following are facts:

1) Above everything stands one force alone.
2) This force called CREATION regulates the laws over all because it is everything in the universe.
3) Real spirituality comes from the understanding of the laws of nature
4) Ritual and ceremony pines away real spirit until it is gone (this is even though the Pleiadian/Plejaren have also promulgated a meditative mantra/chant which is to be ritually performed).
5) A spiritually developed being acknowledges creation in all things
6) Leading a creative life causes fears and doubts to vanish
7) Wisdom is recognizing the existence of spirit and working with the Creational laws.
8) Creative thinking unbinds one from convention and dogma (except for from this convention and dogma).
9) One can never identify God separately from creation because God itself is a part of it.

This is just scratching the surface; Meier has 3,000 pages of such stuff. The Pleiadian/Plejaren did not come to Earth to share an apple pie recipe; they are on a mission to discredit traditional religions and promulgate theirs (which is New Age religion by the way which, in turn, is Old Age occult religion, by the way). Take one example, she firmly asserts that "One can **never**" get it *never* as in *never ever*, "identify God separately from creation" so she is laying out a theology and demanding that it is the one true truth and her theology is pantheism "because God itself is a part of it." This is the sort of theology that resulted in Nichols believing that "we are gods."

Jim Nichols on the Pleiadian/Plejaren Worldview and Theology
In part, the advanced otherworldly revelations of the Pleiadian/Plejaren are nothing new and certainly nothing

that by the 1975 AD had not already been printed in various forms from various points of view. Here is an example, from Nichols along with his recognition that this is nothing new:

> The Pleiadians viewed all Earthly social structures such as governments, corporate economic institutions, religions and the like as self-serving, monolithic, authoritarian, constructs solely designed to exploit humanity, reducing the mass population into mere consumer/materialistic slaves - a truth also perceived throughout history by this world's indigenous peoples as well as ancient Gnostic texts.

Sadly, Nichols is very anti-Bible and pro Gnosticism. He has fallen for the pop-occultural myth that at the 325 AD Council of Nicaea excluded the true gospels (the Gnostic texts) from the New Testament and only kept those parts which would assure that power hungry authoritarians would have their way.

It is as if he, and others like him, think that Christians had no right to determine what was and what was not authentic. Would he allow portions of Anton LaVey's *Satanic Bible* to be added to Meier's 3,000 pages of notes? Then why would Christians allow late dated Gnostic texts into the New Testament? In short, if you take just about any and every biblical doctrine of which you can think and turn it upside down, inside out and backward; you have Gnosticism.

Also, the fact is that by circa 180 AD just about every New Testament book/letter was accepted as apostolic and scripture. The Council of Nicaea did not, in the least bit, deal with canonical issue whatsoever.

More on the Pleiadian/Plejaren view of earthly religion:
> Religion is only the primitive work of
> human beings, in purpose to lead them, to
> suppress them, and for exploitation, into
> which only spiritually deficient life can
> fall…Bring this truth to the light of the
> world and make it known. This is a further
> part of our mission. If this does not happen,
> then mankind will slowly destroy itself and
> fall into complete spiritual
> darkness…religion can suppress a being and
> make him depend on something that stands
> above him and gives him orders and advice.
> The result is a creature no more master of
> himself, but subjecting himself to something
> that remains powerfully above him….
>
> Religions, in the meaning that they exist on
> Earth, are then unique in this Universe, and
> they find no equal. They control the Earth
> human and the whole planet, and retard your
> world thousands of years, in Spiritual
> respect. Every Spiritual evolution is blocked
> by these religions and finds no progress.

So, another part of their mission is doing away with earthly religion (and replaces it with their pantheism). Note that "religion can suppress a being" by making one "depend on something that stands above" but recall that Semjase had stated that "Above everything stands one force alone…CREATION" and that we must adhere to CREATION as it is a combo of god and universe. Moreover, religion suppresses by making us depend on that which is above that "gives him orders and advice." But the Pleiadian/Plejaren are giving us orders and advice which, presumably, they got from CREATION.

Also, note that their concept of CREATION as one force is, actually, exactly what everyone from New Agers to occultists and Star Wars have claimed: that there is one impersonal force (energy, prana, chi, ki, qui, etc.) into which one can tap and which one can bend towards good or evil.

However, let us note that when by "religion" they mean hierarchical authoritarian oppressive man-made systems then, indeed, "religion" is the most corrupt concept humans have ever conceived and there is no greater barrier between God and humans than "religion." In fact, James 1:27 gives the only positive statement on religion in the Bible but note how it defines it:

> Pure and undefiled religion before God and
> the Father is this: to visit orphans and
> widows in their trouble, and to keep oneself
> unspotted from the world.

Billy Meier and His Alien New World Order

Meier has written of himself in terms of his being "the only true contactee of the Pleiadians" and that:

> "It is an urgent necessity that the teachings
> and the Mission are disseminated and
> established throughout the world." (FIGU
> Bulletin 005)

Thus, he is the chosen one and his goals are to be established worldwide. Hereinafter is some of the background of the Meier case as per the book *Contact from the Pleiades* written by Wendelle C. Stevens Lt. Col., USAF (Ret).

In chapter 1 Stevens explains how he got involved:

My Preliminary Investigation Report on this case, published in 1982, began with the commencement of the face-to-face contacts with Semjase and her team of Pleiadians operating from a great mother-ship.

In chapter 2 Stevens relates the real nature of Meier:
Unknown to Meier consciously then was Asket's subsequent statements to him, also later confirmed by Semjase in the Pleiadian contacts, that he was once an IHWH, a Pleiadian expeditionary to Earth, with one of the several earlier occupations of this planet by ancestors of the Pleiadians. He at that earlier time enjoyed his superior status and the obedience of and exploitation of the primitive Earth humans.

Asket and Semjase are two of the aliens with whom Meier had contact. Thus, Meier was on Earth long, long ago; he is an IHWH. Chapter 3 provides the results of that which these "Pleiadian expeditionary to Earth accomplished:
It was they who brought the madness that allowed this aberration here on Earth, as the power hungry IHWHs, who set up their early religious feudalism in order to control and enslave the indigenous survivor remnants of their own earlier ancestry here…Meier…was one of the IHWHs then, as were Semjase, Ptaah, Quetzal and others here now.

Of course, Semjase is the name of a fallen angel in the apocryphal *Book of Enoch* and Quetzal is an equally obvious reference to Quetzalcoatl; the central American feathered serpent god.

But since Meier, Semjase, Ptaah and Quetzal brought madness, allowed aberration, were power hungry and established religious feudalism in order to control and enslave the Earth; why should we disseminate and established their message throughout the world?

Well, in chapter 2 we are told that "Semjase and her team" are "reformed IHWHs." So, they have had a change of heart and are now back to save us from the damage which they themselves caused.

Well, as we set out a basic template whereby to discern alien messages in chapter *The How, What and How of Alien Messages*, they are actually back to, yet again, bring madness and aberration, as they are power hungry and thus, seek to established religious feudalism in order to control and enslave the Earth.

Indeed, the fallen angel and serpent god are back (along with whoever the others may be—if, that is, Meier is in touch with anything but his own fertile mind).

In fact, in chapter 3 Stevens offers more details about "Eduard Meier's Mission":

> …war energies have always been inspired or connected in some way to the advanced extraterrestrials who came here and set themselves up as Gods, Kings of Wisdom, IHWHs, Sons of God, or other similar positions, and exploited the greed and avarice of indigenous Earth men seeking to serve them for the valuable rewards available. From these incentives spring emotional cults and political control systems

out of which have evolved religions again,
the emotional impetus to action.

Thus, Meier and the Semjase team were the ancient false
Gods, Kings of Wisdom, IHWHs, Sons of God, etc. who, so
we are told, were the "self-proclaimed 'Gods' and 'Sons of
God' (The Pleiadian IHWH's) in all mythologies and
religions of the last some 70,000 years of our ancient past."

Stevens also reviews the long and sorted history of the
comings and goings from the Earth of the
Pleiadians/Plejarens:
> Shortly before this time ["50,000 years ago
> in Earth chronology"], 70,000 human beings
> fled (the Pleiades) under the leadership of
> Pelegon. In spacecraft which they took by
> force, they fled through the cosmos and
> settled here on Earth. Under Pelegon were
> 200 subleaders, scientists, competent in
> special fields of knowledge. By these, and
> others, Pelegon was unanimously
> acknowledged as "King of Wisdom"
> (IHWH/God) and regarded as such.

As it turns out, "this went well for only a narrow 10,000
years" until:
"all was destroyed, and only a few thousand human beings
survived (on Earth) while others fled once more into the
cosmos and settled on faraway worlds. For 7,000 years,
none returned to Earth" and "Then descendents [sic] of
those who had settled on faraway worlds returned. They
were again under the leadership of an IHWH, under whose
command they built on Atlantis and Mu."

Then the pattern repeated as "For thousands of years they lived in friendship and peace" until chaos ensued again at which time:

> ...having tired of wars, the nations rose against them, and they occupied spaceships and fled into cosmic space; that being some 15,000 years ago in Earth chronology. For two milleniums, they and their descendants lived in a neighboring solar system.

But then "they left their world about 13,000 years ago and returned to Earth Their highest leader was the scientist 'ARUS', who was also called 'The Barbarian'" who:

> "Like the IHWH 40,000 years before, he also had 200 leaders and subleaders, who were competent in special fields of sciences" and they "succeeded in destroying the civilizations of Atlantis and Mu. The few survivors went into servitude, while many great scientists were able to flee, and return to their homeworlds in the Pleiades."

But what were these scientists up to:

> By mutation and their sciences, they extend their lifespans to some thousands of years....In a forbidden manner and secretly, they went out and caught wild Earth creatures and mutations who were distant descendants of former human beings from cosmic space. Wild and beautiful female beings were tamed and mated with by the leaders who called themselves "Sons of Heaven". Each, according to his own race, created mutated beings, completely new forms of life, who were of dwarf-like stature, gigantic, or animal-like.

We then learn:

> Semjasa, the highest of the subleaders,
> mated with an EVA, a female being, who
> was still mostly human-like and also rather
> beautiful (in feature and form). The
> descendent of this act was of male sex and a
> human being of good form. Semjasa called
> him "Adam", which was a word meaning
> "Earth human being". A similar breeding
> produced a female, and in later years they
> were mated to each other.

So Semjasa (aka Semjase) who, at least in Meier's current incarnation is female mated with a female.

We also get this bit of detail, "With newly appointed subleaders and guard-angels, he [IHWH ARUS] brought three human races under his control"; the "Indians," the "(fair-skinned) inhabitants who had settled around the Black Sea" and "the Gypsies…who were called Hebrews."

And it was IHWH ARUS':

> …son JEHAV who took over his dominion
> was little better, for he too as IHWH
> demanded only blood and death from the
> three enslaved races. The later descendants
> of these "Gods" became more humane and
> developed a degree of spirituality.

Note that IHWH is a borrowed version of what most people spell as YHWH which is the Tetragrammaton; the name which was given to Moses when he asked whom he was to tell the people had sent him to free them from slavery in Egypt (see Exodus 3). This four letter term is better spelled YHVH as there is no "W" sound in Hebrew. In any regard,

JEHAV is really the same as JEHOVAH as JHVH is really YHVH (again, a better version is YHVH because there is no "J" sound in Hebrew) and, of course, JHVH or YHVH is IHVH.

In other words, we come full circle as IHWH is YHWH is YHVH is JEHAV is JEHOVAH is JHVH gets us right back to IHVH. Thus, IHWH is supposed to have a son named JEHAV but this is just applying different forms of the same name to different beings.

"Pleiadians" or "Plejarens"?

We previously touched upon the issue of what the difference is between "Pleiadians" and "Plejarens" (which was originally also spelled "Plejarans"). And what, if anything the difference between these terms has anything to say about those who employ them.[40]

The *Pleiades* aka *M45*, *Seven Sisters*, etc. are a star system within the good ol' fashioned known universe which as accurately represented by supporters of Meier and according to his alien contacts. They note that "solid matter - let alone material life - cannot exist in blue-hot plasma for more than the time it takes to ionize it"

In the *FIGU Bulletin 005* Meier wrote that his alien contact Ptaah stated:

> ...the fact that there exists no intelligent or any other type of life on the Pleiades — hence, neither an energy collective nor any similar terrestrially-invented foolishness — we have received a related confirmation from the Arahat Athersata, who queried the highest of all existing high spirit levels and received a reply to this question to which Arahat Athersata already knew the answer

beforehand: namely, no intelligent energy form, let alone life form of any type, exists on the Pleiades' celestial bodies. The same applies also to Venus, Saturn, Jupiter, Pluto, Neptune and Uranus.

Meier adds:

> ...the Pleiadians/Plejarans...do not come from these stars but from another space-time configuration in another dimension 80 light years beyond the Pleiades. Their constellation is also called the Pleiades/Plejares, just as they are named here.

Even though Meier repeatedly employs the term "Pleiadians/Plejarens," the point of the two terms is to have a manner whereby to distinguish between those in true contact with the aliens, the Plejarens (of which Meier is the only one) and those who are not in contact with them who are identified via their claim to be in contact with Pleiadians:

> People from the Pleiades...do not exist. According to Sfath's Explanation, Billy was told as a young boy that by initially using the term Pleiadian, when referring to the origin of his contactors, the fraudsters and deceivers who would later also claim to be in contact with Pleiadians would and have now have been exposed.
> Billy was told that the Pleiades star cluster in our space-time configuration is too young to support life and the Plejares is the true star system from whence Sfath, Ptaah, Semjase and the other Plejaren originate.

Thus, the disparity between the terms Pleiadians/Plejarans is variously explained and, perhaps, explained away. We knew about the Pleiadians before we knew that of which they consisted. Thus, Meier's early references to his alien contacts being from there could have been his appealing to a named and observed but, as of yet at the time, unknown star system. Later, when we found that no physical life (nor according to Meier's alien contact could spirit) could live there he could have changed his tune, his terms, and simply claim that the change was planned all along.

After all, the first contact (at least in this lifetime of his) was in 1942 AD and yet, it was "1975, when I made my contacts with the Pleiadians/ Plejarans public knowledge."

Other reasons for the correlation, confusion, disparity, etc. are said to be caused by translations:

> ...the fact that the officially designated publisher of the Meier material in English still makes references to the "Pleiadians" and that they departed (!?!) in 1995 – the time they revealed their true origins in the Plejaren system – is more than a little confusing.

Indeed, it is confusing but this excuse is not reasonable since, as already noted, Meier himself writes in terms of "Plejadisch-plejarische" which means that he is perpetuating the correlation of terminology grammatically but not conceptually or, spatially.

In fact, there is a *Plejadisch-plejarische Kontaktberichte Block 1, Seiten 11-20 Pleiadian/Plejaren Contact Reports Volume 1, Pages 11-20* which has the alien Sfath stating (in 141-143) that "many swindlers report worldwide in regard to alleged meetings with me and my successors, and they appear with false and fraudulent messages...these false contact persons" who will "be recognizable as they assert that their physical or telepathic meetings and connections exist with beings from the Pleiades system of this space-time configuration."

This is because "we do not belong to this space-time configuration and thereby also not to this Pleiades system...and is absolutely uninhabited and uninhabitable in every regard, when thermo-bacterial life is disregarded which will disappear again in some tens of millions of years without higher life of some kind ever being able to exist there, subsequently spiritual beings will also never exist on these Pleiades stars."

Thus, "in order to unmask the future swindlers, my successors and you will not name our origins according to our own language-term, Plejaren, rather by the terrestrial-human term, Pleiades, in order that the swindlers will then use this term, whereby they will expose their own fraud and lies as well as slander."

In further contact notes, many such personages are mentioned such as Randolph Winters, George Green, Lee Elders, Randy Winters, Roberta Brooks, "the contact liar Fred Bell," "that other ruthless 'channeller' Jani King."

Then there is Lyssa Royal who claims of herself that "One of the entities that I work with now (Sasha) says she is a physical extraterrestrial from the Pleiadian star system" yet, about whom Meier adherents state, "charlatans and/or fruitcakes like Lyssa Royal and her emergent ilk."

There is also Barbara Marciniak and about whom the alien Ptaah stated the following (in the 252nd Contact, February 14, 1995 AD):

Barbara Marciniak who, in her delusions,
perceives herself as a trance medium, while
she is, truthfully, nothing more than an
obscure person and fantast (WV) of the
same category as Fred Bell. She is engaged
in shady wheeling and dealing regarding
(WV) other people on Earth as well as
herself by purporting to have contacts with
an energy collective from the Pleiadian star
cluster...
All claims made by this obscure person and
fantast (WV) are simply her own inventions
and fantasies and there is not the tiniest
shred of truth in them -- except, possibly, for
a few items she has plagiarized from your
written material...

About such claimants to Pleiadian contact, the Meier camp
has much to say, such as that which follows. Let us begin
with the self-affirmation by Meier that he is the one and
only person in touch with the Plejarens as he writes about
"the lies they spread regarding the contacts they were
supposedly having with the Pleiadians" who spread
"heinous lies and vicious fraud, for not one
Pleiadian/Plejaran maintains contacts with human beings
on Earth --- except for me --- a fact the Pleiadians/Plejarans
have repeatedly and extensively emphasized throughout my
many contact years with them...As the only true contactee
of the Pleiadians."

Supposed Pleiadean contactees are:
            ...all equally "sick in the head" for they are
            simply psychopaths, individuals suffering
            from psychogenic disorders, schizophrenics,
            etc; they may also be deliberate frauds, liars,
            hoaxers or charlatans who wish to project

themselves into the forefront for reasons of
their own image, profit or sectarian faith.

He writes of "their contactee-medium-channeler delusions"
asserts that they are "tortured by sectarian delusions" that
their "claims are pure, unparalleled nonsense" as they "pop
out of the ground like poisonous mushrooms" but are, in
reality, "frauds, liars and deceivers."

Religion and the New Age

Next, consider what Jim Nichols introduces as Wendelle
Stevens' views on the Pleiadian messages":
>...the wave of religious fundamentalism
>sweeping the lands. It is paradoxical that the
>religious fundamentalists, each preaching
>peace and brotherhood, and each blessing
>their great armies marching off to kill in the
>name of "their God", are the ones destined,
>now as always, to bring great bloodshed
>upon this world and even its ultimate
>destruction...

One wonders if Stevens wrote this during the Middle Ages
since, especially as a military officer, he should have
known better. The fact is that the 20th century was, both,
the bloodiest and the most secular in human history.

In fact, *The Encyclopedia of Wars* (New York: Facts on
File, 2005 AD) was compiled by nine history professors
who specifically conducted research for the text for a
decade in order to chronicle 1,763 wars. The survey of wars
covers a time span from 8000 BC to 2003 AD. From over
10,000 years of war 123 wars, which is 6.98%, are
considered to have been religious wars (and half of those
involved Islam).

Moreover:

> Stevens stated that the ultimate message of
> the Pleiadians was that the "Earthman…has
> imprisoned himself in his institutionalized
> fears of confinement, death, ever lasting
> hell…We can change it any time WE
> want…and nobody is ever coming from
> anywhere to relieve us of this responsibility
> - a most enlightening message indeed.

We can clearly discern the anti-Christian message; do not
fear hell and do not look forward's to Jesus' return.

It is also explained that:

> They feared humans would simply worship
> them as "saviors", twisting their "message"
> into yet another monolithic religion. Or, in
> Semjase's words, "then the human beings on
> Earth would again fall in their beliefs and
> remain retarded in evolution. It was far more
> important for "Earth human beings to
> become self-supporting, to think in their
> own way and to begin acting in a right
> manner"…Semjase assured Meier that
> people all over the world would be touched
> and inspired by the teachings he imparted.

It seems as those most taken by the Pleiadian/Plejaren
missionary message are they who, in some or another form,
worship them as saviors. From taking on their theology to
chanting mantras that they have prescribed and much more.

Nichols notes:

> It's been more than thirty years since that
> fateful January in 1975, when a, one-armed
> Swiss security guard was visited by a lady

305

from the Pleiades. We are now well into the
first decade of the New Millennium and
facing a growing threat of Islamic terrorism,
an ongoing ground war in Iraq that could
likely mushroom into a uncontrolled
religious conflict spreading throughout the
Middle East, not to mention, runaway global
warming and the potential for ever more
disastrous storms and weather conditions.
With the human population of Earth now
facing more danger than ever in history -
one cannot examine the Pleiadian
'messages' in light of such events and
dismiss them as delusional fantasies of
yesteryear - in fact they seem more timely
and urgent by the moment!

Without bothering to iron out details; perhaps what
happened is that Meier read the Bible, especially the Book
of Revelation and the Pleiadian/Plejaren had nothing to do
with any such predictions.

The Pleiadian UFO CIA LAPD Rama Peru Case

For some reason, the Meier Pleiadian/Plejaren contact with
Semjase case is often correlated, directly or not, with
Charles Silva's contact with a certain Rama which took
place in Peru in 1974 AD, a year before the Meier case.

The only real correlation (besides their occult messages) is
that both *aliens* were female. If they are the same being
then she decided to dye her hair before meeting up with
Meier as she was a brunette with Silva but a blond with
Meier; perhaps she wanted to have more fun.

However, Semjase claimed to be from the Pleiadian star

system and Rama claimed to be from Ganymede which is one of Jupiter's moons where her people lived underground.

Whilst gallivanting in Peru, Silva, who was supposedly working for a Hollywood related business and also claims to have been a CIA agent, encountered a woman riding around in an LAPD (Los Angeles Police Department) motorcycle. Eventually, she revealed that she was a Pleiadian and takes him on a ride in her spaceship.

Note that Rama told Charles Silva to write a book about their encounter, which he did.

Of course, *Rama* is the name of the seventh avatar of the Hindu god Vishnu (and a king of Ayodhya in Hindu scriptures). Silva was not a "religious" fellow but Rama wanted to discuss the Bible with him and what resulted was basically ancient-astronaut, ancient-aliens and, in reality, ancient-fallen angels and their demonic offspring, theory with her claiming that this and that text was actually a primitive person's description of encounters with UFOs and aliens.

Heavily playing off of the Book of Revelations, she emphasized the references to predicted destructions and the anti-Christ whom she, speaking in 1974 AD, expected to be revealed soon. The specific dates of occurrences which she took upon herself to predict have come, gone and have failed.

She also spoke of cosmology and claimed that the Milky Way galaxy is on a trajectory along with another that, or so it was claimed, is called *Wormwood* in the Bible and is aka *Hercolubus*. One of her failed predictions was that at intervals of 66,666 years the two galaxies come very close to each other and that this would result in the melting of the Earth's ice caps in the late 1980s AD which would lead to worldwide destruction.

Not surprisingly, she taught Charles Silva how to leave his body; out-of-body experiences. And also not surprisingly, she approved of one of the most notorious occultists of recent history: Madame Helena Petrovna Blavatsky.

Silva and Rama think that unmarried sex is a higher, more ascended, spiritual calling as they engaged in just that very act; the sexual devolution at work—again.

In fact, as one reviewer put it, "She used sex to get her message across" and we are back, again, to style temple prostitutes or sex magick (no wonder she approved of Theosophy).

Charles Silva also has a section on the Fatima apparition and message. It is claimed that the (pseudo-Mary) Lady of Fatima was, actually, an alien.
Well, now he may be onto something. On the view that "aliens" are actually demons this appears to be accurate. The original Fatima *revelation* was of a small luminous being only later said to have been Mary (the Roman Catholic faux Mary). Also, the "miracle" of the moving and spinning Sun is thought to have been the movements of a UFO or, in this case, a demonic manifestation.

While, of course, Charles Silva book, *Date with the Gods*, is essentially utterly unknown outside of UFOaltry circles there is an interesting and litigious correlation between it and Shirley MacLaine.

As per the *Federal Circuits* web site, a case was filed when Silva against Shirley MacLaine in a copyright infringement action.[41] Silva "initiated this action against defendants alleging that MacLaine's book, Out On A Limb, and subsequent movie, also entitled Out On A Limb (broadcast in January, 1987), infringed on his copyright of Date With the Gods."

The result was that the "court concludes that, as a matter of law, Silva has not demonstrated that his book, Date With the Gods was substantially similar to MacLaine's Out On A Limb."

Of course, this does not mean that McLaine did not plagiarize the story but only that, if she did so, she, sufficiently, made it her own.

On the Talmud of Immanuel and the Corrupted Bible

Jim Nichols notes that pertaining to the criticism of Earth religion some were concerned that Meier may come across as an "anti-religionist." For this reason, as aforementioned, "sections critical of religion & politics have often been expurgated" from Wendelle Stevens' 4-volume text *Message From The Pleiades: the Contact Reports of Eduard Meier* (MFTP). Well, the combination of occult-mystical practices and contact with "aliens" moved Meier from merely non- or un-biblical views to straight up anti-biblical views as he took aim at the very heart of Christianity.
How so?

With the Pleiadian's/Plejaren's help, of course. Recall that Meier was contacted by the alien *Sfath* aka *Ptaah* at the age of five. This being told Meier, "You are the prophet of the New Age for the entire terrestrial world and all human beings on this planet." Subsequently, Semjase "informs

Meier that he is the prophet of the new age as foretold in the Talmud Jmmanuel."

Many are aware of Rabbinic Judaism's Talmudim; the Jerusalem Talmud aka Talmud Yerushalmi and the Babylonian Talmud aka Talmud Bavli. Well, there is also the *Talmud Jmmanuel* with *Jmmanuel* being a particular transliteration of Jesus's "name." How so? Well, historical and cultural context informs us that in days gone by a name was more than a label but primarily was meant to denote something about the person. Thus, Jesus' name/title was Emmanuel, which means *God with us*, whilst His name/label is *Yehoshua* with His nick name being *Yeshua* (basically *Joshua* and *Josh*) which has been transliterated as *Jesus*.

It is claimed that the reason for not referring to Jesus as *Emmanuel* or even *Immanuel* but rather *Jmmanuel* is that he was directed to spell it as such by his alien handlers. It is easy to imagine that it has something to do with numerology (whether Aramaic, German or English I know not).

Well, as per Research Professor Emeritus Jim Deardorff (Oregon State University) the Talmud Jmmanuel was "discovered in Jerusalem in 1963, ushers in the New Age while exposing the New Testament gospels as being more corrupt than even the Jesus Seminar suspects." If that is not biased enough for you, note that he also has a warning on his website that states, "Scholars beware: the UFO-biblical connections are real." In other words, we are back to ancient-astronauts, ancient-aliens which are, actually, ancient-fallen angels and their ancient-demonic offspring; the descended masters.

One of Prof. Jim Deardorff's claims is that "largely through comparison with the Gospel of Matthew, that the TJ [Talmud Jmmanuel] was the source for that gospel. The TJ informs us precisely which Matthean verses are genuine, which are partly genuine, and which are pure invention." Anyone familiar with the [anti] *Jesus Seminar* can see why Prof. Deardorff makes reference to them.

So, he compared Matthew with the Talmud Jmmanuel but the key question is which came first. One could write a *Document-X* today which differs from the gospels and claim that the gospels corrupted *Document-X* but that would not prove that the gospels are based on *Document-X* because *Document-X* came along long after the gospels.

He is so convinced of his hypothesis that he states that "the arguments pointing to Matthean dependence upon the TJ are seen to be **difficult to reverse**" (emphasis added) and that he holds to "TJ genuineness." However, there is a slight, tiny, little, hiccup in his theory and in a masterful turn of academic-scholarly phraseology, and perhaps a moment of clarity, Prof. Deardorff notes that, "Tests for TJ genuineness are indirect because its original Aramaic scrolls were destroyed" and that "only the German translation survived."

If you look up the Talmud Jmmanuel on Amazon.com the author is listed as "Judas Ischarioth" (as in the betrayer of Jesus and also the star of the apocryphal Gnostic *Gospel of Judas*) and the editor as—drumroll please—"Billy Eduard Albert Meier."

For the journal *Information Sciences*, Kevin Burns wrote the article "Bayesian inference in disputed authorship: A case study of cognitive errors and a new system for decision support" (Volume 176, Issue 11, 3 June 2006 AD, pp. 1570-1589) which noted:

> …the Talmud of Jmmanuel…was discovered in the mid-1960s near Jerusalem by two individuals named [Isa] Rashid and Meier. Rashid translated the original scrolls into German, which is the language of Meier, then in the mid-1970s Rashid was killed and the scrolls were lost, presumably because authorities considered the Talmud to be heretic.

Some refer to Isa Rashid as a *Greek Catholic* priest while others refer to him as a Greek Orthodox priest. It appears that the scrolls destroyed during a 1974 AD Israeli air raid on Lebanon. Reportedly, Rashid had escaped, empty-handed, to Baghdad where he was assassinated.

With particular reference to Deardorff, Kevin Burns writes, "My review of this scholar's analysis found that his mathematical derivations were sound but that his practical application was flawed." This statement pertains to Deardorff's employment of Bayesian methods of comparison but the comparison means nothing without manuscript evidence as regardless of how they compare it may be that Isa Rashid and/or Meier authored the Talmud Jmmanuel in the 1960s.

Meier claims to have, along with Isa Rashid, actually spelunked the cave in which the manuscript was found in 1963 AD and the locale is described as just south of the Old City of Jerusalem (but the location has never been cartographically described in detail and remains unknown and unexplored). Meier is said to have been walking along with Rashid and happened to glance up the slope to notice an opening in the ground which in 1997 AD (34 years later) he recalled was circa one foot wide.

In any case, here is an example of a text of Matthew versus a text of the Talmud Jmmanuel.

Matthew 6:9-13,

> Pray then like this: "Our Father who art in heaven, hallowed be thy name. Thy kingdom come, thy will be done, on earth as it is in heaven. Give us this day our daily bread; and forgive us our debts, as we also have forgiven our debtors; and lead us not into temptation, But deliver us from evil."

Talmud Jmmanuel 6:11-17,

> Therefore pray as one who knows, and thus pray as follows: "My spirit (consciousness), you exist within almightiness. May your name be holy. May your world incarnate itself within me. May your power unfold itself within me, on Earth and in the skies. Give me today my daily bread, that I may recognize my wrongdoings and the truth. And lead me not into temptation and confusion, but deliver me from error."

In part, a note by Deardorff reads that, "The first verse of the Lord's Prayer, Mt 6:9, was criticized by Robert Funk, a leader in the scholar's group called the "Jesus Seminar,' for its lack of logic" and, pray tell, what was this lack of logic?:

> He noted that God's name was considered too holy to pronounce by Jews, while the title of "Father" is not at all holy. "It is difficult to conceive of circumstances under

which Jesus would have referred to God as
'Father' and then turned around and said,
'May your name be sanctified.'"

Well, this is exactly what is to be expected from the Jesus
Seminar and my criticism of it is due to its lack of logic. It
is no wonder that Rabbi Jacob Neusner (University of
South Florida) stated that the Jesus Seminar is "either the
greatest scholarly hoax since the Piltdown Man or the utter
bankruptcy of New Testament studies."

Even granting Robert Funk's assertion note the following:
1) God's name was considered too holy to pronounce.
2) The title of "Father" is not at all holy.
3) Therefore, Jesus would have referred to God as "Father"
in order to not utter YHVH's name but made reference to it
without pronouncing it by stating "May your name be
sanctified."

Also, by the way, while Robert Funk my personally find it
"difficult to conceive of circumstances under which Jesus
would have referred to God as 'Father'" the fact is that—
see if you can unravel this bit of logic—the incarnated
Jesus is God's Son and therefore God is His Father.

Moreover, Deardorff notes:
> Matthew's prayer is a group prayer, as seen
> by "Our Father," "our daily bread" and so
> forth. Yet, its preceding verses, Mt 6:5-6,
> apply to the individual, not to a group, and
> in Matthew they deal with praying in a room
> alone. Hence the collective format of the
> Lord's Prayer is inconsistent with these
> preliminary verses.

How is this even a problem? He is telling individuals how to pray and that when they are to pray they are to speak to the Father collectively as they are all a part of the *eklesia* aka *the church* which means "called out ones" aka the community of Christians.

As for the revised "Lord's prayer" within the Talmud Jmmanuel—which is no longer a prayer to the Lord but to "My spirit (consciousness)"—it is merely indicative of typical New Age phraseology which is either far too majestically spiritually evolved to comprehend or utter malarkey.

The Talmud Jmmanuel asserts that Jesus traveled to India before his ministry began and returned there after not having died on the cross. This is something that has been specifically investigated and is simply unknown to history and to the monks and priests of India.

The claim that Jesus did not die on the cross is in keeping with Islamic beliefs which came about circa half a millennia after the time of Jesus—see chapter *Who Was Abraham Told to Sacrifice, Isaac or Ishmael?* within my book *Is Jesus the Messiah? A Judaism vs. Judaism Debate.* In fact, the text predicts the appearance of Muhammad, by name and details that Jesus stated he would come in 500 years from His own time (which, of course, Meier knew).

Likewise illogical and uninformed is the article "The Author of the TJ Scrolls" which states:

> When Isa Rashid started reading into the
> Talmud of Jmmanuel (TJ) scrolls, he soon
> learned that Judas Iscariot was listed as the
> author. This must have taken him very much
> by surprise, but with the aged Aramaic

> scrolls in front of him, he was in no position
> to doubt its truth.
>
> Further in the TJ, Rashid could translate that
> Judas, who was the only one of the twelve
> disciples who could read and write, had been
> assigned the task of writing down
> Jmmanuel's ministry and teachings as well
> as being their treasurer (as indicated also in
> the Gospel of John).[42]

Note the conclusion that since the now non-existing
manuscript was "aged" Isa Rashid "was in no position to
doubt its truth." Well, this may come as a shock but, even if
there was any such thing as an aged Aramaic manuscript,
even if it dated to the time of Jesus and even if it was
written by Judas; these presumed facts would not ensure
the accuracy of the text's claims—someone could have
written something false long ago.

Also, that Judas "was the only one of the twelve disciples
who could read and write" is inaccurate as Matthew was a
tax collector in His life BC; Rome had appointed him the
task of keeping meticulous records. Also, Matthew wrote
the gospel of Matthew (which the Talmud Jmmanuel seeks
to debunk and replace). Andrew and Peter may not have
kept records but may have as they were fishermen and thus,
businessmen. John wrote books/letters of the Bible. Others
ought to be presumed to have been illiterate based on
arguments from silence and/or arguments for looking down
upon ancient people.

Within a contact with Ptaah on September 1, 2010 AD,
known as contact #501, Meier related the following:

> It was asked, why wasn't it discovered
> earlier, that Isa Rashid had used old,

traditional Christian terms in the translation of the scrolls, whereby things weren't represented correctly. Also, it did, indeed, result that he also omitted important things because these didn't fit into his lay priest concept. From my side, I didn't know all this at that time, when I prepared the "Talmud Jmmanuel" for publication, and I also had no information from your or Arahat Athersata's side.

In other words, even Meier's translation was lacking but how could anyone, having no manuscript to go, concluded that "things weren't represented correctly" and that Isa "omitted important things"?

Note that *Arahat Athersata* is not a person but a level or plane wherein dwells pure spirit and it is said that it requires circa 60-80 billion years reach such a state.

Ptaah replies:

That's right. Of course, we already knew from the outset about the fallibility with regard to the translations and about certain important omissions…But concerning his translation errors and omission errors, it is to be said that we deliberately let the whole thing run in the already executed manner because there would have been too much turmoil at that time and your life would have been endangered even more than it has been, if you had published the entire actual translation of the scroll…we said nothing about this and waited until the aggressiveness had smoothed itself, which has now been the case for quite some time…the time has become ripe to work on the correct translation and to disseminate it…

Assuming that this was the first time that Meier asked about this, and the context indicates that it is; the manuscript was allegedly found in 1963 AD, destroyed in 1974 AD and published in 1978 AD but it was not until 2010 AD that Meier asks about it. He is told that the whole thing was a styled setup. And, indeed, various versions have been published such as by *Wild Flower Press* in 1990 AD, *Bridger House Publishers* in 2005 AD, *Steelmark LLC* in 2007 AD, etc.

Meier actually notes this as the conversation follows with him stating:

…of this, you have never said anything to me. Indeed, I knew that Isa Rashid wasn't able to free himself completely from his faith in God and Jesus, as I have also found out that old, traditional Christian terms were used in the translation of Isa Rashid, but I didn't know why you didn't say anything about this. Due to the silence of you all, I assumed that everything, indeed, had its correctness and that everything corresponded to the contents of the scroll.

Ptaah replies:

That we didn't speak with you about this, our further reason for this lies in the fact that you wouldn't have been in agreement with the publication of the defectiveness of the translation; consequently, you would have insisted on writing and publishing the whole thing very exactly and correctly.

> But this, as I already said, you wouldn't
> have survived, as our possibility forecast
> had yielded. You would have been
> treacherously murdered through one of the
> assassination attempts, of which there would
> have been even more. Noting this in the
> newly revised and edited "Talmud
> Jmmanuel" would certainly be appropriate
> and useful.

In other words; now that you have been pummeled by historians, linguists, reporters, and theologians we will let the alien-cat out of the bad, admit that we allowed publishing faulty info and now tell you to revise, update, edit and publish a new version (*cha-ching!*). But, of course, upon what is Meier to base his revision? There is no manuscript to, presumably, direct revelation from the Pleiadians/Plejarens.

Incidentally, there were a supposed 22 assassination attempts upon Meier over the years.

In the end, Meier states that he will be "making the whole thing clear in an introduction in the 'Talmud Jmmanuel'" and Ptaah reiterates that Billy's reluctance to publish an imperfect text and their fear of his assassination is why "we didn't mention the defectiveness."

Alien Inspired Comments Regarding Christianity

Michael Horn, who considers the Meier information "the most important story in all of human history" posted *Questions To Meier—Answered* wherein Meier (sometimes as consulted by Christian Frehner) answered questions posted to the FIGU which is part of the *Semjase Silver Star Center*.

Michael Horn himself asked Meier:

> Semjase said that the damage from the
> Christian religion had spread to other
> systems and galaxies and even caused their
> destruction. How is this possible when, as
> crazy as things are here, we haven't yet
> destroyed our own world over this, at least
> not to the extent she describes?

The generic answer is:

> The other ones had more sophisticated
> weapons and technology to destroy
> themselves. --- We are still bound to our
> planet (luckily, in this respect). We are still
> in our baby shoes compared to them (in
> technical aspects).

That is interesting since the twentieth century was, both, the most secular and the bloodiest in human history. At that time some 200,000,000 people were murdered, mostly by Atheist Communist regimes, with not much more than bullets—high death rate with low technology.

Someone asked:

> Most Christian believers of Bible
> information are so intensely caught in the
> idea that the So called SATAN figure in
> scriptures still exists in invisible energy
> force. When I come across a Christian
> believer and explain to them certain aspects
> of The PLEJARAN mission and the reality
> behind all history of the world and influence
> which ET groups have input in the world,

they always seems to use the lines of the
Bible which sound something like this:
"SATAN FOOLS US BY MAKING
HIMSELF AND ANGEL OF LIGHT
(UFOs)TO DECIEVE
US INTO THINKING NO GOD EXIST."
I argue the point which is erroneous from
scripture so that they can understand that is a
trick in scripture to condition mankind.
What would be a much better approach to
handling and debating the SATAN idea with
them?? [sic]

The entirety of the answer is:

There's no use to argue with Christian
believers. It's a waste of time. A useless
effort. Besides: Satan simply is some kind of
imagination, a religious invention.

This simple sentence, perhaps beyond any other, is just
about the best summation of Meier's message.

Someone else had a question about Satan:

...it is usually said that 'Satan' was invented
by the evil Chrisitan cult to control people
more easily, which is very logical, but i have
a little doubt . . . the Christian Cult was
created many time after Jmmanuel4s death,
but in the Talmud [which one?] in Chapter
18, he mentions a "Satan" Since it is
supposed that the "devil" was created by
religions distorting the story of Teubel the
guy with horn like growths in his skull and
"god the hunt" of the Celts, Then my
question is:
Was Satan a real person that in the past did

some nasty things, so that his name became a "symbol" of evil and ignorance or is he just another fairy tale to scare kids like "the bogeyman"??? (which i dont think it is the case because then why would Jmmanuel would mention him). [sic]

Answer:

Satan wasn't a real person. It was the personification of "evil", a term he used like "heaven" and "hell", which are no places/locations, but inner states of mind.

Another question:

…What do you mean really happens when a person gets "saved", become baptized spiritually (if it is spiritually, or a loss of human guilt which is manifested in the soul), have a first objective experience with christianity etc etc, which can be manifested completely different in regard of human imagination, or by thinking that "Jesus died for our sins" and so on? What is the reason for such a longlasting relationship to a spiritual force that is not regarded as spiritual by your means? Is this a kind of debuting schizophrenia? [sic]

Answer:

"Being saved" is a matter of pure belief-like imagination from which delusion may develop, and yes, sometimes even schizophrenia etc.

The next question reveals more than the answer, as the answer is simply "No"; here is the question:

> I have reason to believe that the benefactor
> ETs…seem concerned with Christian
> believers who would judge them as devils
> and demons, not to mention humanities
> destructive and deceptive nature at this time
> along with one future possibility that the
> Popes in the Catholic religion could bring
> about a world war 3. Concerning Earth's
> past history, I assume these ETs don't like
> people to be angry or afraid of them. Should
> world war 3 come to past, I hear from
> different sources that these kind of ETs may
> rescue many children from the horrors of
> global war. Is there really a chance that
> children will be rescued from a global war,
> from any one or more groups of ETs?

Well, that was asked in 2003 AD and little did this person
know that by now, 2013 AD, the Vatican considers aliens
to not only be out brethren but will either baptize them or
that they may not have sinned at all.

The next question probably expresses the reaction of a
possessed person to dealing with a Christian who has the
true Jesus living with them:

> I have noticed that when I get into an intense
> discussion with someone about spiritual/
> consciousness related subjects, I often get
> very thirsty and warm in my head and
> sometimes my body gets a bit shaky and
> trembles (perhaps adrenaline pulsing
> through the body). I sometimes feel the
> same symptoms when I try to find words to
> explain spiritual concepts to an interested
> person new to these things.
> These effects are stonger when the one Im

speaking with has a lot of resistance to my
views like a fanatical christian who
aproached me a few weeks ago. This person
claimed that he wanted to hear my opinion
but he really seemed more interested in
preaching Christianity.
After the 10-20 minute discussion I drank
1,5 litres of water to help me back to
balance. Can you explain what happens. Is
this stress (or whatever it is) created by
myself or the other person? Is it my
thoughts, emotions or consciousness that is
behind it? [sic]

The utterly inept reply is:
Thinking is demanding (strenuous).
Thinking sustains itself on the consciousness
and the brain. Thinking burns glucose and
other elements in the brain. Stress is self-
produced.

We all do a lot of thinking every day but do not get thirsty,
warm headed, shaky, tremble, specifically when dealing
with *spiritual concepts* and particularly with Christians.

Question:
Can you tell us exactly what was the
purpose of Jmmanuel's baptism?, as in why
would Jmmanuel need to be baptized by
water in the first place when this sort of act
would only later just fuel the fire of faith in
religious Christian believers?

Good question. While I do not know why Jmmanuel was
baptized, the New Testament tells us about Jesus' baptism:

> Then Jesus arrived from Galilee at the
> Jordan coming to John, to be baptized by
> him. But John tried to prevent Him, saying,
> "I have need to be baptized by You, and do
> You come to me?" But Jesus answering said
> to him, "Permit it at this time; for in this
> way it is fitting for us to fulfill all
> righteousness" (Matthew 3:13-17).

The answer to the Jmmanuel question was:
> It was a symbolic act, some form of
> initiation. It was no exorcism (driving out
> the devil) in the common sense as it is the
> case in Christianity.

But is Biblical baptism about *driving out the devil*? No:
> …baptism now saves you—not the removal
> of dirt from the flesh, but an appeal to God
> for a good conscience—through the
> resurrection of Jesus Christ. (1 Peter 3:21)

It is interesting to ponder what would happen if these folks
actually had a clue as to what the Bible actually states.

Question:
> Jews, Christians and Muslims all believe
> that the Bible speaks of only one God, and
> Muslims say that this God also revealed the
> Quran to them. My question is how many
> gods were there since the time of Adam, and
> was the god Jehovah the only god who
> involved himself in human affairs?

Answer:
> Billy doesn't know the exact number, and
> there have been several gods involved in

human affairs, not only in the Near East, but in other regions and continents too, like Japan, Persia, Africa, North and South America, India, etc. In the case of the Jews there was not just Jehovah involved, but other ones too (Aruseak, Kamagol, ...).

Well, that clears it up.

Question:

This question pertains to the role of ALLAH and where he came from as a inspiring figure for the Prophet Muhammad. ALLAH being an JSHWJSH of the time of the Prophet Muhammad (Peace be upon him), what was the cause of ALLAH's time here and what lineage of ET human race did he come from ??

(The reason I ask this question is because my strong curiousity of knowing about this JSHWJSH who the Muslims name so well and worship in the Qura'an and is part of a segment of the contact notes which are only in German language at this time and I would like to know something more of this JSHWJSH if there is enough information on ALLAH). [sic]

Answer:

The cause was to help Mohammed to correct the false (Christian) teachings that were concocted from Jmmanuel's true teachings. Unfortunately, Mohammed's teachings were distorted and falsified, too.

(Note by CF: Therefore, Mohammed's mission was a failure in this respect.)

Regarding the ET lineage: The JHWH
(Allah) belonged to the Lyrian lineage.

A follow-up question asks:
If Understand correctly ALLAH means
JSCWJSCH, if this being the case then is it
permissible by the Plejarens and yourself to
tell us the name of this JSCHWJSCH. This
ALLAH, what was his name??

Answer:
Allah doesn't mean Jschwjsch/JHWH. Allah
is the name for an imaginary deity just as it
is the case with the Christian God. Besides,
Allah and God are in no way the same as
Creation.

This last portion is important since as it typical of alien
theology; there is no personal God but only an impersonal
and, this is the key, amoral energy (qi, ki, chi, prana, Vril,
the Force, etc.). Meier's alien theology holds to the
(Aleister Crowley sounding) law of love and yet, Creation
is not personal and thus, cannot express or promulgate love.

Question:
In one of your contacts with Asket regarding
the Tunguska Incident, she said to you:
"More than 4,300 life forms of
extraterrestrial origin were destroyed during
this gigantic destruction, which only leads
back to the terrestrial Christian cult, because
the actual reason for this destruction was the
insanity of this terrestrial religion."
Specifically, how did the Christian cult play
a role in the destruction of this
extraterrestrial craft?

Answer:

> About 1160 years ago three races of ET's
> from far away galaxies of this universe came
> to Earth. They got in contact with terrestrial
> priests and studied our religions. After
> several years of study they decided to teach
> their peoples according to the Christian
> religion, a deadly mistake.
> Within 11 years the long peaceful time was
> ended and war broke out between families
> and nations, etc. When one of the three
> worlds was destroyed during the world wars,
> other ET stopped the insanity, and all
> terrestrial religions and especially
> Christianity (Christian faith) was strictly
> prohibited.
> And it was also forbidden to visit Earth
> again, and should a ship get lost on Earth
> and would not be able to get off again, the
> ship and its crew should eliminate
> themselves. This occurred about 1000 years
> after the first visit on Earth, when a ship had
> to land in Russia due to severe technical
> damage.
> The ship was able to rise only a few hundred
> meters above ground, and because within
> the ship a terrestrial epidemic had started, it
> was decided to eliminate the ship in a huge
> atomic explosion, a few hundred meters
> above ground.

Someone else also asked about how Christianity caused an
alien spaceship to blow up:

> About the Christian cult is the cause of the
> Tunguska explosion that killed so many ET

humans. I find it very hard to believe that far far more advanced ET with all the technology for interspace travel would be interested in our human primitive Christian religion!!and then went back home to spread to their far more advanced people of a religion taught by people that are thousands years behind in technology and civilization. This doesn't make sense to me. Can you explain or ask the Pleadians to explain how can this happened?

Yeah, that "far far more advanced ET…would be interested in our human primitive Christian religion!!" that's what's hard to believe in the whole scenario.

Answer:
Being advanced in technical knowledge doesn't protect oneself of foolishness. Technical knowledge and consciousness-related knowledge can be out of balance quite substancially, as has been demonstrated by that IHWH who created the IHWH Mata, the so-called "eye of god", a ring nebula. He destroyed an entire galaxy.

Question:
Because man often repeats his mistakes, the past is sometimes a good indicator of the future. And since Christianity bastardized the teachings of Jmmanuel and Islam bastardized the teachings of Mohammed, what is to prevent a cult from arising in the future and bastardizing your teachings?

Answer:

For the first time in history (since the spirit
teachings originated from Nokodemion and
Henok [Note by CF: billions of years ago]),
the spirit(ual) teachings are presented today
in its original form. Today they are
presented in a form that is clearly
understandable to the human beings.
The teachings are published/given in
German, the only language on Earth that is
suitable to explain all the subtleties in detail.
At the time of the old prophets (Jmmanuel,
Mohammed, Jeremia, etc.) the people were
not capable to understand the teachings.
They were lacking the necessary
understanding and knowledge, etc.
To ensure that there is no cult arising from
the Teachings of Truth, the books must
contain the German original text on the
opposite page of the translation.
Additionally it is FIGUs task to preserve
Billys original teachings in an unchanged
format and to fight against any unauthorized
translation. In order to fully benefit from the
teachings it is necessary to learn German.
Any translation into a terrestrial language
can never be accurate.

Interestingly, Muslims claim that *In order to fully benefit
from the teachings, of Islam, it is necessary to learn Arabic
as that is the only language on Earth that is suitable to
explain all the subtleties in detail* of the Qur'an.

Question:

Since Christianity seems to be working in
regards to its intended purpose (to keep the
people from destroying the world), and

Islam also seems to be working in regards to its intended purpose (to keep Christianity from dominating the world), why is such an inglorious end prophesized for these religions?

Answer:

Because religions are fundamentally wrong. They are purely human-made and, therefore, not lasting eternally. Religions are not in line with the creational laws and the spirit(ual) teachings.

Question:

There's a person which I've heard a number of people talk about called "Jesus Maitreya" who's commonly referred to as the anti-Christ by many Christian believers. Personally I believe it to be all a hoax, however there was a particular individual seeing once in Nairobi Kenya back on June 11 1988 performing so-called miracles for the local residence living in the area from which photos were taken, following of which he was never really seen again despite the many claims by Benjamin Creme. Question and if you know the answer: Who really was this person who appeared in Nairobi Kenya back on June 11 1988? If you don't know then perhaps you can find out for me and others, eh! Also I think all this talk about Helena Petrovna Blavatsky should be finally cleared up as there too exists a group of photos in circulation concerning her involved with 3 individuals who are calling themselves the ascended masters of "Kuthumi, El Myora, and Saint Germain."

Answer:

All this talk about that Jesus Maitreya is nonsense and not in accordance with reality. The same is true with so-called "ascended masters", meaning, that they also don't exist in reality.

Indeed, the question was getting at *lord Maitreya* who is channeled by Benjamin Creme and who reportedly appeared but then went away only to come back again someday with a fleet of spaceships, etc. (Creme was interviewed on *Coast to Coast* by George Noory and Noory became physically ill during the interview, something he claims has never happened before).

Question:

I used to be a Christian and stopped believing it in my teenage years because it seemed illogical. I was raised in the Church by my parents, but I no longer live with them. My parents keep pressuring me to find a church, because ever sinced I moved out of there house, I have never found one because I do not believe in it, but they do not know how I feel.
My Question is: Should I tell them how I feel about it. I feel that I should, but I feel that if I do, they will never talk to me again, and I love them, or should I not interfere with there beliefs by not telling them, because I know they would never accept anything accept Christianity, sadly enough.

> And on top of that I keep having dreams
> about this. What is you advice? [sic]

How sad that a person who stopped believing in
Christianity (not surprising, during their rebellious teen
years) "because it seemed illogical" seeks advice from a
guy who traveled back in time with an alien—'cause that is
logical.

The answer is, firstly, "You shall make a council with
yourself and decide" and secondly to pretend to be asking
his parents about someone else who is experiencing such
issues and judge their reply to see how applicable it is to his
own situation.

Question:

> Sfath [one of the aliens with whom Meier
> dealt] rightly said that people are blinded by
> Christianity. I want to ask, what can we
> adopt to bring down this or any religion?
> What could bring the awareness of the FIGU
> mission to people, I mean there are only a
> few people who know about FIGU. What
> would you (Billy and Christian) suggest to
> raise awareness, coz many people don't want
> to hear such stuff?

Well, one sure way to bring the awareness of the FIGU
mission is to state, on the ***world wide*** web, that you want to
bring down this or any religion.

Answer:

> They are not only blinded by Christianity,
> but also by all other religions. The only
> thing is to learn for, and develop, yourself,
> because each person must individually find

the truth; and through living by the truth,
one is able to change one's genetically
induced religious illness/sickness.

Question:

I wanted to ask you about the aggressor
gene. Did the aggressor gene have a greater
effect on some races than others, if so,
which races. If not, how does it explain the
fact that some races are more war
mongering/racially abusive (of other races)
than others, like the Muslims? Why have
they been in war with us Americans,
Europeans for so long? From the time of the
Crusades, that is and they also justify the
killing of our people?

What good is a question that brings up Muslim aggression
if it cannot be turned around to besmirch Christianity?
Thus, the answer is:

Muslim is no race, but the term for people
who are believing in the religion of Islam,
and Muslim are people who belong to
different races. Btw: It has been Christianity
who was the war-mongering aggressor. The
crusades were a severe act of
crime/aggression against the Muslim, and it
is Christianity who is responsible for the
greatest number of killings in terrestrial
history.
(Note by CF: It is the degenerated and
misguided ones among the peoples who are
terrorists and scum. Among all races and
peoples there are good and bad individuals.)

Well, that certainly is authoritative and dogmatic and sidestepping the question but, is it accurate?
Not in the least bit, in fact, it is the opposite of the facts (see my previous reference to *The Encyclopedia of Wars*).

Meier, OT III, Gen IV & 1 Enoch IV
If you know to what the title refers, you are well ahead of the game. If not…

To make a long story short:
OT III refers to L. Ron Hubbard's *Scientology*'s level known as *Operating Thetan III*.

Gen IV refers to the Bible's book of Genesis at chapter 6.

1 Enoch IV refers to the apocryphal *Book of Enoch*'s (aka *Ethiopic Enoch* aka *1 Enoch*) sixth chapter which means that we are within that *book*'s section known as the *Book of the Watchers* (which ranges from chapters 1-36).

To make a short story long:
OT III was once a top level secret of *Scientology*'s hierarchical mysteries. Warren McShane, president of the *Church of Spiritual Technology* (a subsidiary of Scientology) claimed that OT III "are not trade secrets."

Well, whatever that means, it is a fact that there was much—litigious—ado when that of which it consists was revealed. The, public, revelation occurred via a 1995 AD court case *Religious Technology Center v. F.A.C.T.Net, Inc., et al.* , via a Feb. 2011 AD *New Yorker* article (find a citation to the court documents at this note[43]), via the "Trapped in the Closet" episode of the satirical cartoon show *South Park* (which led to Scientologist Isaac Haze, who was the voice of one of the characters, to quit the show—apparently, besmirching everyone else was acceptable but not once it hits home) and subsequently on innumerable websites, etc.

OT III was conceptualized by L. Ron Hubbard circa 1967 AD and is a history of how psychological trauma came to be within humans—in a manner of speaking. The story goes that 75 million years ago Xenu (aka *Xemu*) was the head of the Galactic Confederation and faced the problem of overpopulation. His final solution was to load circa a billion alien beings into spaceships, deposit them on Earth inside of volcanoes and drop hydrogen bombs on them.

So traumatizing was this that the souls, which Hubbard termed *thetans* (generally pronounced as *thee-tons* and somewhat like *satans*), of these alien beings, fanned out into the Earth and possess, as it were, human beings. These are what Scientology claims to be able to dislodge via their styled form of exorcism.
Of interest may be the fact that they believe that traumatic past life memories can be triggered as to bring the thetans to the surface so as to do away with them. This is why, for example, the book cover of, and commercials for, *Dianetics* features an exploding volcano. It is not an erupting volcano but a volcano that is being exploded by bombs by Xenu.

Keep in mind that the bottom line is that alien beings came to Earth, died a traumatic enough death so that they became disembodied, that they sought to inhabit, or embody, humans and that Hubbard claims the most effective method for removing them. Finally, note that Xenu, the perpetrator, is said to have been imprisoned by his own lieutenants who mutinied and is said to still (75 million years later) be alive and incarcerated here on Earth "in an electronic mountain trap."
Some of this appears to have been derived from Immanuel Velikovsky's theories.[44]

Genesis 6:1-5 states the following:

> Now it came about, when men began to
> multiply on the face of the land, and
> daughters were born to them, that the sons
> of God saw that the daughters of men were
> beautiful; and they took wives for
> themselves, whomever they chose. Then the
> Lord said, "My Spirit shall not strive with
> man forever, because he also is flesh;
> nevertheless his days shall be one hundred
> and twenty years."
> The Nephilim were on the earth in those
> days, and also afterward, when the sons of
> God came in to the daughters of men, and
> they bore children to them. Those were the
> mighty men who were of old, men of
> renown.
> Then the Lord saw that the wickedness of
> man was great on the earth, and that every
> intent of the thoughts of his heart was only
> evil continually.

From this alone, we get the concept that alien beings, the *Sons of God* (who in the Old Testament are *divine beings* consisting of a category of being known as *angels* and perhaps other categories; keeping in mind that Satan is not a fallen angel but a fallen Cherub).

To make some potentially complex stories long; note that this occurred in the pre-diluvian (before the great worldwide flood) world and so what happened to the hybrids (the half Sons of God and half human daughters of men mixtures) is that they died the traumatic death of drowning.

As they were neither 100% divine nor 100% human, they do not fall into one or the other camp (metaphorically speaking). Thus, when they died there was nowhere for them to go, as it were—at least not until the eschaton (the end days, last days, end times, etc.).

Due to this fact, 1 Enoch 6:1-8 states:

> And it came to pass when the children of men had multiplied that in those days were born unto them beautiful and comely daughters. And the angels, the children of the heaven, saw and lusted after them, and said to one another: "Come, let us choose us wives from among the children of men and beget us children." And Semjaza, who was their leader, said unto them: "I fear ye will not indeed agree to do this deed, and I alone shall have to pay the penalty of a great sin." And they all answered him and said: "Let us all swear an oath, and all bind ourselves by mutual imprecations not to abandon this plan but to do this thing."
> Then sware they all together and bound themselves by mutual imprecations upon it. And they were in all two hundred; who descended in the days of Jared on the summit of Mount Hermon, and they called it Mount Hermon, because they had sworn and bound themselves by mutual imprecations upon it. And these are the names of their leaders:
> Samlazaz, their leader, Araklba, Rameel, Kokablel, Tamlel, Ramlel, Danel, Ezeqeel, Baraqijal, Asael, Armaros, Batarel, Ananel, Zaqlel, Samsapeel, Satarel, Turel, Jomjael,

Sariel.
These are their chiefs of tens.

Thus, these traumatized and disembodied souls, now demons, roam the Earth seeking to inhabit, possess, humans.

The perpetrators, the Sons of God, currently find themselves incarcerated. Jude 1:6 refers to "the angels which kept not their first estate, but left their own habitation, he hath reserved in everlasting chains under darkness unto the judgment of the great day." And they are correlated with Sodom and Gomorrha" in verse 7 because those cities "and the cities about them in like manner, giving themselves over to fornication, and going after strange flesh, are set forth for an example, suffering the vengeance of eternal fire."

2 Peter 2:4-5 likewise states:
> For if God spared not the angels that sinned,
> but cast them down to hell, and delivered
> them into chains of darkness, to be reserved
> unto judgment...

Jesus demonstrated His power over demons, the disembodied spirits of the Nephilim (the angel/human hybrids) by commanding them to leave people and they demonstrated His power over them by obeying Him. His Jewish opponents never denied His ability to do this but only questioned whence came His ability.

We have a correlation between OTIII and 1 Enoch 6 with elucidation from Genesis 6. Traumatic deaths resulting in disembodiment. Disembodied spirits seeking embodiment. The incarceration of he/they (Xenu and the sons of God) who caused the fracas.

Thus, we see a ready-made source from which L. Ron Hubbard may have drawn inspiration for OT III.

Or, perhaps due to his consorting with the likes of Jack Parsons and their mutual practice of Aleister Crowley's black magick; he received "revelation" from demons who simply relayed the story to him.

Semjase in the Meier Case and the Book of Enoch: Cosmic Coincidences?

Billy Meier claims to be "the only true contactee of the Pleiadians" aka Plejarens and that, "It is an urgent necessity that the teachings and the Mission are disseminated and established throughout the world." (FIGU Bulletin 005)

Based on the research of Wendelle C. Stevens Lt. Col., USAF (Ret) in his book *Contact from the Pleiades*, we continue noting correlations between Semjase as the main alien within the Meier case and as the main fallen angel in the Book of Enoch.

Recall that *Semjase, Quetzal* (another alien and another form of the central American feathered serpent god Quetzalcoatl) along with Meier himself, another alien named Ptaah, et al brought madness, allowed aberration, were power hungry and established religious feudalism in order to control and enslave the ancient inhabitants of the Earth.

But not to worry, or so we are told, as "Semjase and her team" are "reformed IHWHs" (*IHWH* being a term for these early Earth exploring dictators) who, "set themselves up as Gods, Kings of Wisdom, IHWHs, Sons of God, or other similar positions…self-proclaimed 'Gods' and 'Sons of God' (The Pleiadian IHWH's) in all mythologies and religions of the last some 70,000 years of our ancient past."

Also recall that Semjase is the name of a fallen angel within the Book of Enoch and, in any case, *Pelegon* is said to have had "200 subleaders, scientists, competent in special fields of knowledge" and, later, *Arus* also had "200 leaders and subleaders, who were competent in special fields of sciences."

Well, in Section II of the Book of Enoch's chapter 6 specifies that "the angels, the sons of the heavens, saw and lusted after them [beautiful and comely daughters" of humans, see Genesis chapter 6], and said one to another 'Behold, we will choose for ourselves wives from among the children of men, and will beget for ourselves children."

Indeed, the story notes that Semjase mated with EVA and birthed Adam.

Continuing, "And Semjaza, who was their leader, said to them: 'I fear that perhaps ye will not be willing to do this deed, and I a lone shall suffer for this great sin.' Then all answered him and said:
'We all will swear an oath…and together they were **two hundred**."

Indeed, the story specified that there were **two hundred** under *Pelegon* and later **two hundred** under *Arus*.

In fact, Enoch continues immediately by noting, "And they descended on Ardis, which is the summit of Mount Hermon"; *Arus* in the Meier story and *Ardis* in the Enoch story; they are similar words applied to different people and places. Also, with regards to the term/name *Pelegon*; note that in the Bible *Peleg* means division in Hebrew and was the name of a son of Eber (from whose name we get the term Hebrew). He was named division because "in his days was the earth divided" (Genesis 10:25) via the Tower of Babel incidents (see Genesis 11).

Now, in the Meier story there were 200 scientists and when we again consult with the Book of Enoch we find that it specifies what they did in chapter 7 notes that which these leaders did:

> ...they began to go in to them, and mixed with them, and taught them charms and conjurations, and made them acquainted with the cutting of roots and of woods. And they became pregnant and brought forth great giants...And they began to sin against the birds and the beasts, and against the creeping things, and the fish, and devoured their flesh among themselves, and drank the blood thereof. Then the earth complained of the unjust ones.

To "sin against" animals may mean various things but in updated language, it may refer to the ability to genetically mix. As Wendelle Stevens put it when he retold the Meier story, "By mutation and their sciences....In a forbidden manner and secretly, they went out and caught wild Earth creatures and mutations...created mutated beings, completely new forms of life, who were of dwarf-like stature, gigantic, or animal-like."
And of course, as noted previously the Meier story has the alien Semjase (who was female in the Meier story) mating with "EVA, a female being" who birthed Adam.

Again, recall that in the Meier story the 200 were "scientists, competent in special fields of knowledge" and "competent in special fields of sciences" respectively. This, of course, means that they possessed knowledge which they brought to Earth. In the Book of Enoch's chapter 8 it is specified that which those with such knowledge taught to mankind:

> Azazel taught mankind to make swords and knives and shields and coats of mail, and taught them to see what was behind them, and their works of art: bracelets and ornaments, and the use of rouge, and the beautifying of the eye-brows, and the dearest and choicest stones and all coloring substances and the metals of the earth. And there was great wickedness and much fornication, and they sinned, and all their ways were corrupt.
> Amezarak taught all the conjurers and root-cutters.
> Armaros the loosening of conjurations.
> Baraq'al the astrologers.
> Kokabel the signs
> Temel taught astrology.
> Asradel taught the course of the moon.

These were the seven leaders of the Book of Enoch and not the 200 who fell with them. And yet, the correlation stands as the Meier material and the Book of Enoch coincide in so many places; from similar names to specific references to 200 and from false gods (whom the fallen angles and/or their offspring surely were) to the reference to bringing knowledge from beyond the Earth.

Lastly, within the context of "aliens" and fallen Angels or demons, note that occultist Allen H. Greenfield's wrote the following in his book *Secret Cipher of the UFOnauts* (First Digital Edition, 2005 AD):

...beginning in 1952, [George] Van Tassel
was in communication with a being calling
itself "Ashtar" — the name of a medieval
demon said, in the old magical texts, to have
relocated to America. Ashtar has shown up
in many subsequent cases...As both John
Keel and, in a way, the late Don Elkins have
demonstrated, contactee control names show
up in many cases and are often identical
with ancient deity names. As a prime
example, ASHTAR most likely derives from
Astaroth, a "great duke in 'the infernal
regions,'" according to the ancient magical
text The Lemegeton. The mysterious
Grimorium Verum (the "True Instruction")
in that text informs us that Astaroth "has set
up residence in America."

In his book *Secret Rituals of the Men in Black* Greenfield
notes (December 28, 2005 AD):
> ...the strange words and names that show up
> in Masonic Lodge settings are similar in
> form and purpose to those which show up in
> contact cases. They show up in modern
> cases of Angelic Visitation...They also
> show up in demonology...The occult
> literature has always considered ASHTAR,
> or Astaroth, a fallen angel, that is, a
> malevolent demon.

Meier, Asket, Jmmanuel and Time Travel

The extra-terrestrial alien named *Asket* "was the second
offworlder to contact Billy [Meier]." That which follows
are the notes regarding a time when Asket took Meier back
in time circa 2,000 years to the time of Jmmanuel whom

they claim is the original and actual person who later came to be called Jesus.

Within the notes titled "Asket's Acquaintanceship," Meier writes:

> I stood before Christ's, respectively Jmmanuel's, crucifixion utensils...I stood before everything which was connected with the death of Jmmanuel alias Jesus Christ...I wondered about Sfath's [another alien] words, that everything is only meant to be a deception, that Jesus Christ should never have been called Jesus Christ, rather Jmmanuel, that he was not God's son, and that God is not Creation...[Sfath] had once said to me that the Christian religion is just as much an irresponsible, evil, poor piece of work, for the stupefaction and enslavement of humans, as are all the other terrestrial religions.

You know that you are on the right track, as a Christian, when you learn that aliens despise your faith. On the point of "God" not being "Creation." Note that here Creation is not the material realm which was created by God. Keep in mind that, as is typical of alien theology; there is no personal God but only an impersonal and, this is the key, amoral energy.

Incidentally, In Wendelle C. Stevens' *UFO Contact From The Pleiades,* another Meier related alien named Semjase (also the name of a fallen angel in the Book of Enoch, see here) references the "Cosmic Law of Love."

Yet, *Creation* is not personal and thus, cannot express or promulgate love. Moreover, this is much like Aleister

Crowley's motto which states, "Do what thou wilt shall be the whole of the law. Love is the law. Love under will." Of course, in true satanic form, "love" does not mean that which most think it means.

Moving on to "Asket's Explanations - Part 1" we learn that "84 The terrestrial religions, brought there through the expeditions, and the destruction-releasing Christianity, were strictly forbidden to any life forms." This is part of the infamous manner in which Meier and his alien cohorts blamed Christianity for blowing up a spaceship...see below.

We are going to focus on what the notes have to say about the Bible, Jesus, and Christianity in general.

> 183-184 You thought that Sfath told you an
> untruth and that Jmmanuel, alias Jesus
> Christ, could indeed be the son of God
> because the utensils brought you into
> confusion. But Sfath spoke the truth,
> because even as with all other religions, the
> Christian religion is also only an evil and
> wrong enslaving, poor piece of work of
> Earth people, who, in their establishment of
> religions, found the wealth promised to
> them, and power over fellow men, and
> found that they would be addressed by a
> degenerated group of extraterrestrial
> intelligences if they would spread the
> erroneous religious teaching...
> 210 the alleged universal validity of
> Christianity...
> 259 You will learn the truth about
> Jmmanuel, who you wrongly call Jesus
> Christ.

In "Asket's Explanations - Part 3" "Asket, Billy and [Illyitch Ustinov aka] Jitschi travel back in time to 13th century France and encounter a man of that period, named Jechieli." Note that the notes refer to "Eduard" which is in references to *Eduard Albert Meier* who is more popularly known by his *Billy the Kid* inspired name. Thus, below we will replace *Eduard* with *Billy* for the sake of cohesion.

Meier refers to Jitschi as "an innocently trusting son of Christ, and a Bible-twerp."

> **Jitschi** "…I am a good Christian and very devout, even if I am a roughneck and walk around here armed. Here - I even always carry a small Bible with me."

> **Asket** "10. Unfortunately I have to disappoint you. 11. I am neither an angel nor do I come on a mission from God. 12. These stories about us are deliberate mis-directions by evil elements who want to conjure up malevolent things in a religious form. 13. If you are a religious believer then you have succumbed to evil, false teachings."

> **Jitschi** "You blaspheme God. That is indeed monstrous."

> **Asket** "14. That is really not the case, because you are the one who has been misled by religion…"

Meier states the following to Jitschi:
"But you said you are a good Christian. Then do Christians have a fear of death?

Jitschi "You ask funny questions. Every human does indeed fear death. Besides, I find that I am not yet mature enough to actually go to heaven. Indeed, Jesus said ... [ellipses in original]"

Asket "20. That is precisely what he did not even say. It is all a deliberately falsified tradition. 21. Besides, the man never bore the name Jesus. 22. He was plainly and simply called Jmmanuel."

Meier "I find your behaviour also not exactly correct and courageous, and besides, I believe I know that you are basically wrongly orientated in regard to heaven."

Jitschi "Do you think so? - You two have somewhat peculiar views. I trust in God and Jesus Christ."

Meier "If you trust in them, then indeed you do not need to be afraid of the spaceship. - Is it rather not the case that your beloved Christian religion leaves you in doubt?"

Jitschi "I am devout and not in doubt."

Meier "That appears to me to be exactly the case – if I reflect on everything. Here you have to make your own decision, because dear God and Jesus Christ, who you can simply load off on and burden with your responsibility, are not here. It is unfortunately the case with the believers that they always shift their own responsibility onto a saint or onto dear God because they are not able to bear their own responsibility. Therefore they also cannot make any of their own decisions and conclusions which are really important for them. Do you want to assert something else and do you belong to this sort of believer?...

In "Asket's Explanations - Part 4":

Billy describes the experience of travelling through time and how his companion Jitschi became irrational and developed fanatical tendencies against the Christian religion through his experience of time travel discoveries of our true past, even though he was previously a devout Christian before the journey.

Meier notes:

I caught him cursing while furiously scratching out entire chapters of his Bible with a red pen. Having found reality completely different from the way it was described in the Bible must have made a great deal of work for him. From time to time I heard him talking to himself and issuing threats against those who, "still preach such nonsense today". I slowly developed serious concerns that he could become an anti-religious fanatic and that, after the final return into our normal time, he would go quite mad.

But the remainder gave him the truth about the life and work of Jmmanuel when Asket led us back to the year 32 in order to, there and then, examine those events which are described so wrongly and counter to reality in the New Testament of the Christian Bible…the events concerning Jmmanuel, which, during two thousand years, were so malevolently falsified that a mass psychosis arose from it, as did a further religion, Islam, as well as many sects which were able to be constructed from it.

This convenient tale is about how traveling through time acquainted a once devote Christian with the truth which the aliens were showing him; that Jesus, actually Jmmanuel, was that whom the Bible claims and was crucified but did not die, etc. Via this tale, Meier takes occasion to show how, specifically, his claims can overcome Christianity and thus, how Christians can be converted to alien theology.

"Asket's Explanations - Part 5" continues along these lines:
> **Jitschi** "Damn. The year 32 would indeed have to be the year of the crucifixion of Christ. Or?"

> **Asket** "…7. I have to determine that your manner of expression has indeed changed a lot in the last few days. 8. It is no longer so strongly orientated towards religion as it was at the beginning of our acquaintanceship."

> **Jitschi** "Holy smoke. Is that so surprising?…I was a slave to damned religion and this idiotic Christianity my whole life long. Now you suddenly turn up with your mad friend and drag me out into outer space and far back into various past epochs. Everywhere I have to see and

recognise that the damned religions are only mean and filthy machinations of mad or power-greedy humans and that everything is only a quite damned idiocy for the purpose of the exploitation of us dumb commoners. And now you even want to drag me back to the time of the crucifixion in order to actually prove to me the goddamned idiocy of these power-mad swine. Then I am still supposed to keep quiet there, eh?"

Meier "Jitschi, I advise you to talk to Asket somewhat more politely, otherwise I will punch you in the nose…you allowed yourself to be misled by the false religious teachings…each one was transformed into a cult by irresponsible humans and is ruled by delusional dogmas which lead humans into error. But in itself each religion possesses many good and correct things which point many people to the correct path and are able to help them in many sorts of matters. Religion, in and of itself, is therefore not bad, rather only that which is made of it in association with the unreal dogmas and many erroneous teachings of irresponsible, delusional believers and profit-sharks, and so forth.

In "Asket's Explanations - Part 6" *Eduard* aka *Billy* meets *Jmmanuel* aka *Jesus*.

Meier "…people made you into a superman with a divine function."

Jmmanuel "10. You are very wise and

quick thinking…14. You are very connected to reality."

We find out that, in a manner of speaking, via a clairvoyant exercise of the power of consciousness one can "wander through the ages and can explore them."

Jmmanuel also says of the *scribes* that "30. From the spiritual teaching, they have made a false teaching, and they have abased Creation to a human entity which they call God." Which could refer to a denial of a personal God and/or a denial of Jesus' divinity. In 34 he references "a human, such as I."

Apparently, Meier is getting bored with Jmmanuel's ramblings and interrupts him to state, "…it appears to me that I can recognise, from that, that you, in a certain sense, have succumbed to weltschmerz, and thereby digress from the actual questions." Interestingly, the word *weltschmerz* is not translated from the German original. It refers to world-weariness or world-pain and denotes a "mental depression or apathy caused by comparison of the actual state of the world with an ideal state."
Jmmanuel then states:
> 72. Truly, your evolution is about 2000
> years further advanced from my time, which
> I did not take into account. 73. It is therefore
> not fitting that I converse with you in the
> same way that I do with my contemporaries.
> 74. Truly, I had not considered this. 77.
> Truly, I had not considered all that.

Jmmanuel then states that he "spent long years in the distant land of Kush (note from Billy: today part of North India), where I was permitted to experience further learning." This plays off of the, thoroughly debunked claim that Jesus learned occult practices (by any other name) in India from Buddhist monks or Hindu priests, some claim that He learned such things whilst in Egypt as a child and on it goes.

Jmmanuel goes on to state:

> 91. Among my followers, I have a literate man named Judas Iscariot, who writes down the most important parts of the teaching and events, which later, well preserved, shall outlast the time in order to hand down the actual truth to posterity.

This may sound like the *Gospel of Judas* but it is not. Rather, it is in reference to the Talmud of Jmmanuel:

> 92. With the help of an ex-priest, these texts will be found by you, in your time, in Jerusalem and you will spread them again, true to their meaning, and make them accessible to the humans.

Meier asks if that means "that your teaching really remains preserved and then it will also be found by me somewhere?" and gets a reply in the affirmative. Thus, according to what Meier writes, it is Meier who is the only one who has presented to the world the real, actual and truly accurate teachings of Jmmanuel / Jesus.

As it turns out:

> 97. Juda Ihariot, a son of a Pharisee, secretly took it out of Judas Iscariot's bag in order to sell it to my persecutors for 70 pieces of silver, in order, thereby, to be able to charge me with blasphemy against God. 98. But Judas Iscariot has been ordered by me to write the text once again and now to keep it

quite safe whereby its purpose will outlast
the ages.

Next, Meier plays into the satanic deception of turning
Judas into the good guy by asking:
>   You speak of Judas Iscariot, who is
>   supposed to be your betrayer, as the texts of
>   my time still convey, nonetheless falsified!

Jmmanuel tells him:
>   99. Truly, I speak of him. 100. But he will in
>   no way be the guilty one. 101. He who will
>   hand me over to the persecutors is the same
>   one who stole the texts and sold them.

Thus, Jmmanuels' true betrayer is not Judas Iscariot but
Juda Ihariot. Well, as unimaginative as this is, it leads to a
further conspiracy as:
>   103. But his father will spread the lie that
>   Judas Iscariot is the betrayer, because the
>   Pharisee name Ihariot must not be soiled.

And, of course, the one who hanged himself was not Judas
but Juda. Moreover, Jmmanuel notes:
>   119. So then, in your time, they call me 'the
>   Anointed One' and they thereby wander far
>   from every truth, through deep darkness
>   engendered by belief.

Well, this leads to one of the big deals for Meier's which is:
>   But how is it now with yourself - I mean
>   with your name? It is indeed Jmmanuel, but
>   in spite of that, in my time you are called
>   "Jesus Christ". That is the way it is in the
>   New Testament anyway.

He does not seem to know that in the time of Jesus titles were names and names were titles. That is to say that a "name" was not just a label but something that said something about a person and their character.

The New Testament states:
> Behold, a virgin shall be with child, and
> shall bring forth a son, and they shall call his
> name **Emmanuel**, which being interpreted
> is, God with us. Then Joseph being raised
> from sleep did as the angel of the Lord had
> bidden him, and took unto him his wife: and
> knew her not till she had brought forth her
> firstborn son: and he called his name **Jesus**
> (Matthew 1:23-25)

It is not as if no one noticed this until Meier came along, it is just that people have understood it via historical, cultural and grammatical context. *Jesus* comes from *Yehoshua* which is what we today pronounce *Joshuah* and whom many call *Yeshua* (or *Y'shua*) which is *Josh*. The Greek is *Iesous* and it means *YHVH is salvation*.

Well, to this issue Jmmanuel states that it is "127. Truly, that is an evil vituperation, which is foreign to every truth." Vituperation refers to an outburst of violently abusive or harshly critical language.

He also takes the opportunity to debunk another Christian claim that is based on the well evidenced and well preserved Bible:
> 130. He will also bear the blame for me
> being designated as Creation and for the lie
> that I am omnipotent.

This leads to a favorite of anti-Christians; Paul bashing, as Jmmanuel states, "131. All this will happen this way through Paul, who currently is still one of my worst enemies and is still named Saul." And receives an affirmative reply when he asks whether "through the construction of Christianity, he will found his own erroneous religion; a Paulism."

In the end, Meier asks, "You mean, that only a misled human calls you 'Jesus Christ'?" to which the reply is, "139. Truly, that is what I said, because every human who knows the truth will call me by my correct name, because, for him, the truth signifies life and knowledge."

In "Asket's Explanations - Part 7" the *Jmmanuel vs. Jesus Christ* issue continues as Jmmanuel states, "154. If one, however, associates me in any kind of manner with this name then one accuses me of wrong and of lying" to which Meier, hilariously, states, "You are very sensitive, Jmmanuel."

And on it goes as he also states that "172....the name Jesus Christ, malevolently given to me":

173. It will be asserted that I, Jmmanuel, would not be falsely named Jesus Christ, so it is supposed to appear that I, Jmmanuel, and the person of Jesus Christ, who I am imputed to be, have been two different people.

Meier takes an opportunity to declare himself, via these writings, to be more advanced than Jmmanuel (keeping in mind that Meier traveled back in time):

You thereby mean that in regard to your development, and so on, calculated in your time, you live in my future time, therefore

roughly calculated as about the year
2000?...But you have spoken of more than
3,000 years in regard to me. I am supposed
to be advanced, by this number of years, in
spiritual development in relation to the real
time of the year 1953. Is that not quite
grossly underestimated for you?

Jmmanuel replies:
204. From this time, in which I live here, I
am advanced in my spiritual evolution
already by about 2,000 years, while you are
about 3,000 years advanced of your real
time. 205. So therefore our spiritual
development is truly not the same in my
current and in your normal time. 206. You
are, in real life, about 2,000 years further
advanced than myself, and are indeed
already 3,000 years advanced of your own
time in your spiritual development. 207.
Truly it is calculated in such a way that you,
in your time, and I in my time, do not
display a common level of spiritual
development.

But, of course, during Jmmanuel's time Meier is more
advanced since he came from the future but when Billy
returns to the future then Jmmanuel will be more advanced
as he will have 2,000 years on Billy but then Billy should
have lost 2,000 when he went back in time and thus been
less advanced than Jmmanuel...oi vey, time travel's
grandmother paradox has nothing on this.

On the other hand, a "Note from Billy" on this text states:
"Billy" Eduard Albert Meier, in this time, on
his part, is already again more than 3,000

years further advanced and consequently again more than 3,000 years in advance of Jmmanuel's spirit form in overall spiritual evolution.

In "Asket's Explanations - Part 8" Meier asks Jmmanuel "how things stand with your teachings" since "It is indeed said in the New Testament that you are the son of God; and that God himself embodies Creation."
Well, the New Testament refers to Jesus as the son of God but not that *God himself embodies Creation*. In fact, as per above, the Meiersian concept of Creation is nothing like the Bible's concept of creation.

Meier also states:

> ...in these testament texts, God is always even spoken of as the Heavenly Father and you are spoken of as the redeemer of mankind, and so forth. Everything is quite confused and often even absolutely illogical and paradoxical.

Jmmanuel agrees, "213. Truly, you say it" and reiterates that Judas wrote the original and accurate version. He also states that within the New Testament:

> ...mendacious words [prone to lying at any time, deliberately untrue, etc.] are put into my mouth, and I am supposed to have spoken of a father in heaven, the gathering of a host of angels and many other false things [that] do not correspond to the truth...an evil deception and abominable falsification on the part of the twisters of the texts and false teachers...falsifications lies...slander.

Jmmanuel states, "221. God was never put on a level with Creation by me, because God is a creature of Creation as are you and I and every other human." So, according to the Meier definition, Creation created God and thus, in a manner of speaking, Creation is God's God.

One thing that Meier has going for him is that he never bothers distinguishing *relation*—as in what we are to have with Jesus—and *religion*—understood as an authoritative hierarchy. In other words, he makes a good point about the corrupt nature of man-made *religion* and then takes his readers/listeners down the road towards alien theology.

Yet, man-made religion is not Christianity and true Christianity is not man made religion. Recall the only positive statement about "religion" in the New Testament:
> Pure and undefiled religion before God and
> the Father is this: to visit orphans and
> widows in their trouble, and to keep oneself
> unspotted from the world. (James 1:27)

Meier asks "But how is it then with religion in general?" and makes an attempt to define that of which he speaks, "And when I thereby speak of religion, then I mean really the religion itself, not, for instance, the dogmas and other false teachings."

He also states that the dogmas and false teachings are make up the modern day "cult."

Jmmanuel replies, "231. Truly, you are not inferior to me in my teachings" and promulgates a dogma, "235. But these religions must be free of misleading cults, from dogmas and false teachings." It is dogmatic to demand that "religions must be free...from dogmas."

Recall that within *The How, What and How of Alien Messages* I provided a template for understanding, reading between the lines of such messages and how they all lead to the establishment of a new world order with a one world religion.

Case in point, Jmmanuel goes on to say that when "the truth is again purified" then "religion and relegeon can again be united." Well, this is because he had previously noted that "239….religion is fundamentally wrong, and only relegeon alone can be useful."

This segment of Meier's notes are the end of the "Asket's Explanations" and although, as Meier notes, "further reports of the contacts with Asket must be interrupted here.

The reason for that is that I can no longer locate the old reports from the year 1953/1964, as I have obviously hidden them too well." Don't you hate it when an alien takes you back in time to meet Jmmanuel but you misplace some of your notes about it?

Erich Von Daniken and the Ancient Astronauts

While in his cell, he claims, he experienced an intense vision. Von Daniken won't discuss the nature of the vision…
—Timothy Ferris referring to when Daniken was incarcerated for embezzlement, fraud and forgery

Playboy of the Gods

In 1974 AD Erich Von Daniken—of ancient (alien) astronaut fame (or, *infamy*)—was interviewed by Timothy Ferris for *Playboy* magazine and yet, one that no one seems to have transcribed it as of yet which is why we will provide much of the text within this series. I decided to review this article rather than various books since it includes fascinating back and forth discussions and was not merely a platform from which Von Daniken could claim that which he willed in an unchallenged manner—FYI: since it was, after all, published in *Playboy* I did not exactly check the primary source material—capiche?—but found a scan of just the article alone.

Ferris did a great job in digging into the issues pertaining to Von Daniken many claims. Von Daniken shows an ability to attempt good answers which, if left to themselves, would fly (pardon the pun) and yet, which Ferris all but dismantles by digging deeper.

Let us begin with some statements about Von Daniken background beginning with what his views are:

> Von Daniken speculates that Earth was explored at least twice in prehistoric times by intelligent beings from another world. According to him, the mated with humans,

bestowed the gifts of intelligence and civilization and may have helped build such monuments as the pyramids…

Now, quoting Von Daniken:

…we have been visited from outer space in ancient times but that those visitors had sexual intercourse with our ancestors…and altered, by artificial mutations, our intelligence…we are the products of them. This does not deny Darwin and his theory: I fully admit that we came from apes. My question is just why and how we became intelligent. *To this question each mythology, each old religion gives the same answer: The gods created man after their own image.*

Von Daniken is asked, "When did you become convinced that these theories were true?" and replies:

I guess only in recent years. I wrote *Chariots of the Gods?* in 1966 so for me it's an old book. When I wrote it, I was not at all convinced. By the second book, *Gods from Outer Space* I was more certain, but not absolutely. The basic thing is to be convinced that the fundamental theory is right, that we have been visited from outer space and those visitors altered our intelligence by artificial mutations. Of this I have felt certain for the past four years or so.

What is interesting about the whole ancient astronaut alien issue is that it is yet another corruption or, a materialist rewriting of, the Bible's Genesis chapter six, et al.

Note that "that Earth was explored at least twice in prehistoric times by intelligent beings from another world" mirrors Genesis chapter six's *Sons of God* who came to Earth. These are *alien* beings, not from another planet but from another dimension: EDs and not ETs.

That they "mated with humans, bestowed the gifts of intelligence and civilization and may have helped build such monuments as the pyramids" also mirrors the Genesis text as the extra dimensional *aliens* married and mated with the *daughters of men* and their children (the *Nephilim*) became mighty (Hebrew *gibbowr*) men of old renown. In post flood history we find that Nimrod was mighty/gibbowr and set out to build the tower of Babel and various cities.

The main premise obviously differs, such as that "we came from apes," (see what we meant by materialism: Atheism, by any other name) and yet the story line lines up at certain points.

The reason is that the real events of creation, Eden and its garden, an original couple or humans, the *Sons of God* mating with the *daughters of men*, the flood, the ark, etc. survive as stories in every ancient culture is that these are our most ancient histories.

These would have been carried across the Earth by the people groups who separated according to language groups after the tower of Babel event. Henceforth, this history would be subject to variation, changes in names, etc., and yet maintain the basic premises and come to be called *legend* or *myth*.

Fact, Fraud or Fiction?

Within the article, Von Daniken is referred to as an "ex-convict" as he has been convicted of embezzlement, fraud, and forgery. It is noted that the legal system's "Examining psychiatrist said he displayed a 'tendency to lie'" and that "a count appointed psychiatrist described him as a liar and a criminal psychopath."

Without getting into the details of his convictions, it may be of interest to note Von Daniken's statement on the issue:

> I have never committed fraud or embezzlement, although it is true I have been convicted of those things. I was improperly convicted three times…People don't ask if Christ was convicted of a crime. What has that to do with the message Christ brought? What does my having been in jail, guilty or innocent, have to do with my work?

In a way, his reply is a good one as strictly speaking saying something to the likes of "Well, Von Daniken is an ex-convict so his ancient astronaut alien must be false" would be to commit an *ad hominem* aka *genetic fallacy*: bypassing a counter argument by seeking to discredit the source of the argument. And yet, if a person has been thrice convicted of embezzlement, fraud, and forgery and displays a tendency to lie then his claims can be rightly thought of as suspect. Yet, to be *suspect* is not to be debunked which is why Ferris actually digs into the specific claims made by Von Daniken.

> Critics say…he plays fast and loose with the truth. "Shilling the rubes," *The New York Times* has called his work. "A fine unscrupulous 12-year old mind," said *Esquire*. "The Clifford Irving of the Cosmos"—*The Miami News*. And an

> archeologist familiar with Von Daniken's
> work said, flatly: "He simply lies."
> But that kind of talk doesn't seem to bother
> Von Daniken. "I'm the only author who has
> really frightened the critics," he says. "Other
> writers sit at home and wait for miracles,
> I'm making the miracles"…scientists
> dismiss him as a con man, but to millions of
> readers what he writes is close to gospel.

While he surely did not mean it this way, his statement "I'm making the miracles" is actually true; in a manner of speaking as he simply invents his evidence and thus, *makes the miracles.*

Another interesting fact about Von Daniken's background is provided:

> …he grew up under the twin shadows of a
> stern father and the Catholic Church,
> eventually rebelling against both. At Saint
> Michaels…[a] Catholic school in Fribourg,
> he soon ran into trouble, he says today,
> because he refused to accept Church
> interpretations of the Bible…["]I did have
> difficulties with my father and with my
> Catholic upbringing, but it's not true that
> because of this I am now, an adult, trying to
> defeat Christianity. That's not so.["]

Well, rebelling against and refusing to accept (the Roman Catholic) Church's interpretations of the Bible is not only understandable but commendable. Although, of course, he is, consciously or not, trying to defeat Christianity with everything from his belief that "we came from apes" to his main theory that "we have been visited from outer space" by "visitors [who] had sexual intercourse with our ancestors" and that "we are the products of them." So, aliens had sex with apes and here we are—not exactly Christian theology.

And just what was that "intense vision" and who bequeathed it unto him? "Von Daniken won't discuss the nature of the vision."

The Lucrative Changing of Youthful Minds

With pride in his voice, Von Daniken explained that he had just paid off the mortgage on the house. It's not a large place and the boast seemed a bit odd coming from an author who had sold some 25,000,000 books [as of 1974 AD] world-wide, but in fact he isn't a very rich man.

Rights to "Chariots [of the Gods]" have been sold over the years to a series of publishers in a system that works out like a writer's nightmare. Each partner in his elaborate bucket brigade skims off 50 percent of the money and what's left may take as long as three years to reach Von Daniken. So whatever else he can be accused of, he is not profiteering from his theories.

Well, overall, while he *may not* have made much money from his books—as he is rich but not "very rich"—he has, for decades, made money from presenting lectures, given interviews and has been involved in all sorts of projects related to various forms of media. Thus, he most certainly is *profiteering from his theories* (a fact that does not discredit his claims, this was just a point about accuracy).

Note the following, revealing, statement made by Von Daniken:

> There are only a few of us working on my
> theory and it's like a war we have to win.
> First we must change the minds of the
> public, especially the young girls and boys
> in high schools and universities, so that
> when they come to the scientists they will
> look at the facts with new eyes. One or two
> generations will pass; maybe today's truth
> will no longer be the truth of tomorrow.

So just what was that "intense vision" and who bequeathed
it unto him? "Von Daniken won't discuss the nature of the
vision." But it has led him to seek to "change the minds of
the public, especially the young girls and boys" so that they
will believe that "we came from apes" to his main theory
that "we have been visited from outer space" by "visitors
[who] had sexual intercourse with our ancestors" and that
"we are the products of them."

Until such a time as "today's truth will no longer be the
truth of tomorrow." Well, if something is true/truth then it
was, is and will be true/truth as, by definition, truth is
absolute. This means that something is what/how it is
whether we like it or not, whether we would prefer it be
different or not, whether we disagree or not, whether we are
aware of it or not; truth is true.

And what is his "truth" based upon, these "facts" here is
one simple example of Von Daniken's modus operandi:

> ...he rummaged through books and papers
> in search of material to back up his claims.
> He seemed satisfied even if the books
> yielded no evidence at all: He is a man who
> enjoys the trappings of scholarship—at least
> as much as scholarship itself.

Ezekiel's UFO vision

I dealt with this issue above but will touch upon it again as Von Daniken brings it up as he states:

> Mr. Josef Blumrich, chief of the systems-
> layout branch of NASA has published a
> book, *The Spaceships of Ezekiel*. He comes
> to the definite conclusion, with scientific
> methods, that the Old Testament prophet
> Ezekiel described the landing of a spaceship
> in 592 B.C.

Apparently, when traversing the vast distances
Of space it is a best practice to use propellers.

The following exchange takes place:

> [Ferris] Ezekiel also says he saw a heap of
> dry bones turned into an army of living men.
> [Von Daniken] Oh, really? I don't remember
> this passage. It must have been a miracle. As

wild speculation, I could say maybe he saw
a movie or something.

Well, the main issue is the allegedly supposed "Spaceships
of Ezekiel" which is in chapters 1 and 10 of the Book of
Ezekiel whilst the dry bones are found in chapter 37 so let
us set it aside (might as well quote 37:1, "The LORD took
hold of me, and I was carried away by the Spirit of the
LORD to a valley filled with bones").

The interview continues:

> [Ferris] If the creature who spoke to Ezekiel
> was an astronaut, why did he keep insisting
> he was God?

> [Von Daniken] I have just the opposite
> recollection, that he did not say he was God.
> I guess it depends on the translation you use.

> [Ferris] In the King James version of the
> Bible this being repeats many times, very
> clearly, that He is God and Ezekiel had
> better listen to Him.

> [Von Daniken] Well, if I came down to a
> primitive people they would look upon me
> as God. Everything I did would make me
> God in their eyes, because I did would make
> me God in their eyes, because I could fly,
> kill animals with a single shot, and so forth.
> So maybe Ezekiel called him God. But I
> definitely do not think the commander of the
> spaceship said he was God. If he did, it
> would be proof for me that he was a liar.

[Ferris] This being is quoted as saying "I am the Lord" over and over again.

[Von Daniken] But what is the Lord? The commander.

Step one in unpacking this is the claim that "the creature who spoke to Ezekiel…keep insisting he was God. Focus on Von Daniken's reply which is that, that is not the case but it "depends on the translation" which brings the reference to "the King James version" which makes it "very clearly, that He is God."

But the issue is **not** translation because we can simply check the underlying Hebrew text. Yet, in any regard let us check the KJV translation for good measure.

The term "God" appears in:
     1:1, "I saw visions of God."
     10:5, "the sound of the cherubims' wings was…as the voice of the Almighty God."
     10:19, "the glory of the God of Israel [was] over them [the cherubim] above."
     10:20, "This [the cherubim] [is] the living creature that I saw under the God of Israel."

The term "LORD" appears in:
     1:3, "The word of the LORD came expressly unto Ezekiel…and the hand of the LORD was there upon him."
     1:28, "This [was] the appearance of the likeness of the glory of the LORD."
     10:4, "Then the glory of the LORD went up…and the court was full of the brightness of the LORD'S glory."

> 10:18, "Then the glory of the LORD
> departed."
> 10:19, "the cherubims...stood at the door of
> the east gate of the LORD'S house."

Not all of these identify the "creature who spoke to
Ezekiel" as being God or the LORD but some do and so the
case is closed.

But it is not closed for Von Daniken:
> [Von Daniken] Well, if I came down to a
> primitive people they would look upon me
> as God. Everything I did would make me
> God in their eyes, because I did would make
> me God in their eyes, because I could fly,
> kill animals with a single shot, and so forth.
> So maybe Ezekiel called him God. But I
> definitely do not think the commander of the
> spaceship said he was God. If he did, it
> would be proof for me that he was a liar.
>
> [Ferris] This being is quoted as saying "I am
> the Lord" over and over again.
>
> [Von Daniken] But what is the Lord? The
> commander.

Note what we have repeatedly emphasized which is that the
ancient astronaut alien theory is materialistic/Atheistic.
After all, he is explaining away an appearance of God/the
LORD as being some sort of technologically more
advanced alien.

But what, then, of the fact that "This being is quoted as
saying 'I am the Lord'"? Well, "the Lord" is not "The
commander" although the LORD God is a commander, of

sorts. Rather, the word LORD is capitalized in the text in order to denote that the Hebrew term does not translate directly as ruler, commander, etc. but that it refers to YHVH which is the term/name that the LORD God revealed to Moses in Exodus chapter three.

This particular discussion ends thusly:

[Ferris] So you're saying the text is letter perfect when it describes the so-called spaceship but completely inaccurate when it records what the pilot had to say. Isn't that an inconsistent position?

[Von Daniken] I'm very sorry, but theologians are in the same position. **It's true that I accept what I like and reject what I don't like**, but every theologian does the same. Everyone accepts just what he needs for his theory, and to the rest he says, "Well, that's a misunderstanding." [emphasis added]

[Ferris] Except that you claim to be offering science, not theology, and you say you don't have much regard for theologians.

[Von Daniken] I have regard for theologians if they are really honest in their hearts. I have some theologian friends and we have long discussions into the night, and they are nice persons. But in the depth of their hearts they are believers. Theology would be science if they would study all religions, not just the one they believe in.

Well, he is scurrying away again by admitting that he accepts that which he can use to attempt to buttress his theory but then asserts that "every theologian does the same."

Of course, the assertion that "Theology would be science if they would study *all* religions, not just the one they believe in" is generic and, of course, misses the point that theologians most certainly tend to study *all* religions and yet, base their worldviews upon the one upon which they have settled.

This particular interview did not delve into the details of Ezekiel chapters 1 and 10. If you are interested in this issue perhaps the soberest and evidence backed source on this issue is ancient languages scholar Michael Heiser's article "Ezekiel's Vision: Why it Wasn't a Flying Saucer."

In short, the supposed spaceship is a Babylonian style thrown and the point is to show that Marduk may be the "god" of Babylon but that, in reality, YHVH is on the throne and rules all.

This came about because during Ezekiel's time the Israelites were captive in Babylon and so YHVH was showing them that He is in control, He is on the throne as the Lord of lords and King of kings.

"Half Truth" About the Cave He (Never) Explored

In this part of the interview, the following issue is raised:
> ...in a third book, "The Gold of the Gods,"
> he returned to punchy sentences and
> sensational claims—including the discovery
> of a huge cave in Ecuador allegedly holding

a treasure in gold artifacts left behind by
visitors from outer space.

It is into this cave that the discussion descends:
[Ferris] Let's talk about some of the
mysteries you say the archaeologists ought
to be studying. In your book *The Gold of the
Gods*, you describe taking a voyage through
enormous caves in Ecuador where you claim
to have seen ancient furniture made of
plastic, a menagerie of gold animals, a
library of imprinted metal plates and other
evidence of a great early civilization.
You Call this "the most incredible, fantastic
story of the century" and say you were
guided through the caves by a South
American adventurer named Juan Moricz.
But Moricz says he never took you into any
such caves. Which of you is telling the
truth?

[Von Daniken] I guess we both are telling
half truth.

[Ferris] Which half is yours?

[Von Daniken] I have been in Ecuador
several times. I have met Moricz several
times and we have been together at the side
entrance to those tunnels. But before we
went into that entrance, Moricz made it a
condition that I would not be allowed to give
the location or to take photographs inside. I
could understand that because he didn't
want people going in there. So I agreed, we
shook hands and we left. And, as a matter of

fact, in my book I have not told the truth
concerning the geographic location of the
place, not about some various other little
things.

In German we say a writer, if he is not
writing pure science, is allowed to use some
dramaturgisch Effekte—some theatrical
effects. And that's what I have done. But
finally, the whole controversy over whether
I have been down there in those caves or not
seems ridiculous. The main question should
be: Does the library of gold plates exist or
not? This should be the main question, not
whether Mr. Von Daniken has seen them or
not.

But just where, when and how is this dramaturgisch Effekte
employed in his works?:

    [Ferris] Are you saying you have never
    been inside the caves?

    [Von Daniken] I have been inside the caves,
    but not at the place where the photographs in

the book were taken, not at the main entrance. I was at a side entrance. And we were down there for six hours.

[Ferris] Did you, in fact, see the things you describe? Seven chairs made of a plasticlike material, a zoo of solid-gold animals, a library of gold plates?

[Von Daniken] Definitely. No doubt. Though I must say I am not at all sure anymore, if the so-called zoo is made of gold. It could be something different.

[Ferris] In the book you say Moricz led you in darkness then gave the command "Switch on your torches!" You write, "We are standing dumbfounded and amazed in the middle of a gigantic hall." Is that what really happened?

[Von Daniken] No, that is not true. It is what I call theatrical effect.

[Ferris] Were you and Moricz even in the caves?

[Von Daniken] Yeah, sure. He saw everything.

[Ferris] Moricz says, "Von Daniken was never in the caves: when he states he has seen the library and the other things himself, he is lying. We never showed him these things."

[Von Daniken] I know those statements because he has written to me the same thing and I can well understand it. In 1969 Moricz organized and expedition down there.

All the crew members signed documents promising to say nothing about whatever they might find. This was reported in the Ecuadorian press.

So when *The Gold of the Gods* appeared, I think members of the 1969 expedition must have told Moricz, "Listen, this isn't fair. Von Daniken has made the thing public. We could have made money with it, but we were pledged to silence."

I feel this was the main reason though there were others, why Moricz now says the whole things is a hoax. But again, to me the min point is not if I have seen these things or not. I just don't care. The question is, do they exist?

[Ferris] Didn't your German publisher finance an expedition to the caves in order to decide just that question?

[Von Daniken] Yes. They sent a leading German archaeologist to Ecuador. He was there more than six weeks.

He had been to Ecuador many times before and his purpose was to organize an expedition into the caves, but he came back and said it was impossible.

He could not find Mr. Moricz and the archaeologists in Ecuador knew nothing of this discovery.

[Ferris] Why not lead an expedition into the caves yourself?

[Von Daniken] I cannot. I'm a little afraid to go there now. Mr. Moricz, under Ecuadorian law, is something like an owner of the caves together with the government and he has the right to defend his property. After this controversy, I have the feeling I should not go there and I really don't care too much anymore.

The conversation speaks for itself. Note how as the conversation progresses Von Daniken's interest fades. He goes from "The main question should be: Does the library of gold plates exist or not?" and "The question is, do they exist?" to finally "I really don't care too much anymore."

But why would such a treasure trove of evidence for his theory not matter anymore?

China's Dropa Disks

Are we previously noted Von Daniken may "I really don't care too much anymore" about the cave in Ecuador but what about the cave in China?:

> [Ferris] You seem to have bad luck when it comes to caves. In your second book Gods from Outer Space, you tell of a cave in China explored in 1938. You say an archaeologist discovered odd, thin-boned skeletons there, along with a set of stone

disks bearing inscriptions. According to your story, these inscriptions, deciphered in 1962 say spacemen have crash-landed on Earth and been hunted down and killed by Earth people.

When the book appeared, Dr. Kwangchil Chang of Yale University investigated your story. He says that, as a specialist in Asian archaeology, he knows personally every dig conducted in China in or around 1938 but has never heard of this one. He says there has never been a Chinese archaeologist named Chi Pu Tei, the one you say discovered the skeletons, nor a Peking professor named Tsum Um Nui, whom you identify as the translator of the inscriptions. In fact, there are no such names as Tei and Nui in the Chinese languages: Dr. Chang says they sound to him like words made up by a Westerner trying to sound Chinese.

[Von Daniken] When I wrote that story, I didn't have enough background information; I had only a discussion with a friend in Moscow and two or three publications. Since then an Austrian journalist named Peter Krassa has investigated further. He visited Russia and China several times and he had only one thing in mind—to find out about this story.

He found out definitely that it is true. The stones exist, the skeletons also, but the names and some of the dates are wrong. Krassa has written a book about it…and he has a letter from a Chinese minister proving it is the definite, absolute truth.

This is a messy subject and one that seems to have been first reported by another ancient astronaut alien proponent, Robert Charroux. The *Dropa* or *Dzopa* disks (which look like weight lifting *plates*) have what is said to be an unknown language written in a line which spirals outwardly and then back in towards the center/hole. Two decades after their discovery, some text was translated and told of the crash of alien spacecraft at the mountains of Baian-Kara-Ula 12,000 years ago. While the aliens "came in peace" the local Han tribe did not understand this and hunted them down.

However, they also interbred with them. This is actually the easy part of the story as the Han are a petite people of circa 4 feet tall and so it is convenient to claim that they mirror the diminutive stature of the typical gray alien.

Bodies are said to have been recovered but their current location is unknown. Likewise, 716 disks are said to have been discovered but their location is also unknown.

Some have noted that Tsum Um Nei is a Japanese name written down in Chinese. In other words, a mixture of Chinese and Japanese.

Some more problems are that there is no such thing as a *Beijing Academy for Ancient Studies* nor any records of Chu Pu Tei being associated with the Academy. The name Chu Pu Tei itself could be aka Qi Futai or Qifu Tai.

It has also been noted that the disks with their holes and spiral text are known to be related to ancient snake cults wherein there are known as *Bi discs*.

This was noted in relation to Peter Krassa and Hartwig Hausdorf's discussions with Dr. Karyl Robin-Evans who claims to have been shown a stone disc, by a certain

Professor Lolladorff, that appears to have been found in Northern India and that was used during certain religious ceremonies.

At least this is what Krassa and Hausdorf say that Evans said that Lolladorff said.

All of this mystery and missing evidence is nicely wrapped up in tales of a Chinese hush-hush of the whole affair including missing museum curators, etc.

Alien/UFO Cave Painting in Uzbekistan

The issue of the Uzbekistanian cave painting is a really odd one, let us consider the discussion first:

> [Ferris] …What about the so-called prehistoric cave painting from Uzbekistan that appears in the film version of Chariots of the Gods? It shows vividly a modern-day astronaut and a flying saucer and if it's prehistoric, as the script says, it would be very solid evidence for your theory.

> [Von Daniken] You have a wonderful way of touching on every point which is uncertain. I feel like I'm being prosecuted. I'll tell you, about 95 percent of the things I write about I have seen with my own eyes. But there are a few things, especially in Russia and China, which I couldn't have seen. This is one such case. I never seen the painting, never been there. Dr. Saizev, a philologist at the Lenin State University, published thing painting in the Soviet magazine Sputnik, April 1, 1968, and I took the story.

The film crew went to Moscow and interviewed Dr. Saizev. He showed them the picture and told them the same thing, that the painting was ancient. I wasn't there with the crew. Then the funniest thing, Peter Krassa, the journalist I was telling you about, wrote to Dr. Saizev and Saizev answered that the picture was actually modern, not prehistoric. Now, that's really fantastic, don't you think? First he published an article saying it was old, then he told the movie crew the same thing, and only now does he say it is not old at all.

[Ferris] When did you discover that the painting was a hoax?

[Von Daniken] I'm still not sure it is. I have had some interesting experiences with people in Russia and China. You can never be sure when they tell you something that they really mean it. They sometimes have reasons to say one thing in private and another in public.

[Ferris] People all over the world have seen the film and they haven't been told that the origin of the painting is doubtful or that it might be a hoax. They're being told it's genuine. Isn't that irresponsible?

[Von Daniken] The film starts with questions and ends with question, not answers. In the film you see Dr. Saizev being interviewed, you see him give this picture to the movie crew. I'm very sorry but the interview is a fact. And the commentary says simply, "Dr. Saizev showed us this…" [ellipses in original]

[Ferris] Reading from the film script, it says: "We must look and look again to grasp the significance of this prehistoric drawing. A creature wearing the headgear of an astronaut." And so on.

[Von Daniken] Here I'd like to say that the commentary to the film was not written by me.
Also, there are many things in the film that I would never have said in that way. For example, concerning Nazca, Peru, where there are great lines laid out in the desert, the film commentary says something like, "No doubt, it must have been an airfield." I never made such a statement. I said, "It looks like an airfield." There's quite a difference.

The great oddity is that not one has a photo of the ancient astronaut alien graffiti in a cave in Uzbekistan but what we do have is that which it actually is. And that is nothing more than an illustration drawn for the referenced *Sputnik* magazine dated to 1968 AD.

Let us conclude with a wrap up of this whole affair as elucidated by the (self-confessed possessed) professor Jeffrey Kripal who notes:

> ...the ancient-astronaut theory. This is the idea that UFOs are not recent appearances, but have been interacting with humans for millennia, if not actually millions of years, guiding and shaping our biological and cultural evolution. Some versions of this theory are very abstract and leave things largely unexplained...Some versions of this theory have it that the human species is a literal biological hybrid of early primates and visiting aliens (a theme, already present in the theosophical literature, that was given a dramatic new life in the abduction narratives and hybridization theory of the late 1980s and '90s).
>
> Other forms function as popular theories of religion, focusing on how such ancient visitations were recorded in myth and legend and the ancient visitors thus became our "gods."
> Sometimes this is read in a fascinated, positive light. Other times-and this is when it gets really gnostic—it is read in a very negative light, that is, as a millennia—long deception or control mechanism...
>
> One very obvious example will suffice for now. This is *Marvel Preview* #1 and its cover story, "Man-Gods from beyond the Stars," written by Doug Moench, the same writer with whom we began this book.

The cover of *Marvel Preview* certainly
suggests that the ancient-astronaut theory is
more than a theory. "Impossible- or true?" is
ambiguous enough, but the question mark is
effectively rendered null in the next lines:
"Photos, fantasy, and facts about the starmen
who walked the earth before time began."

The Moench story is followed by, among other things, a bibliographic essay that correctly identifies Charles Fort as "the Great-Grandaddy of all the modern flying saucer broo-ha-ha" and a number of supporting essays about the cultural phenomenon of Von Daniken's Chariot of the Gods, which was clearly the real catalyst for this particular issue.

Von Daniken, previously a hotelier by profession, is a Swiss enthusiast of ancient history. His megabestseller, which argued that much of the ancient history of religion was really a history of human contact with spacefaring aliens, was originally published in Germany in 1968, a year later in English in Britain, then in America in 1970.

It is easy, and all too common, to dismiss popularizers and so miss entirely the important, and often very subtle, roles that they play in the history of ideas.

It is also all too easy to dismiss an idea by naively equating it with an easily dismissible popularize, as if the popularizer was not popularizing a complex and nuanced idea that was already there in the culture. This is precisely the case with the ancient-astronaut idea. There were certainly earlier, more nuanced, and more elite versions of the same thesis.

To take a single example, von Daniken's comparison of a photograph of an American

Apollo astronaut and an ancient drawing from the Sahara, which could be construed as a one-eyed alien in a spacesuit, was almost certainly inspired by Carl Sagan's earlier discussion of the ancient-astronaut theory, which appeared in 1966 (and there were many other authors. in England. France, and the U.S., who preceded and followed Sagan in these provocative waters).

Sagan had imagined "colonies of colonies of colonies" in outer space (which echoes his signature line, "billions and billions" and-much like Charles Fort-he deftly used the mythical memories of contact with European colonizers from North America and sub-Saharan Africa in order to suggest that other "contact myths" may encode ancient encounters with galactic astronauts, who "would probably be portrayed as having godlike characteristics and possessing supernatural powers."

After teasing his readers with the aforementioned ancient fresco from central Sahara depicting, in the words of a French archaeologist, "the great Martian god," Sagan zeroed in on a series of Sumerian myths as particularly suggestive of extraterrestrial contact. "Sumerian civilization is depicted by the descendants of the Sumerians themselves to be of non-human origin" he wrote, "A succession of strange creatures appears over the course of several generations.

Their only apparent purpose is to instruct mankind. Each knows of the mission and accomplishments of his predecessors. When a great inundation threatens the survival of the newly introduced knowledge among men, steps are taken to ensure its preservation."

As for the gods themselves, they were associated with individual stars, the cuneiform symbols for "god" and "star" being identical.

Sagan, of course, is offering this as a thought experiment, not as the truth or things, although it is also clear that he considers such scenarios to be real historical possibilities.

He even speculates about a possible interstellar base on the far side or the moon (remember *The Fantastic Four* #13?) and suggests one possible reason for intervening in another planet's evolution: "to head off a nuclear annihilation."

These, of course, are all standard tropes in the contactee and ufological literatures, not to mention science fiction and the later alien abduction literature.[45]

The Piri Reis Map

Another problematic claim of Von Daniken pertains to a supposedly absolutely accurate and yet allegedly impossibly old map:

> [Ferris] Another ancient mystery you write about, no so old, is the 16th Century map put together by the Turkish cartographer Piri Reis. You write, "There is no doubt that the maps must have been made with the most modern technical aid—from the air…whoever made them

must have been able to fly and also take photographs!" [ellipses in original]
You went on to call the map "absolutely accurate" and you said it coincides with a view of the Earth from a spaceship in orbit above Cairo. The trouble is that the Piri Reis map is not "absolutely accurate," nor does it coincide with a view from space.

[Von Daniken] I'm not so sure about this, really. According to my information, it does.

[Ferris] We can take out a copy of the Piri Reis map and a modern globe and look at the two of them and see that they don't agree.

[Von Daniken] Yes, the movie crew did something similar. But for the whole map to coincide with a view from a great height is impossible, because from Cairo you cannot at the same time see the North American continent and Antarctica.

[Ferris] Here's a copy of the Piri Reis map. If you look at the way it represents South America, for example, you'll find that whole section of the coast are missing. Yes this is the map you call absolutely accurate.

[Von Daniken] Look, the Piri Reis map is not one map. It was composed by Piri from several other old maps. So we have to deal with a mixture of several things and some of it, such as the Antarctic coast line looks as it would from a great height. I don't have other information.

[Ferris] You had a copy of the map when you wrote your book, didn't you?

[Von Daniken] Sure, I had one.

[Ferris] And you had access to a globe of the Earth. All you had to do was compare them.

[Von Daniken] It's not so easy. Really, it's no. Look here on the map, we have a connection between Chile and the Antarctic Continent. There is no such connection today, but maybe there was 12,000 years ago. Who knows? And there are islands off Antarctica. You explain to me how they knew about those islands.

[Ferris] It's a fascinating question, but not one that necessarily requires ancient astronauts to answer. Do you have any qualms about telling your millions of readers that this is an absolutely accurate map, when, in fact, some parts of it ware accurate and other parts are wrong?

[Von Daniken] I really don't know. I must find out about what you say. If I find that what I've written is wrong, then I will be the first to correct it. At least in my next book, I'll say this was wrong. At the time I wrote the passage, that was my information: I never invent anything.

[Ferris] Is it your opinion today, as it was when you wrote the book that the Piri Reis map could have been drawn only from the air?

[Von Daniken] No, absolutely not. My opinion is that some parts of the map, especially Antarctica and the island, are a great mystery.

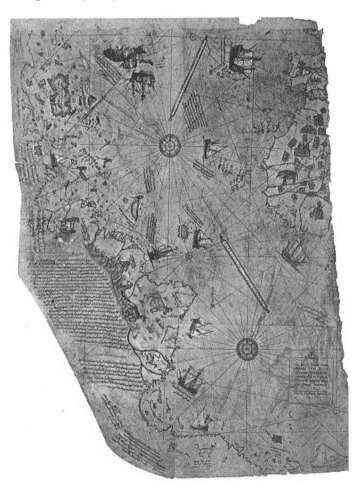

Note how Von Daniken goes from utter confidence, "There is no doubt" to "I'm not so sure about this." Note further that he makes this move; only when called out on it. In other words, he does not publish a rebuttal or correction but only backs off his claims when put on the spot.

India's Un-Rust-Able Iron Pillar

[Ferris] What about the iron column in Delhi, India, which you write has resisted rust for thousands of years and is made of "an unknown alloy from antiquity." In fact, that column does have rust on it and the process by which it was made is well understood. Do you still find it mysterious?

[Von Daniken] No, not anymore. But when I wrote Chariots of the Gods? The information I had concerning this iron column was as I presented it. Since then, I have found that investigations were made and they came to quite different results, so we can forget about this iron thing.

[Ferris] Those investigations had been made even before you wrote the book, hadn't they?

[Von Daniken] I didn't know of them. Even if they were made, other authors who are listed in my bibliography said the same thing I did and some of those authors are very serious, quite well known.

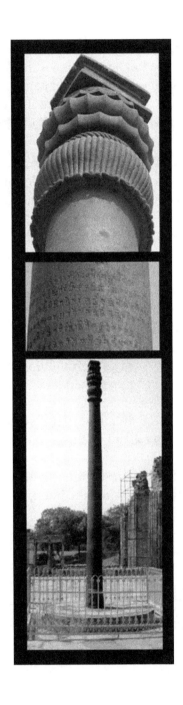

The pillar is circa 98% (wrought) iron and its corrosion resistance has been explained in the 1963 AD paper A.K. Lahiri, T. Banerjee and B.R. Nijhawan, "Some Observations on Corrosion-Resistance of Ancient Delhi Iron Pillar and Present-time Adivasi Iron Made by Primitive Methods," *NML Tech. J.*, 5, 46-5.

Another early source is the 1971 AD paper T. Misawa, T. Kyuno, W. Suetaka, S. Shimodaira, "The mechanism of atmospheric rusting and the effect of Cu and P on the rust formation of low alloy steels," *Corrosion Science*, 11, 35–48.

Other sources are Prof. Ramamurthy Balasubramaniam's "On the Corrosion Resistance of the Delhi Iron Pillar," *Corrosion Science*, Volume 42, 2000 AD, pp. 2103–2129. Also the same professor's "On the growth kinetics of the protective passive film of the Delhi Iron Pillar," *Current Science*, vol. 82, no. 11, 10 June 2002 AD and "On the Origin of High Phosphorus Content in Ancient Indian Iron" written in conjunction with Vikas Kumar, *International Journal of Metals, Materials and Processes*, vol. 14, pp. 1–14. 2002 AD.

Also, Matthew V. Veazey, "1600 Years Young, Materials Performance, July, 2005," *Chemistry International*, Vol. 27 No. 6, November-December 2005 AD.

Lastly, Kamachi Mudali, U.; U. Kamachi Mudali and Baldev Raj, "Insitu corrosion investigations on Delhi iron pillar," *Transactions of the Indian Institute of Metals*, 62 (1): 25–33, February 2009 AD.

On Extra-Terrestrial Alien Bananas

Ferris asked, "in *Gold of the Gods* in which you suggest that the banana was brought to Earth from space? Were you serious?"

He was referring to this bit of text:

> The banana, a delicious item of food, has been known in every tropical and subtropical region of the earth for many thousands of years. The Indian saga tells of the "wonderful Kandali" (= banana bush) which the "Manu," the loftiest spirits and protectors of mankind, brought to our planet from another star which was much further along the path of evolution than our earth. But a banana bush or banana tree simply does not exist! The banana is an annual plant which does not multiply by seeds, which it does not possess, but by suckers. Looked at in this light, the banana is a problem. It is found on even the most remote South Sea islands.
> How did this plant, which is so vital for the nourishment of mankind, originate? How did it make its way round the world, seeing that it has no seeds? Did the "Manu," of whom the Indian saga tells, bring it with them from another star-as an all-round foodstuff?

Apparently, not only did extra-terrestrial-alien seed bananas upon the Earth (directed pan*banana*ia?) but they subsequently returned in order to bequeath upon us the knowledge of making ice cream Sundays!

Well, maybe not and also maybe they did not gift us with bananas as Von Daniken's reply to Ferris was, "No, and not many people realize that":

> [Ferris] That leads us to ask if all your writing is a put-on. Are you, as one writer suggested, 'the most brilliant satirist in German literature for a century'?
>
> [Von Daniken] The answer is yes and no. We have a wonderful term in German: jein. It's a combination of *ja* and *nein*, yes and no. In some part, absolutely not; I mean what I say seriously. In other ways, I mean to make people laugh.
>
> [Ferris] Well, you've succeeded in both aims.

BOOM! seems like an appropriate common parlance term to insert at this point. Yet, while the particular issue of the banana may be very simple to refute it makes one wonder in just how many areas Von Daniken was not serious, employed the *jein* and no one knows about it simply because he has never been asked.

Carl Sagan and First Contact

> [Ferris] …you write, "Our radio astronomers send signals into the universe to make contact with unknown intelligence." But, in fact, no such experiment has ever been performed.
>
> [Von Daniken] Oh, it has. [Carl] Sagan should know this very well.

[Ferris] Well, we asked Sagan about it. He
called it a common misconception. He
added, as an opinion of your work: "The
kindest thing I can say about Von Daniken is
that he ignores the science of archaeology.
Every time he sees something he can't
understand, he attributes it to extraterrestrial
intelligence and since he understands almost
nothing, he sees evidence of extraterrestrial
intelligence all over the planet."

Well, if Carl (Mr. Non-Sequitur) Sagan was against it then
perhaps there was some merit to it. But he had a point here.

On the other hand, it is well known that our radio
astronomers send signals into the universe to make contact
with unknown intelligence—ever hear of SETI? SETI
stands for *Search for Extraterrestrial Intelligence.*

Also, as the *Smithsonian* reported:
By the 1970s, astronomers Carl Sagan and
Frank Drake already had some experience
with sending messages out into space. They
had created two gold-anodized aluminum
plaques that were affixed to the Pioneer 10
and Pioneer 11 spacecraft. Linda Salzman
Sagan, an artist and Carl's wife, etched an
illustration onto them of a nude man and
woman with an indication of the time and
location of our civilization.[46]

In fact, Ferris himself wrote the article "Voyagers' Never-
Ending Journey" for the Smithsonian and stated:
Voyagers will wander forever among the
stars, mute as ghost ships but with stories to
tell. Each carries a time capsule, the

"Golden Record," containing information about where, when and by what sort of species they were dispatched. Whether they will ever be found, or by whom, is utterly unknown. In that sense, the probes' exploratory mission is just beginning.

Ancient Nuclear War, the Bible, and the Mahabarata

Von Daniken claims that the Indian *Mahabarata* (oldest preserved parts are not much older than around 400 BC, may have originated 8th-9th centuries BC) and in the *Epic of Gilgamesh* (the *Old Babylonian* version dates to the 18th century BC, the *Standard Babylonian* version dates from the 13th to the 10th centuries BC) some, such as Gilgamesh's Engidu, die due to a "hot wind" which he takes to be some sort of nuclear weapon.

But it is *hot wind* from ancient nuclear weapons or merely *hot air* from Von Daniken?

An example of that to which ancient nuclear weapon usage believers hold is elucidated by Jason Colavito:
> [Ancient astronaut/alien] Believers maintain that in the distant past either extraterrestrials or a lost civilization like Atlantis detonated nuclear weapons, producing terrible devastation. This disaster was recorded, they say, in the Bible, Hindu scriptures, and world mythologies. Sodom and Gomorrah felt the sting of nuclear weapons when "the LORD rained down burning sulfur on Sodom and Gomorrah—from the LORD out of the heavens." (Genesis 19:24-25, New International Version)...[47]

As you will see, there is a short distance from Genesis 19's fanciful misinterpretation to Von Daniken:

> ...the Soviet mathematician and ethnologist Matest M. Agrest, who argued in 1959 that Sodom and Gomorrah had been destroyed by nuclear bombs from alien spaceships...This claim was brought to the attention of the other side of the Iron Curtain through The Morning of the Magicians (1960), a French work by Louis Pauwels and Jacques Bergier which outlined one of the earliest complete (nonfiction) versions of the modern ancient astronaut theory...
>
> It was von Daniken who introduced mainstream audiences to the idea (borrowed from the French writer Robert Charroux, as well as Pauwels and Bergier) that the "aliens" had blown up Sodom and Gomorrah with atom bombs. Pauwels and Bergier quote what they say is a description from the Dead Sea Scrolls about the nuclear effects of the Sodom bomb.

But the aliens were quite busy back in the day and were blowing up all sorts of sites:

> From the very beginning of the ancient astronaut movement, Hindu mythology, exotic to Western eyes, has been a mainstay of ancient astronaut theories. Ancient Vedic epics, running into the hundreds of thousands or even millions of words each were perfect for out of context quoting since ancient astronaut writers could be fairly certain no one would be able to find and check their accuracy.

One ubiquitous quotation in this regards was a simple, and frightening, statement:

> J. Robert Oppenheimer, the father of the atomic bomb, used a line from ancient Indian epic the Bhagavad Gita to reflect on the enormous power of the Bomb: "Now, I am become Death, the destroyer of worlds." He spoke these words not at the time of the detonation in July 1945, but twenty years later, on a television documentary, The Decision to Drop the Bomb.

From specific sites of Sodom and Gomorrah we move to more exotic sites:

> ....believers hold that deposits of 28-million-year-old glass found buried in the deserts of Libya are the result of ancient atomic bombs that melted the desert sand. In fact, according to geologist Evelyn Mervine, the glass (while still not completely understood) is likely the result of either a meteorite impact or volcanic action.

Also, David W. Davenport and Ettore Vincenti claimed that "an archaeological site they investigated in India, the famous city of Mohenjo Daro, was destroyed in ancient times due to a nuclear blast" within their 1979 AD book, *2000 A.C. Distruzione atomica /Atomic Destruction in 2000 BC.*

Back to the Ancient Vedic epics' millions of words, Colavito notes that one such quotation:

> ...is translated into English from an 1889 German translation of the Sanskrit original, with no indication of where in the 1.8 million words of the epic the quotation

came, or in what context this amazing weapon worked. In Book 7, I found what I believe to be the same passage in a standard translation:

The very elements seemed to be perturbed. The Sun seemed to turn round. The universe, scorched with heat, seemed to be in a fever. The elephants and other creatures of the land, scorched by the energy of that weapon, ran in fright, breathing heavily and desirous of protection against that terrible force. The very waters being heated, the creatures residing in that element, O Bharata, became exceedingly uneasy and seemed to burn.

From all the points of the compass, cardinal and subsidiary, from the firmament and the very Earth, showers of sharp and fierce arrows fell and issued, with the impetuosity of Garuda or the wind. Struck and burnt by those shafts of Acwatthaman that were all endued with the impetuosity of the thunder, the hostile warriors fell down like trees burnt down by a raging fire. Huge elephants, burnt by that weapon, fell down on the Earth all around, uttering fierce cries loud as those of the clouds.

Other huge elephants, scorched by that fire, ran hither and thither, and roared aloud in fear, as if in the midst of a forest conflagration. The steeds, O king, and the cars also, burnt by the energy of that weapon, looked, O sire, like the tops of trees burnt in a forest fire. […] Burnt by the energy of Acwatthaman's weapon, the forms of the slain could not be distinguished. (Ganguili Vol. 7, 678-679)

In Morning, two passages from the Mahabharata are cited as proof of ancient atomic warfare. In later works, like those of David Hatcher Childress, these two passages are interpolated into a single block of (out of context, mixed together) text. Here is the passage as it is frequently given online and in the works of Childress, somewhat different than in Morning:

Gurkha, flying a swift and powerful vimana, hurled a single projectile charged with all the power of the Universe. An incandescent column of smoke and flame, as bright as ten thousand suns, rose in all its splendor. It was an unknown weapon, and iron thunderbolt, a gigantic messenger of death, which reduced to ashes the entire race of the Vrishnis and Andhakas.

The corpses were so burned as to be unrecognizable. Their hair and nails fell out. Pottery broke without any apparent cause, and the birds turned white.…After a few hours, all foodstuffs were infected…to escape from this fire, the soldiers threw themselves in streams to wash themselves and all their equipment. ([David Hatcher] Childress Lost 72-73)

This passage does not appear in the 1.8 million words of the Mahabharata. Instead, it appears to be carefully and purposefully rewritten from genuine passages, combining texts at will to create a misleading paragraph that seems to indicate anomalous knowledge of nuclear bombs. Childress did not do the rewriting; it seems that Pauwels and Bergier were the first to record the variant version, though few seem to seek out the actual Vedic original, relying instead on Pauwels and Bergier or Childress rather than primary sources. When we look at the source texts, we can see how this material has been altered dramatically:

Gratified with him, the holy one then showed Utanka that eternal Vaishnava form which Dhananjaya of great intelligence had seen. Utanka beheld the high-souled Vasudeva of universal form, endued with mighty-arms. The effulgence of that form was like that of a blazing fire or a thousand suns. It stood before him filling all space. It had faces on every side. Beholding that high and wonderful Vaishnava form of Vishnu, in fact, seeing the Supreme Lord (in that guise), the Brahmana Utanka became filled with wonder.
Acwamedha Parva, Section LV (Ganguili Vol. 16)

As it turns out, the context bares out that this description pertained to an appearance of Vishnu. Here is some more:
When the next day came, Camva actually

brought forth an iron bolt through which all the individuals in the race of the Vrishnis and the Andhakas became consumed into ashes. Indeed, for the destruction of the Vrishnis and the Andhakas, Camva brought forth, through that curse, a fierce iron bolt that looked like a gigantic messenger of death. The fact was duly reported to the king. In great distress of mind, the king (Ugrasena) caused that iron bolt to be reduced into fine powder.
Mausala Parva, Section 1. (Ganguili Vol. 16)

Here it is clear that the iron bolt, known also as the rod of chastisement, is not envisioned as a bomb but as a type of scepter. But more importantly, this passage does not describe events that happened, but rather a prophecy of events to come. The king destroyed the bolt before it could be used. The actual destruction of the Vrishnis came three decades later when they became drunk and killed one another with pots and pans.
Day by day strong winds blew, and many were the evil omens that arose, awful and foreboding the destruction of the Vrishnis and the Andhakas. The streets swarmed with rats and mice. Earthen pots showed cracks or broken from no apparent cause. At night, the rats and mice ate away the hair and nails of slumbering men. […] That chastiser of foes commanded the Vrishnis to make a pilgrimage to some sacred water. The messengers forthwith proclaimed at the command of Kecava that the Vrishnis

should make a journey to the sea-coast for
bathing in the sacred waters of the ocean.
Mausala Parva, Section 2 (Ganguili Vol. 16)

It is also noted that Childress:
...uses material from the Lemurian
Fellowship lesson manual to tell how the
Ramas and the Atlanteans fought a great war
which resulted in nuclear holocaust. Never
mind that Lemuria was a failed 19th century
scientific theory designed to explain the
appearance of lemurs in both India and
Madagascar in the years before plate
tectonics showed that the animals walked
from one to the other when both were
linked.

Kripal elucidates the part that an imaginary continent
played:
Through clairvoyant, telepathic, and other
occult channels (a stock staple of human-
alien communication in the later UFO
accounts), Theosophy claimed further to
offer an account of "the ascent of man" that
was really more of a "descent of man," that
is. A descent or emanation from the Divine
Mind. In this vision, we are all avatars,
literally "descents" of the divine. And
Lemuria played a key role here. It, after all,
was the land of the first civilization, which
the Lemurians developed with the help of
some divine teachers from the planet Venus,
the Lords of the Flame who arrived in the
chariot of the Sons of the Fire in order to
breed the next Root Race, the Atlanteans,
from the stock of the Lemurians.

The notion of alien intervention in human evolution was in fact a staple of the theosophical imagination, and it worked on many levels. As Theosophist Alfred P. Sinnett—one of the first to popularize the terms "occultism" and "occult" for the English-speaking world-put it: "The evolution of man is not a process carried out on this planet alone. It is a result to which many worlds in different positions of material and spiritual development have contributed."

This notion of a Venusian-Earth hybrid civilization would come to play a major role in science fiction, pulp fiction, and the UFO contactee cults of the 1950s and '60s, as would Theosophy's central assertions around some "occult dimensions to human evolution of which material sciences were barely cognizant." In short, before there was science fiction, there was Theosophy.[48]

But Childress add more confusion to the mix as he:
> …cites L. Sprague DeCamp's assessment of ancient oil-based weapons like Greek Fire to bolster the claim of sophisticated stone-age weapons. DeCamp, it should be noted, was one of the disciples of the American horror author H.P. Lovecraft, whose mythos of Great Cthulhu helped spawn the ancient astronaut theory when Pauwels and Bergier used him as inspiration for Morning of the Magicians (see my eBook, The Origins of the Space Gods and my Cult of Alien Gods).

Childress then brings in another ancient astronaut supporter, Robin Collyns, to testify that on the authority of another Indian epic, the Vymaanika-Shaastra, ancient peoples had plasma guns powered by electrified mercury.

Though the Atlantis legend has its origins in an unfinished work by Plato written more than 2,500 years ago, the modern version of the Atlantis legend begins with Ignatius Donnelly, an American politician who wrote Atlantis: The Antediluvian World in 1882 to prove that the lost continent was very real and was the origin of all European, Asian, and Native American civilizations. Donnelly was the first to equate Atlantis with the destructive power of advanced weaponry.

Yet, beyond all of this; even the descriptions of alleged ancient atomic/nuclear weapons do not match reality:
When atomic bombs go off, the majority of their destructive power derives from the blast wave—a wall of wind that knocks down all around it. No mention of this blast wave—the most prominent effect of a nuclear blast—shows up in Genesis. Theoretically, with Lot so close to the site of the destruction, he should have felt the blast. While nuclear weapons can set off fires, this is entirely dependent on the amount of flammable material and the distance from the blast site; whereas in the biblical description the dominant motifs are first, a rain of burning sulfur and second, heavy smoke and fire lasting into the next day....

Unlike an actual nuclear weapon, which produces a mushroom cloud, vaporizes the area beneath it, and then dissipates, this weapon is specifically said to be like a "smokeless fire." It causes the sky to fill with clouds that rain blood, but instead of vaporizing those it hits, instead, it causes the air to boil, setting alight all around it. In an actual nuclear explosion, the blast force is the force that kills once one passes the hypocenter. And anyone who survived to describe the blast would by definition have been in the region where the blast wave overtook any flame.

Outside the small area where the actual explosion occurs, the thermal radiation from a nuclear blast is intense, but brief, lasting perhaps one or two seconds. It can cause severe skin burns (but not light a person aflame). Thermal blasts can ignite highly flammable materials, though these do not include elephants or trees; nor would it boil the rivers and seas.

Within the show *Ancient Aliens* it was stated:
After those blasts, people who survive started to lose their hair and nails started to fall out. I mean, right there, we have a concise reference to radiation poisoning; nuclear fallout – and those texts are thousands of years old.

However, note that which the actual text *Mahabharata, Mausala Parva*, 2, actually states:

> The streets swarmed with rats and mice;
> earthen pots showed cracks or broken from
> no apparent cause. At night, the rats and
> mice ate away the hair and nails of
> slumbering men.

Rats and mice, not nuclear fallout.

Ancient Alien UFOs, the Vimanas

No discussion of ancient nuclear weapons, ancient
technologies or ancient alien astronauts is complete without
dealing with Vimanas.

The (pseudo) *History Channel* show *Ancient Aliens* has
claimed that references to Vimanas are found within,
"Ancient Sanskrit texts dating back as far as 6,000 BC"
which are notable for "describing vivid detail flying
machines called Vimanas."

Of course, in reality, as Chris White has noted, "the oldest
of these texts would be the Vedas, which date to between
500-1500 BC":

> The word Vimana literally means "having
> been measured out." It was related to the
> king's palaces and was referring to the
> intricate construction. Later on, as a result,
> the word became synonymous with palaces
> in general. And because of that, it was used
> to refer to the palaces of the gods as well.

> And yes these palaces of the gods were in
> the heavens, and they could fly, but as we
> look into this it will be clear that some of the
> Vimanas of the gods really were huge
> palaces, with gardens and terraces and
> golden staircases.

Then, because the palaces of the gods flew,
the word gradually became used for
anything that could fly, either in mythology
or in reality.[49]

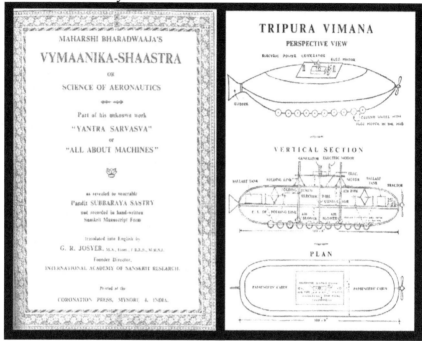

Vimanas are sometimes referred to, in the related literature,
as anything from airplane powered by jet engines to
spacecraft powered by some high tech power source. As
Ancient Aliens put it, "Elephants ran away in panic; grass
was thrown out because there was a lot of pressure from
behind those Vimanas, so we can say that this was a
description of spaceships."

Note that, "almost everything that *Ancient Aliens* says
about Vimanas comes from a totally bogus text called the
Vimanika Shastra" which "is not an actual ancient text.

It was channeled, or dictated, to the author from the spirit world in 1918":

> The spirit who supposedly dictated the text claimed to be an ancient seer named Bharadvada, who is prominent in some ancient writings, so I guess that is what is supposed to give this text credibility – that is, the idea that the ghost of someone ancient supposedly dictated it.

> But they're not even sure if that version of the story is true, because the first mention of any of this is in 1952 by the guy who supposedly found and translated this text from 1918, so as far as anyone knows he could have made the whole channeled by a famous ghost story up in 1952.

> The text itself reads like a technical manual, describing the details of how Vimanas operated. It includes the description of what must have sounded like a really technical idea in 1918 or 1952 called a mercury-vortex engine...It even includes very technical drawings.

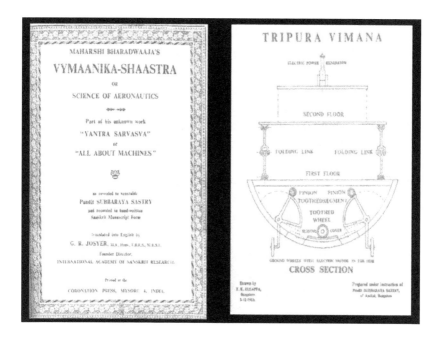

As *Ancient Aliens* put it, "The Vimanika Shastra, or science of aeronautics, indicates Vimanas used a propulsion system based on a combination of gyroscopes, electricity and mercury."

Considering that the time frame ranges into the early 1950s; there is plenty of time for the author of the *Vimanika Shastra* to have become aware of Nazi experiments with a device known as the *Bell*. As elucidated by Jim Wilhelmsen:

> ...in Greek mythology...The symbol of Hermes staff shows a disk on either end of a central shaft, with two inter-twined serpents, with wings of flight above their heads. The intertwining could indicate the vortex principles understood by Victor Schauberger. The dual disks on the shaft representing the electro-magnetic energy

generated from the mercury through a vortex implosion as symbolized by the intertwining serpents.

The final result produced rapid flight, as represented by the wings. Although you might think this strange, this is the very methodology used which led to new technology the Nazis are claimed to have obtained by this unorthodox view of mythology...evidence of an unusual use of mercury was discovered in April of 1944. The ill-fated submarine U-859 left Germany and was sunk off the straits of Malacca in Indonesia. This sub had a cargo of 33 tons of mercury! This was strange cargo in such a huge amount and being treated as an important military cargo! In 1944 mercury was used for thermometers and switches, with no known military purpose. Some sort of unconventional use can only explain this strange cargo...

Another curious note was the death of Jack Parsons. He was the American Rocket scientist who invented solid rocket fuel. He died in a fire while working with mercury. And yes, he was involved with occult societies that had Nazi connections during the war. There does seem to be more to Mercury than just switches, thermometers and mythology! This is only one small example of how the Nazis approached legends and myths and attempted to extract a physics from them.[50]

Yet, in any regard, "in 1974, a study was done on the texts and the drawings by the *Aeronautical and Mechanical Institute of Science* in Bangalore, India (H.S. Mukunda, S.M. Deshpande, H.R. Nagendra, A. Prabhu, and S.P. Govindraju, "A critical study of the work 'Vyamanika Shastra,'" *Scientific Opinion*, 1974, pp. 5-12).

About this study, Will Hunt, an American freelance writer based in India, wrote:

> As thoroughly as it had been written, the committee just as thoroughly dismantled the study in an essay called A Critical Study of the Work Vymanika Shastra. They questioned whether the author (whoever that may have been) had any grasp of basic physics, chemistry and electricity, not to mention the "disciplines of aeronautics: aerodynamics, aeronautical structures, propulsive devices, materials, and metallurgy." Their conclusion: "None of the planes has properties or capabilities of being flown; the geometries are unimaginably horrendous from the point of view of flying; and the principles of propulsion make them resist rather than assist flying.

Sacred Text Archive writer, JB Hare, also noted that they are, "absurdly non-aerodynamic...brutalist wedding cakes, with minarets, huge ornithopter wings and dinky propellers."

In any regard, the fact is that Vimanas:

> ...were not even mentioned in the earlier texts, and when they were finally mentioned, the next thousand years of their being mentioned always included them having

wheels and being drawn by horses…Then, around 500 BC, the chariots lose their horses and are depicted as flying on their own.

Let us consider one actual reference to these mighty spaceships from *Ramayana, Sundarakandam 9*:

> And the mighty monkey ascended the splendid car Pushpaka, containing figures of wolves,—made of Kart taswara and Hir anya; graced with ranges of goodly pillars; as if blazing in splendor; throughout garnished with narrow secret rooms and saloons, piercing the heavens, and resembling Meru or Mandara, and like unto the flaming Sun; skillfully reared by Vic wak arma; with golden staircases and graceful and grand raised seats, rows of golden and crystal windows, and daises

composed of sapphires, emeralds and other
superb gems; embellished with noble vid-
rumas, costly stones, and round pearls, as
also with plastered terraces; pasted with red
sandal, like unto gold, and furnished with a
sacred aroma; and resembling the sun new
risen.

In other texts, they are referred to as being filled with fruit
trees and are not powered by jet engines or mercury
vortexes but by geese.

Overall, we have a huge concoction of mistranslated
contextual misinterpreted statements which are mixed and
mashed into a theory which explains just about nothing at
all except how some go about justifying their preferred
theories.

Did Von Daniken Plagiarize HP Lovecraft?

Charles Garofalo and Robert M. Price (see their article
"Chariots of the Old Ones?") are two more in the long line
of people who recognize that Von Daniken, "may be guilty
of the worst case of pseudoscientific overkill in the
twentieth century" as he asserted that "beings from outer
space once visited the Earth and inspired all the myths of
gods and heroes" and that humanity "rode to civilization on
the backs of more advanced races."

What they specify is that "There are some remarkable
parallels in Von Daniken's and Lovecraft's work" as "H. P.
Lovecraft expounded the same theories in his Cthulhu
Mythos stories back in the nineteen thirties."

In their article *Crypt of Cthulhu*, Charles Garofalo and
Robert M. Price note:

In Lovecraft's first major Cthulhu Mythos
story "The Call of Cthulhu", a researcher
discovers the cult of the Old Ones, a star-
spanning race that once ruled the world, and
now sleeps in sunken cities and underground
caverns....Later Mythos tales ("The
Dunwich Horror", "The Whisperer in
Darkness", "The Curse of Yig", "The
Mound", "Medusa's Coil", and "Out of the
Eons")...Cthulhu and similar Old Ones are
supposed to have influenced...religions...
Lovecraft also believed the alien races could
be reproductively compatible with
humanity. Hybrid offspring...Cthulhu and
his kin are one of many races from many
planets.

Some descriptions of Lovecraft's creatures are that Cthulhu
is "a giant man with an octopus for a head, scales like a
dragon, huge claws, and vestigial [bat-like] wings"
(possibly the inspiration for the *Davy Jones* character in
Pirates of the Caribbean).

Cthulhu

Davy Jones

The *Mi-go* are "winged lobster-like critters," there is also
the "star-headed Old Ones" there are also "spawn of Dagon
and the Deep Ones, semihuman fishmen" and many others.

Charles Garofalo and Robert M. Price point out that:
>Von Daniken and other proponents of the
>"ancient astronauts" hypothesis...are quick
>to seize upon fortuitous passages in the
>Bible and other ancient texts...In pretty

much the same way, Zecharia Sitchin plays
fast and loose with ancient Babylonian,
Akkadian, and Sumerian texts.

And yet, with regards to the H. P. Lovecraft connection:
Von Daniken and Sitchin force us to raise
the question of who influenced whom.
Von Daniken was once actually asked if
Lovecraft had been the source of any of his
ideas. He not only denied it, but seemed
never to have heard of HPL.

It is not, shall we say, required that Daniken plagiarized or
was merely influenced, by Lovecraft but his mere denials
do not suffice as they are coming from a thrice convicted of
embezzlement, fraud, and forgery. Of course, that he has
been thrice convicted of embezzlement, fraud and forgery
does not guarantee that he is being dishonest in this case.

Thus, at this point we should consult with Jason Colavito
who researched this specific point:
ONE OF THE MOST dramatic ideas found
in the Cthulhu Mythos is the suggestion that
extraterrestrial beings arrived on earth in the
distant past, were responsible for ancient
works of monumental stone architecture,
and inspired mankind's earliest mythologies
and religions…

Lovecraft provided a number of different
explanations for the arrival ancient visitors
on the primeval earth…In At the Mountains
of Madness, Lovecraft presents his most
complete vision of the extraterrestrial
origins of human life…Lovecraft described
his ancient visitors as maintaining a

presence on the modern earth, and like the
Nephilim of the Bible, they begat children
with earth women...

Human knowledge of these aliens is
fragmentary and obscure. Evidence exists in
the form of anomalous ancient artifacts of
pre-human manufacture, garbled folklore
and mythology, and written texts.[51]

It is also noted that Jacques Bergier, a chemical engineer,
former Resistance fighter and practicing alchemist, and
Louis Pauwels editor, publisher, and self-confessed mystic:

...wrote Le Matin des magiciens (1960)
(published in English as The Morning of the
Magicians) and presented the first fully-
fledged modern ancient astronaut theory. In
it, they presented the themes found in
Lovecraft as nonfiction, speculating about
such alternative history touchstones as the
"true" origin of the Egyptian pyramids,
ancient maps that appear to have been drawn
from outer space, advanced technology
incongruously placed in the ancient past,
and the other staples of later ancient
astronaut theories. They note that ancient
mythologies are replete with gods who visit
earth in fiery chariots and return to the sky.
These, they state, may have been alien
visitors in spaceships.

Here is the key point:

Morning of the Magicians became one of
the most important sources for Erich von
Däniken...a lawsuit forced him to disclose

the sources he closely paraphrased in
Chariots.

Also, "Other authors were inspired by von Däniken's
theories, including Robert Temple...and Zecharia Sitchin."

Richard L. Tierney also mentioned:
> ...the potential correlations between
> Lovecraft's story "The Mound" (with Zealia
> Bishop) and actual Mesoamerican and
> Native American legends and traditions, and
> he identifies Yig, father of serpents, with the
> Aztec god Quetzalcoatl, the feathered
> serpent. At Teotihuacan, the Mexican city so
> old and mysterious that even the Aztecs
> themselves knew it only as a ruin belonging
> to the gods who descended from the sky,
> Tierney humorously identifies the sculptures
> of tentacled Tlaloc the rain god and
> serpentine Quetzalcoatl on Quetzalcoatl's
> temple as representations of Cthulhu and
> Yig.

> *These viscous masses were without doubt what*
> *Abdul Alhazred whispered about as the "Shoggoths"*
> *in his Frightful Necronomicon, though even that mad*
> *Arab had not hinted that any existed on earth except*
> *in the dreams of those who had chewed a certain alkaloidal*
> *herb*
> —H. P. Lovecraft, *At the Mountains of Madness* 1931 AD

Kripal offers some more background on Bergier and
Pauwels:
> It was Jacques Bergier's alchemy and his
> enthusiasm for quantum physics that made
> Pauwels finally realize that traditional

mystical ideas could be married to modern science, that modern physics is modern magic-in short, the mytheme of Radiation.

It was physics again that convinced him that the fantastic was not "out there" in some other transcendent world, but right here, in the very heart of matter and the world as it evolved toward a future superconsciousness and what the two authors called, rather beautifully. "That Infinity Called Man."

Significantly, *The Morning of the Magicians* was rooted in the authors' own mystical experiences of the fantastic as real, or, better, the real as fantastic. Pauwels thus freely confesses that the book would not likely have been written "if Bergier and I had not on more than one occasion had an impression of being in contact-actually, physically—with another world."

This certainly helps explain their attraction to such impossible ideas as contact with alien intelligences and the existence of parallel universes. This also explains their obvious affection for Charles Fort, science fiction, and Superman allusions. The book positively swims with traditional Fortean, sci-fi, and superheroic themes.[52]

Incidentally, it is also noted that it is also noted that "Admittedly, in his earlier stories, HPL treated the Old Ones as demons or evil gods."

In short, the bottom line is that this story has been told and retold and revamped and updates, etc. ever since the events recorded in Genesis 6 took place. Recall that, "the sons of God came in to the daughters of men, and they bore children to them. Those were the mighty men who were of old, men of renown."

It appears that, as time progressed, these mighty men of old renown were misidentified as gods or aliens (or alien gods), passed themselves off as such, etc. and eventually we end up with the modern day ancient alien / ancient astronaut theories/theologies:

> Von Daniken makes much of the recurrent theme of a powerful god who uses a lightning bolt as a weapon and begets demi-gods on mortal women. He believes the being was a more human-looking spaceman who was somehow reproductively compatible (perhaps because of some artifice) with Earth women.
>
> He must have been trying to improve the human race by begetting superior hybrids, as mythical demi-gods are usually depicted as incredibly strong, smart, magical, and given to discovering fire, founding cities, developing the art of weaving and similar useful things.

Robert Temple and the Sirius Mystery

Dagon and the Dogon: the Background

This chapter regards a serious mystery behind "The Sirius Mystery" but the mystery is not that which one may generally think. "The Sirius Mystery" is a book first published by Robert Temple in 1976 AD. Its premise pertains to ancient astronauts or as the term has been updated, ancient aliens or actually in this case, ancient extraterrestrial amphibians.

It is called "The Sirius Mystery" because the claim is that "the Dogon people of Mali, in west Africa, preserve a tradition of contact with intelligent extraterrestrial beings from the Sirius star-system." That is, the Dogon have knowledge of the Sirius system embedded with their ancient mythologies and traditions; knowledge they had no Earthly way of knowing, "Sirius B, the white dwarf companion star of Sirius A, invisible to the naked eye." I end this chapter with a list of research sources whence come all of the quotes which follow. However, I will note some citations along the way when they seem immediately relevant.

> Though anthropologists failed to find a genuine Sirius B tradition among the Dogon outside what they had gleaned from recent contact with Europeans…and skeptics refuted Temple's extraterrestrial conclusions, *The Sirius Mystery* continues to serve as a standard reference work in the New Age and alternative archaeology movements…The internet, too, is a hotbed

of Temple-derived Sirius theories. And, of course, Temple continues to publish books…

Moreover:
> Temple's book and the debates that followed its release publicized the existence of the Dogon tribe among many New Age followers and proponents of ancient astronaut theories. Speculation about the Dogon on numerous websites is now mingled with fact, leading to wide misunderstanding among the public about Dogon mythology.

Also:
> Robert Temple…claims to be able to trace the Sirius-B myth back through Egyptian mythology to Sumerian mythology, thus establishing the certainty that the informants were extraterrestrials.

Making first contact "5,000 or more years ago" the fish/frog humanoid amphibians:
> …are hypothesized to have taught the arts of civilization to humans, are claimed in the book to have originated the systems of the Pharaohs of Egypt, the mythology of Greek civilization, and the Epic of Gilgamesh, among other things.

The following references are to H. H. Adams' *African Observers of the Universe: The Sirius Question* and Ivan Van Sertima's *The Lost Sciences of Africa: An Overview*:
> Claims that the Dogon knew these things for at least 700 years (not 500) and that the

ancient Egyptians also possessed this
knowledge were first made in Adams
(1983a) and endorsed by Van Sertima
(1983). The sole source this information
about Dogon astronomical knowledge is the
research of two French anthropologists,
Marcel Griaule and Germaine Dieterlen...[53]

One, main, issue is:

...the Dogon legends about a companion to
Sirius **are claimed to** originate before any
terrestrial astronomer could have known of
the existence of Sirius B, let alone its 50-
year orbit or its nature as a tiny, condensed
white dwarf star, all of which the Dogon
allegedly knew. (emphasis added for
emphasis)

Ogotemmêli, the sole source of data used in
The Sirius Mystery...Griaule first published
this data [along with Germaine Dieterlen] in
Dieu d'eau: entretiens avec Ogotemmêli
("God of water: Conversations with
Ogotemmêli", 1948), in which he records
his conversations with a blind hunter,
Ogotemmêli, who claimed to have extensive
knowledge of Dogon lore, much of which
was restricted to certain tribal elders.

Moreover,

Griaule's original data, on which this whole
edifice is built, is very questionable. His
methodology with its declared intent to
redeem African thought, its formal
interviews with a single informant through
an interpreter, and the absence of texts in the

Dogon language have been criticized for years.

To state it in more detail, "The sole source this information about Dogon astronomical knowledge is the research of two French anthropologists, Marcel Griaule and Germaine Dieterlen" and the sole source of the anthropologists' knowledge was Ogotemmêli.

The Book

What set Temple on the path of researching the Dogon was the work ethnographers Marcel Griaule and Germaine Dieterlen, "Temple's theory was heavily based on his interpretation of" their work.

The point is:

> Griaule and Dieterlen…worked among the Dogon from 1931 to 1952. Between 1946 and 1950 the Dogon head tribesmen unfolded to Griaule and Dieterlen the innermost secrets of their knowledge of astronomy. Much of this secret lore is complex and obscure, as befits ancient legends, but certain specific facts stand out, particularly those concerning the star Sirius, with which their religion and culture is deeply concerned…the superdense nature of white dwarfs was not realized until the 1920s. But the Dogon Sirius traditions are at least centuries old.

> A substantial bulk of *The Sirius Mystery* consists of comparative linguistic and mythological scholarship, pointing out resemblances among Dogon, Egyptian and Sumerian beliefs and symbols. Greek and

Arab myths and words are considered to a
lesser extent…

Temple did not argue that the only way that
the Dogon could have obtained what he
understood to be accurate information on
Sirius B was by contact with an advanced
civilization; he considered alternative
implausible possibilities, such as a very
ancient, advanced, and lost civilization that
was behind the sudden appearance of
advanced civilization in both Egypt and
Sumeria.

Isaac Asimov has been quoted by Temple as
having said that he found no mistakes in the
book; but Temple did not know that the
reason for this, according to Asimov, was
that he had found the book too impenetrable
to read!

This is noted because in the essay, "The Dark Companion,"
found within Asimov's book *Quasar, Quasar Burning
Bright*, "he says" says the Ridpath article editor, "he is
embarrassed by his stupidity in not specifying that his
comment, made only 'to get rid of him and to be polite,'
not be quoted. 'I assure you I will never be caught that way
again.'"

As Asimov elucidated:

Robert Temple on three different occasions,
by mail and phone, attempted to get support
from me and I steadfastly refused. He sent
me the manuscript which I found
unreadable. Finally, he asked me point-
blank if I could point out any errors in it and

partly out of politeness, partly to get rid of him, and partly because I had been able to read very little of the book so that the answer was true, I said I could not point out any errors. He certainly did not have permission to use that statement as part of the promotion, I'll just have to be even more careful hereafter.

Arthur C. Clarke encouraged Temple's research but opted for the "modern influence" theory, see below.

Dr. Philip C. Steffey did an in-depth analysis of Dogon astronomical traditions in "Some Serious Astronomy in the 'Sirius Mystery,'" which criticized Temple's book as "inadequate and full of factual errors and misrepresentation of critical material.'"

In 1998, Temple republished the book with the subtitle "new scientific evidence of alien contact 5,000 years ago." The book's reputation was first dented in 1999, when Lynn Picknett and Clive Prince published *The Stargate Conspiracy*, in which they allege that Temple's thinking had been heavily influenced by his mentor, Arthur M. Young.

Young was a fervent believer in "the Council of Nine," a mysterious group of channelled entities that claim to be the nine creator gods of ancient Egypt. "The Nine" became part of the UFO and New Age mythology and many claim to be in contact with them. "The Nine" also claim to be extraterrestrial beings from the star Sirius.

See chapter *Pop-Occulture: Gene Roddenberry and The Psychic (Deep Space) Nine* chapter herein.

As for Temple's book:
> As Picknett and Prince have been able to show, Temple's arguments are often based on erroneous readings of encyclopædia entries and misrepresentations of ancient Egyptian mythology. They conclude that Temple was very keen to please his mentor, who believed in extraterrestrial beings from Sirius.

Another aspect is anthropological:
> In 1976 Robert Temple published the Sirius Mystery…These claims were dealt with in an article in The Skeptical Inquirer (Ridpath 1978)…the Afrocentrist movement has revived and expanded these claims…Adams (1990: 60) briefly presents the current claims:…The Dogon with no apparent instrument at their disposal, appear to have known these facts for at least 500 years.

Temple on Life in the Universe - The Serious Mystery

Herein, we will consider a statement made in a chapter titled, "The Knowledge of the Dogon":
> Any people who still believe human beings are unique as intelligent life in the universe are seriously out of touch with reliable and informed estimates by scientists and astronomers. An attitude which asserts that

man is the only intelligent life form in the
universe is intolerably arrogant today,
though as little as twenty years ago it was
probably common belief.

But anyone who holds such an opinion
today is, fortunately for those who like to
see some progress in human conceptions,
something of an intellectual freak equivalent
to a believer in the Flat Earth Theory. I
mention that theory because I once met a
woman who appeared quite sane and yet
who was a member of a cult who believe the
Earth is flat.

This was one of the more startling
experiences anyone can have, and a salutary
education to me. It taught me never to
underestimate the power of the human mind
to believe what it wants to believe despite
any amount of evidence.

Let us consider this statement in segments:
1) *"Any people who still believe human beings are unique
as intelligent life in the universe are seriously out of touch
with reliable and informed estimates by scientists and
astronomers."*

If you "still," mind you, believe that "human beings are
unique as intelligent life in the universe" you are **_not_**
necessarily "seriously out of touch with reliable and
informed estimates by scientists and astronomers."

You may believe, still, that "human beings are unique as
intelligent life in the universe" even whilst being perfectly

aware of "reliable and informed," and here is the key word, "estimates."

You can believe that humans are unique while affirming estimates against your view and withholding a conclusion that there are other intelligent lifeforms in the universe until such a time as we have actual evidence and not merely estimates.

2) *"An attitude which asserts that man is the only intelligent life form in the universe is intolerably arrogant today, though as little as twenty years ago it was probably common belief."*

It would only be "intolerably," mind you, "arrogant" if it is not true. If it is true, then it is a mere fact.

Also, note that he is not claiming that it was "intolerably arrogant" twenty years ago (that was written in 1976 AD) but it is so "today"—such are the ways of the moral zeitgeist which is tentative and can quickly go from zeitgeist to poltergeist.

3) *"But anyone who holds such an opinion today is, fortunately for those who like to see some progress in human conceptions, something of an intellectual freak equivalent to a believer in the Flat Earth Theory."*

This is, somewhat, reminiscent of Richard Dawkins correlating those who doubt his chosen version of Charles Darwin's theory of evolution to Holocaust deniers (Dawkins actually stated that those who doubt that humans are related to bananas and turnips are like Holocaust deniers[54]).

So, if you believe that humans are the only intelligent life in the universe despite mere estimates; you are "an intellectual freak equivalent to a believer in the Flat Earth Theory."

That the Earth is not flat is not based on estimates but on reproducible science. Moreover, the other problem in believing in the flat Earth is that the concept of a flat Earth is a secular myth; it was invented in order to make religious people look like freaks, sans that intellect.

4) *"I mention that theory because I once met a woman who appeared quite sane and yet who was a member of a cult who believe the Earth is flat."*

Well, there is a reason why it is a cult.

5) *"This was one of the more startling experiences anyone can have, and a salutary education to me. It taught me never to underestimate the power of the human mind to believe what it wants to believe despite any amount of evidence."*

And now we come to the nut, the main point, the key, the rub, etc.

If you *still believe human beings are unique* you *are seriously out of touch with reliable and informed estimates* and are *intolerably arrogant* and also *an intellectual freak equivalent to a believer in the Flat Earth Theory* some of whom formed a *cult*.

Yet, Temple believes that extra-terrestrial chimeras consisting of some combination of fish-frog humanoids flew their spacecraft to Earth in order to impart their knowledge, and some lack of knowledge as they got much wrong, about the universe. They spent their nights on Earth in the water and the days amongst certain civilizations, such as the Dogon of Africa upon whom Temple focuses his, debunked, book, "The Sirius Mystery."

In fact, he titled one chapter, "The Nommo – the Amphibian Race from Sirius."
It is easy for Temple to point his finger but, when he does so, three fingers are pointing back at him.

Serious Sirius Mystery - Nommo and Oannes

A Dogon legend, similar to many other tales by primitive people of visits from the sky, speaks of an "ark" descending to the ground amid a great wind. Robert Temple interprets this as the landing of a rocket-powered spacecraft bringing beings from the star Sirius. According to Dogon legend, the descent of the ark brought to Earth an amphibious being, or group of beings, known as the Nommo. "Nommo is the collective name for the great culture-hero and founder of civilization who came from the Sirius system to set up society on the Earth," Temple explains…

Much of Temple's book is devoted to establishing that the Dogon share common roots with Mediterranean peoples. This explains the central place occupied by Sirius in Dogon beliefs, because the ancient Egyptians, in particular, were also preoccupied with Sirius, basing their calendar on its yearly motion.

Nommo is supposed to have come from the Sirius system even though, "astronomical theory virtually precludes the possibility that Sirius is a suitable parent star for life or that it could have habitable planets."

Also note that "the Sumerian Oannes" is identified by George Michanowsky "as a Hellenized version of the Sumerian name Ea" in his book *The Once and Future Star: The Mysterious Vela X Supernova and the Origin of Civilizations* (Hawthorn Books, 1977 AD).

Also, Oannes, "is thought to be the Uan (or Uanna) of Babylonian myth, sometimes identified with Adapa, the equally mythical first king of Eridu, also identified by some with Atrahasis, the hero of the Babylonian version of the flood legend."

> Temple claims that bas-reliefs of the Sumerian demigod Oannes, which depict a "fish man," prove Nommo, whom the author identifies as the ancestor of the Dogon Nommo myths, was an amphibious extraterrestrial. Unfortunately he neglects to mention other bas-reliefs which show "fish-deer" and "fish-lions" and which consequently suggest that the fish motif was symbolic, not descriptive.

Since there is supposed to be a correlation to ancient civilizations, let us consider an ancient Assyrian tale of Oannes; an amphibian who imparted knowledge to humanity. This is from Berossos / Akkadian Belreušu (early 3rd c. BC) *Babyloniaca*, Book I.

Fragments of Chaldœan History, Berossus: From Alexander Polyhistor, section: "Of the Cosmogony and Deluge":

> BEROSSUS, in the first book of his history of Babylonia, informs us that he lived in the age of Alexander the son of Philip. And he mentions that there were written accounts, preserved at Babylon with the greatest care, comprehending a period of above fifteen myriads of years: and that these writings contained histories of the heaven and of the sea; of the birth of mankind; and of the kings, and of the memorable actions which they had achieved...

> In the first year there appeared, from that part of the Erythræan sea which borders upon Babylonia, an animal destitute of reason, by name Oannes, whose whole body (according to the account of Apollodorus) was that of a fish; that under the fish's head he had another head, with feet also below, similar to those of a man, subjoined to the fish's tail. His voice too, and language, was articulate and human; and a representation of him is preserved even to this day.

> This Being was accustomed to pass the day among men; but took no food at that season; and he gave them an insight into letters and sciences, and arts of every kind. He taught them to construct cities, to found temples, to compile laws, and explained to them the principles of geometrical knowledge. He made them distinguish the seeds of the earth,

and shewed them how to collect the fruits; in short, he instructed them in every thing which could tend to soften manners and humanize their lives. From that time, nothing material has been added by way of improvement to his instructions.

And when the sun had set, this Being Oannes, retired again into the sea, and passed the night in the deep; for he was amphibious. After this there appeared other animals like Oannes, of which Berossus proposes to give an account when he comes to the history of the kings. Moreover Oannes wrote concerning the generation of mankind; and of their civil polity; and the following is the purport of what he said:

"There was a time in which there existed nothing but darkness and an abyss of waters, wherein resided most hideous beings, which were produced of a two-fold principle. There appeared men, some of whom were furnished with two wings, others with four, and with two faces. They had one body but two heads: the one that of a man, the other of a woman: and likewise in their several organs both male and female.

Other human figures were to be seen with the legs and horns of goats: some had horses' feet: while others united the hind quarters of a horse with the body of a man, resembling in shape

the hippocentaurs. Bulls likewise were
bred there with the heads of men; and
dogs with fourfold bodies, terminated
in their extremities with the tails of
fishes: horses also with the heads of
dogs: men too and other animals, with
the heads and bodies of horses and the
tails of fishes.

In short, there were creatures in which
were combined the limbs of every
species of animals. In addition to
these, fishes, reptiles, serpents, with
other monstrous animals, which
assumed each other's shape and
countenance. Of all which were
preserved delineations in the temple of
Belus at Babylon."

Berossus: From Apollodorus, section: "Of the Chaldæan
Kings":
THIS is the history which Berossus has
transmitted to us. He tells us that the first
king was Alorus of Babylon, a Chaldæan: he
reigned ten sari: and afterwards Alaparus,
and Amelon who came from Pantibiblon:
then Ammenon the Chaldæan, in whose
time appeared the Musarus Oannes the
Annedotus from the Erythræan sea. (But
Alexander Polyhistor anticipating the event,
has said that he appeared in the first year;
but Apollodorus says that it was after forty
sari; Abydenus, however, makes the second
Annedotus appear after twenty-six sari.)

Then succeeded Megalarus from the city of
Pantibiblon; and he reigned eighteen sari:
and after him Daonus the shepherd from
Pantibiblon reigned ten sari; in his time (he
says) appeared again from the Erythræan sea
a fourth Annedotus, having the same form
with those above, the shape of a fish blended
with that of a man.

Then reigned Euedorachus from
Pantibiblon, for the term of eighteen sari; in
his days there appeared another personage
from the Erythræan sea like the former,
having the same complicated form between
a fish and a man, whose name was Odacon.
(All these, says Apollodorus, related
particularly and circumstantially whatever
Oannes had informed them of: concerning
these Abydenus has made no mention.)
—Syncel. Chron. 39.—Euseb. Chron. 5.

Berossus: From Abydenus, section: "Of the Chaldæan
Kings and the Deluge":
...Amillarus from the city of Pantibiblon,
who reigned thirteen sari; in his time came
up from the sea a second Annedotus, a semi-
dæmon very similar in his form to
Oannes...Daos, the shepherd, governed for
the space of ten sari; he was of Pantibiblon;
in his time four double-shaped personages
came up out of the sea to land, whose names
were Euedocus, Eneugamus, Eneuboulus,
and Anementus: afterwards in the time of
Euedoreschus appeared another
Anodaphus...

—Syncel. Chron. 38.—Euseb. Præp. Evan. lib. 9.—Euseb. Chron. 5. 8.

Sirius' Place in Dogon Astrology

The Dogon are also supposed to know that Sirius B orbits every 50 years. But what do they actually say? Griaule and Dieterlen put it as follows: "The period of the orbit is counted double, that is, one hundred years, because the Siguis are convened in pairs of "twins," so as to insist on the basic principle of twinness." The Sigui ceremony referred to is a ceremony of the renovation of the world that is celebrated every 60 years (not 50). And the "twinness" referred to here is an important Dogon concept which explains why they believe Sirius must have two companions.

Also, note that "observations reported in 1973 by Irving W. Lindenblad of the U.S. Naval Observatory, Washington, D.C., showed no evidence of a close companion to either Sirius A or Sirius B":

But what can we make of the Dogon statement that Sirius B is the smallest and heaviest star, consisting of a heavy metal known as sagala?...hundreds of white dwarfs are known, not to mention neutron stars, which are far smaller and denser. Any visiting spaceman would certainly have known about these, as well as black holes.

Note the following:

Nowhere in his 290-page book does Temple offer one specific statement from the Dogon to substantiate his ancient astronauts claim.

> The best he does is on page 217, where he
> reports that the Dogon say: "Po tolo [Sirius
> B] and Sirius were once where the Sun now
> is." Of this ambiguous statement, Temple
> comments: "That seems as good a way as
> any to describe coming to our solar system
> from the Sirius system, and leaving those
> stars for our star, the Sun."

Thus, the Dogon state that Po tolo and Sirius used to be
within our solar system but moved away from it and
Temple (mis)understands this to mean that this means
"coming to our solar system from the Sirius system"?!
Again, the Dogon state that the movement was **from our**
solar system **to outside of it** and Temple states that this
means the movement **to our** solar system **from outside of
it**. This is not delving into the minutia of astrophysics; this
is just understanding words in the right order.

But Dogon astronomy goes beyond supposed speculations
about Sirius (by the way, "the sketches used to illustrate the
Sirius secrets are also used in puberty ceremonies"):

> The Dogons hold that Jupiter has four
> moons when in fact it has at least 12, plus a
> ring, as any true extraterrestrial would have
> known. Saturn is not, as the Dogons insist,
> the farthest planet in the solar system. At
> least three are farther and at least one of
> them has rings too.

> [Marcel] Griaule…took star maps along
> with him on his field trips as a way of
> prompting his informants to divulge their
> knowledge of the stars…The Dogon were
> well aware of the brightest star in the sky
> but, as Van Beek learned, they do not call it

sigu tolo, as Griaule claimed, but dana
tolo...To quote James and Thorpe: "As for
Sirius B, only Griaule's informants had ever
heard of it."

The following quote references the research of the Belgian
anthropologist Walter van Beek wrote "Dogon Restudies.
A Field Evaluation of the Work of Marcel Griaule, *Current
Anthropology* 12: 139-167 (1991 AD) who spent 11 years
among the Dogon:

Is Sirius a double star? The ethnographic
facts are quite straightforward. The Dogon
of course, know Sirius as a star [it is after all
the brightest star in the sky]...Knowledge of
the stars is not important either in daily life
or in ritual. The position of the sun and the
phases of the moon are more pertinent for
Dogon reckoning.

No Dogon outside of the circle of Griaule's
informants had ever heard of sigu tolo or po
tolo...Most important, no one, even within
the circle of Griaule informants, had ever
heard or understood that Sirius was a double
star [or according to Renard Pále, even a
triple one, with B and C orbiting A].
Consequently, the purported knowledge of
the mass of Sirius B or the orbiting time was
absent' (van Beek 1991).

Van Beek points out that Griaule's data was
developed in long intense sessions with one
primary informant, Ambara. In this process,
Griaule probably reinterpreted statements
from his informant in the light of his own
knowledge about Sirius and its heavy

companion, which had been much in the news at the time he began his field work. In turn, the Dogon, because Griaule was extremely respected and liked and because the Dogon culture places enormous importance on consensus and in avoiding contradictions, would have accepted his analysis as if it were theirs (van Beek 1991: 152-155).

As an example of the process, van Beek points out a Dogon tale which explains the differences between white people and the Dogon, but which, in fact, is taken from the Bible.

"Thus the story of the drunken Noah [Genesis 9: 21-27] has found its way into the stories of the se Dogon [sic], who emphatically denied that this was a 'white' story."…In many other instances the process was discernible: foreign elements were adopted and in a single generation became "traditional."

It might be argued that the knowledge given to Griaule was very secret and known only to a few, including Ambara. Van Beek points out that "neither the myths nor the song texts—though they are sacred—are secret. In fact, the tem [collective knowledge] is public knowledge…if the secrets revealed to Griaule are part of Dogon culture, one should be able to retrace them to some extent."

Another anthropologist named Jacky Boujou spent a decade with the Dogon and agrees with van Beek's assessment ("Comment," *Current Anthropology*, 12: 159, 1991 AD):

> I am struck by the degree to which van Beek's analyses coincide with those I have gradually arrived at...I would underline the obvious desire of the Dogon for collective harmony and consensus that is striking to the participant observer.

Yet another anthropologist named Paul Lane agrees ("Comment," *Current Anthropology* 12: 162, 1991 AD):

> Many of van Beek's substantive claims come to me as no surprise...I found little evidence for the complex but nonetheless allegedly unified symbolic ordering of daily life described by Griaule.

Cultural Transference Theory

The above mentioned "modern influence" theory is aka "Cultural Transfer":

> Noah Brosch "Sirius Matters" cultural transfer could have taken place between 19th century French astronomers and Dogon tribe members during the observations of the solar eclipse on 16 April 1893. The expedition, led by Henri Deslandres.

Such transfer is considered likely because the "Dogons' astronomical information resembles the knowledge and speculations of European astronomical knowledge of the late 1920s" and "their mythology was recorded in the 1930s." As an FYI: "Sirius B was first observed in 1862, and had been predicted in 1844 on dynamic grounds."

Specifically, "doubts have been raised about the reliability of Griaule and Dieterlein's work" for which you can see Bernard R. Ortiz de Montellano, *The Dogon Revisited* and Philip Coppens, *Dogon Shame*.

> ...anthropologist Walter Van Beek, who studied the Dogon after Griaule and Dieterlen, found no evidence that the Dogon considered Sirius to be a double star and/or that astronomy was particularly important in their belief system...

> Others, such as Marcel Griaule's daughter Genevieve Calame-Griaule and an anthropologist, Luc de Heusch, came to criticize Van Beek's dismissal as "political" and riddled with "unchecked speculation", demonstrating a general ignorance of Dogon esoteric tradition.

> Astronomer Carl Sagan...believes that because the Dogon seem to have no knowledge of another planet beyond Saturn which has rings, that their knowledge is therefore more likely to have come from European, and not extraterrestrial, sources.

> Astronomer Ian Ridpath observed..."The whole Dogon legend of Sirius and its companions is riddled with ambiguities, contradictions, and downright errors, at least if we try to interpret it literally.

Thus, it may simply have been a case of the Dogon relating their beliefs about Sirius to researchers, having the researchers offer new info about the system and, finally, having the Dogon simply incorporate the new info into their ancient cosmology. In fact:

> As anthropologists have known for a long time, primitive tribes have a remark able talent for absorbing interesting new stories into their traditional mythology.

Note that "Temple's book mentions the absorption of a Christ-figure into the traditional Dogon Pantheon, obviously a recent addition." How recent? It is difficult to say with specificity, however, "Missionaries from the White Fathers made contact with the Dogon in the 1920s."

Also, the Dogon's Sirius related beliefs, "are reminiscent of European Sirius speculations of the late 1920s" for example, "Europeans too talked about the discovery of a third star in the Sirius system; later investigations, however, ruled out that possibility."

In fact:

> ...the Dogon are not isolated...Dogon tribesmen could have journeyed to the coast, where they might have met astronomically informed seamen. The Dogon have been in contact with Europeans since at least the late nineteenth century...Peter and Roland Pesch of the Warner and Swasey Observatory in Ohio have pointed out that French schools have existed in the Dogon area since 1907. Dogon tribesmen wishing to pursue their education have been able to do so in nearby towns.

"Dogon descriptions of Jupiter, Saturn and Sirius remind one of Jonathan Swift's uncanny description of the two undiscovered moons of Mars" within his 1726 AD *Travels into Several Remote Nations of the World in Four Parts, by Lemuel Gulliver* aka *Gulliver's Travels.*

> But that isn't the only parallel. Swift appears to have taken the idea of two close (although not necessarily small) moons of Mars from Voltaire's novel Micromegas in which an extraterrestrial visitor tells earthmen about the undiscovered Martian moons. And from what star system does the visitor come? You guessed it — Sirius!

Voltaire wrote *Micromegas* in 1752 AD.

Thus, even fictional tales which reference Sirius could have been related to the Dogon and note:

> The Dogons were not isolated. Many served in the French army in World War I and some of them could have returned years later with colorful embellishments for their native legends.

> From the findings of Van Beek and the authors of Ancient Mysteries, it is clear that Griaule himself was responsible for the creation of a modern myth; one which, in retrospect, has created such an industry and near-religious belief that the scope and intensity of it can hardly be fathomed. Nigel Appleby – whose book Hall of the Gods was withdrawn from publication – has admitted to being tremendously influenced by Temple's Sirius Mystery.

The full title of the Nigel Appleby book is *Hall of the Gods: The Quest to Discover the Knowledge of the*

Ancients and some also claim that is it basically a plagiarism of Ralph Ellis' book *Thoth Architect of the Universe.*

You can find this chapter's research resources at this endnote.[55]

Travis Walton and the Fire in the Sky

I refer to Travis Walton within the context of the movie "Fire in the Sky" which is based on his experience for the sake of recognizability and yet, as we shall see, Walton notes that some of that movie is Hollywood myth making and does not accurately reflect his claimed experiences. Yet, he went on to write a book by the same title.

Walton, and fellow US Forest Service loggers, claim that he was abducted by aliens into a UFO on November 5, 1975 AD in the Apache-Seagreaves National Forest in Arizona. As noted above, eventually, in 1993 AD, a movie was produced; it is "based on the true story." Of course, "based" is a very wiggly word.

In the movie, Walton runs across a gray alien on the UFO; typical almond shaped head and almond shaped eyes yet, a moment later, realizes that it is merely an alien's spacesuit. The movie aliens look like E.T.'s evil twin; much smaller eyes than grays and not gray but brown.

Walton notes that what the aliens he saw were quite unlike those depicted in the movie and the spacesuit scene is simply movie fiction. This is a great example of my *fifty shades of gray aliens* concept which seeks to trace the typical gray alien form and figure to speculation about future humans via fiction, sci-fi and fantasy literature, TV shows and movies.

Walton has taken many, many polygraph tests which conclude that he believes in that which he is claiming. What is of interest, within this context, is the differentiation between his story and the Hollywood depiction—but that is not all.

Well, Hollywood is that which it is and they will do that which they will do. The point is that for some unknown reason, even though they were supposed to have been depicting a true story, they decided to disregard Walton's description. The *that is not all* portion is that Walton states that he saw **two kinds** of aliens. Firstly, he saw and interacted with aliens that were transformed into the evil E.T.s in the movie but also some that were just good ol' fashioned good looking humanoids or, simply, humans.

Walton went on to write a book about his experience that is titled *Fire in the Sky: The Walton Experience.*

Within the chapter titled *The Aliens*, he described the aliens as:

…a horrible creature…

…huge, luminous brown eyes the size of quarters…

…puny physique…more like fat than sinew. The creature was light [as in "not heavy"] …

…horrid entities…

…monstrous trio of humanoids…

…creatures…

…They were a little under five feet in height. They had a basic humanoid form: two legs, two arms, hands with five digits each, and a head with the normal human arrangement of features. But beyond the outline, any similarity to humans was terrifyingly absent. Their thin bones were covered with white, marshmallowy-looking flesh…

…they had very small feet, about a size four by our measure…

…they had no fingernails. Their hands were small, delicate, without hair. Their thin round fingers looked soft and unwrinkled. Their smooth skin was so pale that it looked chalky, like ivory.

Their bald heads were disproportionately large for their puny bodies. They had bulging, oversized craniums, a small jaw structure, and an underdeveloped appearance to their features that was almost infantile. Their thin-lipped mouths were narrow; I never saw them open. Lying close to their heads on either side were tiny crinkled lobes of ears. Their miniature rounded noses had small oval nostrils.

The only facial feature that didn't appear underdeveloped were those incredible eyes! Those glistening orbs had brown irises twice the size of those of a normal human eye's, nearly an inch in diameter! The iris was so large that even parts of the pupils were hidden by the lids, giving the eyes a certain catlike appearance. There was very little of the white part of the eye showing. They had no lashes and no eyebrows.

In the chapter mentioned next, he also refers to them as "those awful creatures."
He told the TV show *Phenomena Television* "these eyes blinked" and confirms that they had a pupil and iris.

During Walton's first interview, on November 11, 1975 AD, he stated that he saw "men leaning over me. They weren't really men, they were a lot like men but they weren't quite human." He states that they had underdeveloped features, no hair and were slightly shorter than he. He notes that they were a "brownish orange" which more so matches the movie alien color than the ones depicted in his book that had white skin. The other human aliens were "Just like you and I."

During an April 23, 1980 AD interview with Page Bryant and Jack Kennicutt, Walton stated that the first thing he saw was "aliens" and recalls "those eyes were very large…they blinked" and were "extremely large." He could not tell if they were male or female.

Another chapter of *Fire in the Sky* is titled *Human?*, wherein he described the other aliens(?) as follows:

> There, standing in the open doorway, was a human being!...He was a man about six feet two inches tall. His helmeted head barely cleared the doorway. He was extremely muscular and evenly proportioned. He appeared to weigh about two hundred pounds.

> …three other humans! Two men and a woman were standing around the table…they had no helmets. The two men had the same muscularity and the same masculine good looks as the first man. The woman also had a face and figure that was the epitome of her gender. They were smooth-skinned and blemishless. No moles, freckles, wrinkles, or scars marked their skin. The striking good looks of the man I had first met became more obvious on seeing them all together. They shared a family-like resemblance, although they were not identical.

What this all mean, was it really real and other questions are, ultimately, left not altogether answered. Our purpose was to provide some of the relevant information about that which he claims about the beings with whom he interacted and how it fits into my concept of the *Fifty Shades of Grey Aliens*.

Jeff Wells was a member of *The National Enquirer*'s team that originally covered the Walton case and, along with six other reporters, wrote the story "Arizona Man Captured by UFO" that was published on December 16, 1975 AD. He then wrote "Profitable Nightmare of a Very Unreal Kind" for the Melbourne, Australia paper *The Age*, January 6, 1979 AD.

Therein, he referenced, "The so-called facts, the carefully-woven tapestry" and that "We were to present a bold front for good footage of dedicated reporters sparing no expense to bring the public the true story of one of the most amazing incidents in recorded history." Eventually:

> ...I sat down to detail everything that had happened in a 16-page memorandum designed to kill the story. It was all over...A few weeks later I picked up the paper I worked for and found that with the help of the professor it had turned my memorandum into a sensational front-page story...

An organization that is favorable to the UFO hypothesis, *Ground Saucer Watch*, noted that "The Waltons 'sold' their story to the National Enquirer and the story was completely twisted from the truth."

He notes, "My paper had offered tens of thousands of dollars to anybody who could positively prove that aliens had visited our planet" and that is was just "five days later" when "the young man we came to call 'the kid'" Walton "stumbled into a small western town, phoned his brother and claimed he had been kidnapped by the crew of an alien spacecraft we were ready":

> It was a tale of little men with heads like fishbowls and skin like mushrooms...

The kid was a wreck and it was all the
psychiatrist could do to get him ready for the
lie-detector expert we had lined up. The test
lasted an hour…The kid had failed the test
miserably. The polygraph man said it was
the plainest case of lying he'd seen in 20
years but the office was yelling for another
expert and a different result.

To head that off we had the psychiatrist put
the cowboy and the kid through a long
session of analysis.

Their methods were unique. The next day
the four of them disappeared into a room
and soon a waiter was headed there with two
bottles of cognac. At the end of it the
psychiatrists were rolling drunk but they had
their story…

…the professor had talked the brothers out
of taking the sheriff's polygraph test and into
an hypnosis session in his room
immediately…

Not only did this transpire five days after the offering of a
reward but also, two weeks before the Walton event, NBC
had aired a movie based on the experiences of Barney and
Betty Hill. The movie, *The UFO Incident*, depicts the aliens
as having large eyes but with whites and pupils, just like
Walton's and not like that which has become the standard
description of large all black eyes. Also, like Walton's
aliens, the Hill's wore clothes which are also unlike the
standard.

The failed test was the one with John J. McCarthy, a test that was not mentioned in the *National Enquirer* story. This is covered in chapters 18-23 of Philip J. Klass' book *UFOs: The Public Deceived*.

An interesting point is that "It seemed that the kid's father, who had deserted them as a child, had been a spaceship fanatic and all his life the kid had wanted to ride in a spacecraft." In fact, Walton's brother previously "began to talk about his own UFO experience when he had been chased by a flying saucer through the woods as a child." During a *UFOAZ* interview, v stated that his brother's had been a "pretty dramatic sighting."
Moreover, GSW interviewed Walton's family beginning whilst he was *missing* (they did so along with Dr. J. Allen Hynek of the *Center for UFO Studies*). One of their investigation's eventual conclusions is that "The entire Walton family has had a continual UFO history. The Walton boys have reported observing 10 to 15 separate UFO sightings (very high)."

Furthermore, during a November 8, 1975 AD interview with Fred Sylvanus, Walton's brother Duane stated that he had regularly seen UFOs for the previous "ten or twelve years. I've been seeing them all the time." So focused on UFO was the Walton clan that, as Duane put it, he and Walton had a general agreement that if the occasion ever presented itself they would "immediately get as directly under the object as physically possible." At that time, he thought that Walton was "having the experience of a lifetime."

Despite all of this, at one point, Duane told Arizona's *Daily Star*, "I'm not a UFO buff and neither is my brother."

> He had seen something out there in the
> woods, some kind of an eerie light which
> had triggered a powerful hallucination
> which might recur at any time. There was no
> question of any kidnap by any mushroom
> men…
> Reports began to filter in that the witnesses'
> lie detector tests were not much help either -
> they supported the story that they had all
> seen the strange light but not that the strange
> light was identifiable as a spaceship…

The problem with hypnosis is that after a session who can tell what was real and what was not. In other words, the crew that worked with Walton can attest to having seen a "strange light," (five of Walton's crew passed the polygraph question, "Did you tell the truth about actually seeing a UFO last Wednesday when Walton disappeared? with the sixth result being inconclusive) a basic story was related to McCarthy and resulted in a failed polygraph, Walton underwent hypnosis and suddenly, subsequent polygraphs result in Walton having told the truth about his experiences aboard the craft.

However, this only means that he believes that which he is stating and does not mean that he actually underwent the experience. What we do know that he did undergo is hypnosis. Thus, perhaps he has passed polygraphs because he is retelling hypnotically suggested false memory events.

In fact, the *Ground Saucer Watch* report concludes that "Walton never boarded the UFO. This fact is supported by the six witnesses and the polygraph test results."

Another interesting note is that the GSW report has it that Walton's brother stated "I have a feeling, a strong feeling" that "Travis will be found" because the "UFO's are friendly." When asked "If the UFO 'captors' are going to return Travis, will you have a camera to record this great occurrence?" he replied, "No, if I have a camera 'they' will not return."

Also, Walton's mother "showed no outward emotion over the 'loss' of Travis and stated that UFOs would not harm her son and that he would be returned" and stated, "Well, that's the way these things happen." She noted that UFOs had been seen by her family, including by herself, many times. His sister, Grant Neff, also took the news in a strangely calm manner.

The promoter of the Barney and Betty Hill case, Karl Pflock noted, within the January 15, 2000 AD issue of James Moseley's UFO gossip newsletter Saucer Smear, Vol. 47 No. 1, a statement by Steve Pierce, part of Walton's crew, made during a recorded June 20, 1978 AD interview. When asked "What did you see?" by Philip Klass, he answered:

> Uh, well, I thought it was something a deer
> hunter, you know, rigged up. You know,
> 'cause it was deer season, you know, so he
> could see. You know? And, uh, and, but I
> couldn't see the bottom or a top or sides, all's
> I could see was the front of it, you know.
> You couldn't tell if it had a bottom to it or,
> you know, or a back to it or anything.

This is of interest as some claim that Walton could have rigged up some light source in the trees. Within this scenario, Mike Rogers, the driver, was also in on it and would have sped off once Walton neared the source of light so as to allow Walton to abscond to wherever he hid away for five days. This would have the convenient byproduct of removing the witnesses from being able to witness anything further; they saw a light and sped off.

The "Yes" answer to "Did you tell the truth about actually seeing a UFO last Wednesday when Travis Walton disappeared?" is true as they did see an object that they thought was flying but could not identify.

Whitley Strieber
and the Visitors

*For Strieber, in any case, what the visitors are probably
about is not invasion, but a profound and sufficiently
gradual change in our worldview and our souls.*
—Jeffrey Kripal

Even the typical person on the street may very think of
Whitley Strieber if asked about UFOs and aliens. This is
because Whitley Strieber is one of the most well-known
personages related to such topics. In fact, the cover of his
book *Communion* depicts an alien which has become more
popular than any other and adorns everything from guitar
picks and drug/head shop paraphernalia to drawing of many
alien abductees, contactees and experiencers and crop
circles.

Strieber has been the poster child for UFO and alien related
subjects of decades just as much as the gray alien has been
the poster child for the same. However, those who are
much more well aware of Strieber than is the typical non-
gender specific personage on the street will already be
shaking his and/or her heads because the fact is that
Strieber has never claimed that his experiences had
anything to do with aliens when we define aliens as
typically conceived of extra-terrestrial beings who were
born on another planet, etc.

Rather, Strieber is basically the Bertrand Russell of
UFOlogy, for lack of better terms (keeping in mind that
there is UFOlogy and then there is UFOlatry). Russell is
well known to have held to just about any and every
philosophy at one point or another during his life and

likewise, seeking diligently to understand his experiences Strieber has entertained a myriad of explanations.

Strieber has experienced many things which are typical of people who claim to have had experiences with extra-terrestrial aliens; abductions, experimentations, sexual encounters, telepathic communications and yet, even the good ol' probe. He has referred to these beings as *visitors* and perhaps the most interesting views he has held about them are his original one and his most recent one.

But before getting to the alpha and omega of his views let us note that some seem to think that he, just like many others who have similar experiences, were just minding his own business and all of a sudden they are being accosted by unusual beings. Yet, the fact is that he, just like many others who have similar experiences, had a prior history of engaging in occult practices—by any other name.

For example, the place within the visitors manifested was his meditation room, "he had made a meditation room in the upstairs of his cabin. Indeed, it was there, while he meditated, that the visitors would come as the encounters developed and deepened...I meditated with them" (pp. 306-307).

Also, he "had been involved for some time" with the "work of contemporary mystic Gurdjieff" who teaches a "bizarre synthesis of alien intervention and Tantric Yoga." Is it any surprise that he ends up involved with non-human beings who engage him in psycho-sensual/sexual relations ("sacred" sex/Tantric yoga)? I mean, there is a one-to-one correlation; this ain't rocket surgery!

Moreover, Jeffrey Kripal notes that Strieber:

> ...invokes childhood and sexual abuse as possible triggers of the visitor experiences, something that the broader ufological literature would support. (p. 320)

These quotes were from the self-professed possessed professor Jeffrey Kripal's book *Mutants and Mystics*.

In short, Strieber's initial discernment of the experience was accurate as he wrote about in his book *Transformations* (pp. 44-45, 172, 181):

> Increasingly I felt as if I were entering a struggle that might even be more than life and death. It might be a struggle for my soul...so far the word demon had never been spoken among the scientists and doctors who were working with me...I worried about the legendary cunning of demons...I wondered if I might not be in the grip of demons, if they were not making me suffer for their own purposes, or simply for their enjoyment...I felt an absolutely indescribable sense of menace. It was hell on earth...I couldn't move, couldn't cry out, couldn't get away. I'd lay as still as death...Whatever was there seemed so monstrously ugly, so filthy and dark and sinister. Of course they were demons. They had to be...

Kripal further notes (p. 299):

> Strieber is very clear that, whether derisive or dangerous, the basic worldview of the dogmatic scoffers worked in the exact same way as that of the dogmatic believers. Each excluded—"damned"...what did not, what

could not fit into its particular system and
assumptions. The official critics 'were
promoting a religion of skepticism that was
as belief-based as the demonization of me
that was going on among fundamentalist
Christians.' Both damned him.

But *fundamentalist Christians* were not damning what
could not fit into their particular system and assumptions.
Rather, they were reacting to Strieber 1) based on his own
claims and 2) because that which Strieber claimed **did** fit
into their particular system and assumptions.

His most recent conclusion is one shared by many now a
days (see chapter *Time Travelling Aliens?*) which is that so
called aliens, Strieber's visitors, are technologically
advanced highly evolved humans who travel back in time
from the future in order to help us evolve so as to realize
that, as Kripal put it, "human beings...are gods in
disguise...the angels and aliens, gods and demons are us."

Kripal quotes an interview as follows:
"No," [Whitley] Strieber jumps in, "I didn't
say aliens. I never said that. I don't use the
word aliens because I don't know what they
are. My impression is that the physical
beings that are involved are from the Earth.
They are an evolutionary leap of some kind,
but that they are primarily Earth-oriented.
That's my impression. We are not looking at
aliens. We are looking at our replacements."
(p. 46)

Kripal chimes in with:
We are all future butterflies who think,
wrongly, that we are just slugs. And we are

evolving, whether we admit it or not, into something else. Something with wings. (p. 56)

Kripal is personally acquainted with Strieber and thus, wrote much about him and so in this series we will consider some of these statements.

On p. 315 Kripal notes something which Strieber shared with him in person:

…his vision of a Gray [alien/visitor] rushing through the forest behind his New York cabin. As he described the being zipping in and out of the trees, avoiding each tree trunk as if it too were physical, with "blinding speed."

Kripal chimes in so as to make a point relevant to his book's context which is:

I could not help but think of all those drawings of the Flash [the comic book superhero] I had seen as a kid doing, well, exactly that. In this same superhero spirit, I might also mention the recurring metatheme of the alter ego, the secret identity that we all possess…

And he continues directly with:

…that we all secretly are: "Not psychiatry, not religion, not biology could penetrate that depth," Strieber writes. "None of them had any real idea of what lives within. They only knew what little it had chosen to reveal of itself. Were human beings what we seemed to be? Or did we have another purpose in another world?"…

Strieber at least came to realize that his "conscious life was nothing more than a disguise for another reality, another secret life," that "we very well may be something different from what we believe ourselves to be"

...Strieber's books are meant as catalysts, as triggers of awakening from this state of amnesia in which most all of us exist at the moment...They are meant, that is, to awaken us into our own secret lives.

Beyond anything else, this is a correct assessment of that which Whitley Strieber refers to as "The Secret School" (which is for "Preparation for Contact"). In other words, Strieber has gone from identifying the alien/visitors as demons to urging humanity to attend their secret school and prepare to make open contact with them.

Kripal continues thusly:

So too with the Communion letters. A certain Dr. Colette Dowell, for example, had experienced a disappearing pregnancy with no obvious miscarriage at fifteen, and she had experienced UFO dreams since about the same time. During a camping trip in 1988, "a vibrating energy permeated my vehicle and continued through my body with the focus being my third eye or pituitary region." This resulted in "an even greater sense of clairvoyance." Since she was a teenager (the age of the Mutation, as we have seen). "I felt there were two Colettes, one from this planet and one up in the stars..."

The reference to "the age of the Mutation" is Kripal's correlation between what he reads in comic books (and various forms of sci-fi) and that which occultists claim. In fact, the point of his book is that occultists are the ones, by in large, writing comics and sci-fi (although he is very much in favor of it all).

Thus, it is true that occultists consider puberty to be not only a physical change but also a time when a person's occult abilities begin to emerge and must be nurtured—this is why so very many occult stories of all sorts are geared towards teens, such as the current vampire craze.

To illustrate this, Kripal goes on to note:

> It is very difficult at such moments not to recall Otto Binder, who thought, of course, that the entire human species is a primate-alien hybrid. Or Frederic Myers, who wrote of our double "terrene" and "extraterrene" nature. Or Jacques Valle, who wrote extensively about the paranormal effects of UFO encounters. Or Philip K. Dick, who knew himself as a homoplasmate. Or...well, you get the point by now.

It would take us well beyond out context to unpack Philip K. Dick but note that in his *Tractates: Cryptica Scriptura* he wrote:

> The Immortal One was known to the Greeks as Dionysos; to the Jews as Elijah; to the Christians as Jesus. He moves on when each human host dies, and thus is never killed or caught...This is the Immortal One whom we worship without knowing his name...I term the Immortal One a plasmate, because it is a form of energy...The plasmate can

crossbond with a human, creating what I call a homoplasmate.

The (Alien) Goddess

It is interesting that Kripal admits being possessed by the Hindu goddess Kali. Likewise, Strieber has undergone the same basic experience with another goddess.

One of the most well-known and influential depictions of an *alien* is that of the gray *visitor* on the cover of Strieber's book *Communion*. It bears an amazing likeness to another (in)famous illustration; such as that of *LAM* by Aleister Crowley.

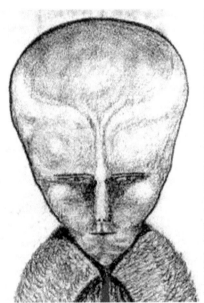 

Within Strieber's tale, this being is a female whom he describes as being "spider-like." He has also noted that after his initial experience with visitors such as she, he felt "a state of extreme terror and excitement" and this "somehow involved a provocative, even devastating, female figure." Also, "Strieber often compares the old bald gray goddess who could both inspire and sexually arouse him to a bug, and, later in his work, to a spider" (p. 311).

And he has much more to say about her such as that related by Kripal (p. 310) as he notes that Strieber described "the nonhuman woman as old and bald with bulging eyes, floppy lips, and yellow-brown skin":

> Strieber confesses that he does not know if the being is even a woman, and yet he continues to call her a woman, sometimes, not always, even capitalizing her presence as "Her." A bit later in the book, now back in his cabin, he reflects before the fireplace on his hypnosis session and the memories of this female presence that the session called up in him. Seven hymnlike pages follow.

> She appears, staring at him with those astonishing eyes: "Sitting before me was the most astonishing being I have ever seen in my life, made the more astonishing by the fact that I knew her. I say her, but I don't know why. To me this is a woman, perhaps because her movements are so graceful, perhaps because she has created states of sexual arousal in me....She had those amazing, electrifying eyes…the huge, staring eyes of the old gods."

Thus, already we have the manifestation of a non-human being, perceived as female, about whom Strieber writes hymn-like pages referring, having the term her generally capitalized (as is often done in referring to God and Jesus) and she starred like the old gods.

This is theme upon which Kripal focuses as, he too, was taken with Kali's large bug eyes (which, he notes, also are mimicked in Spiderman; recall that the visitor is "spider like"):

> Strieber wonders whether there are any connections between his experiences "and the mystic walk of the shaman, or the night ride of the witch." There are. The owl, he notes, was the personal symbol of the Greek goddess of wisdom, Athena. The owl's Latin designation, moreover, as strix is also related to later European words for witch...Even further back. Strieber will associate the owl with the wisdom of Ishtar, the ancient Mesopotamian "Eye-Goddess" with the huge, staring eyes. He wonders out loud about what Ishtar really looked like, and if these ancient gods and goddesses were not similar to the semidivine beings imagined by the very modern visionaries who have formed the contactee cults.

And this all comes to a point as Kripal continues:

> It is at this point that Strieber traces the origins of the alien and the UFO back not to contemporary pulp fiction, but into the furthest reaches of the history of religions, complete with possible memories of a past life (or lives); that is, in my own terms now…"The closest thing I have been able to find to an unadorned image of these beings is not from some modern science-fiction movie, it is rather the age-old, glaring face of Ishtar. Paint her eyes entirely black, remove her hair, and there is my image as it hangs before me now in my mind's eye, the

ancient and terrible one, the bringer of
wisdom, the ruthless questioner. Do my
memories come from my own life, or from
other lives lived long."

That "Strieber traces the origins of the alien and the UFO
back…into the furthest reaches of the history of religions"
is very telling as the very same demons who disguised
themselves as ancient gods and goddesses may very well be
doing the same today but in the guise of aliens instead.

Note the very telling statement on p. 300:

It is as if the visitors. Strieber suggests, have
decided that the U.S. government (which,
since the late 1940s, has treated them as
targets to shoot down), our religious
institutions (which, with precious few
exceptions [including Strieber's own initial
identification], have treated them as
"demons"), and our media (which has
chosen, with the professional scoffers, a
strategy of public ridicule) are more or less
incompetent.

In such a situation, Strieber speculates,
direct one-on-one intervention would
become a reasonable strategy to effect
specieswide change. This is why, Strieber
suggests, the visitors quickly ceased to rely
exclusively on their, theatre in the sky, and
began to interact with the human
unconscious via the deposits of dream,
myth, and out-of-body experience.

Put in my own terms, the visitors (which,
again, may be us) are ignoring our left-brain

reason and working instead on our right-
brain mythmaking, that is, on our Super-
Story. They are not, convincing, us. They
are rewriting and retelling us.

Well, both Kripal and Strieber had experiences with
goddesses with whom they had sexual experiences and who
rewrote them (Kripal claims to have devoted all of his
works subsequent to his possession to her will—and he is a
college professor, by the way).

Furthermore, Kripal writes (pp. 304-305):
I am also, frankly, drawn to his land my own
Roman Catholicism. [Strieber's book]
Communion, after all, can be read as a most
unusual and most original Roman Catholic
mystical text. His major abduction occurred
just after Christmas, and there is no more
Catholic a title than Communion. But if it is
a Catholic mystical text, it is one that turns
the orthodox sexual structures of traditional
Roman Catholic mysticism on their head.

How? Through an erotically charged
communion with an alien "Her."
Remarkably, there is no Christ as
bridegroom of the feminized soul here,
which is precisely what, one would expect in
a traditional Catholic mystical work. Nor is
there a Blessed Virgin Mary, whose
blessedness resides primarily in her
immaculately white virginity.

But there is, as we shall soon see, an Ishtar
and a long history of sacred sex with subtle

beings, be they fairies, elves, or alien visitors.

It is this deep (hetero) sexual structure. I want to suggest, that constitutes Whitley Strieber's deepest heresy and his most original spiritual move. It is also, I suspect, why he originally turned to the ancient pre-Christian world of Mesopotamian religion, and to Asia, to find precedents for his remarkable experiences. There is, after all, no divine feminine in Catholicism with whom a male mystic can unite. None. Where else could he turn, then?

Well, within Catholicism there may not be any sacred sexual union with Mary but there most certainly is a *divine feminine in Catholicism with whom a male mystic can unite*; the Catholic Mary. The real, historical and biblical Mary is not the Catholic Mary; the former was a natural born humble servant of God who recognized her need for salvation and the latter was born immaculate, was sinless her entire life, was assumed into heaven, can hear prayers, grants petitions, dispenses graces, etc. and, most importantly is the Queen of Heaven.

Queen of Heaven is an Old Testament and historical term for an abominable idol. Essentially, Catholicism has turned Mary into a goddess and likely got influenced to do so via a long history of goddesses whose name is basically changed throughout history. This time around she is celibate but, well, then again, largely, her priests are not so; there is that to consider. For more on all of these points and more, see the chapter on the Queen of Heaven within my book *In Consideration of Catholic Doctrines, Traditions and Dogmas*.

Lastly, it may be of interest to note that "Strieber suggests, the visitors…interact with the human unconscious via…out-of-body experience." Well, it just so happens, as long as we are talking about correlations between alien/visitors and gods/goddesses: according to the Qur'an, Allah essentially abducts us while we sleep as per Surah 39:42:

> It is Allah that takes the "Nafs" (of men) at death [nafs is the self, psyche, ego or soul]; and those that die not (He takes) during their sleep: those on whom He has passed the decree of death, He keeps back (from returning to life), but the rest He sends (to their bodies) for a term appointed. Verily in this are Signs for those who reflect.

On the Buddhist, Taoist, Horus, and Face on Mars Connection

On pp. 293-294 Kripal wrote:

> In my own term's now, we might speculate that any deep encounter with the sacred involves a temporary dissolution of the ego. If the psyche is ready for such an ego death, the encounter will tend to be experienced positively, even ecstatically. If the psyche is not ready, however, the encounter will tend to be experienced negatively, even demonically. The angel can quickly become the demon, and the demon can just as quickly turn into an angel.

This is actually very much like that which many Satanists will tell you about their view of Satan. Many will claim to not actually believe that there is any such personal being as Satan but that Satan, demons and various other such beings, are merely reflections of their psyche. Kripal and others have simply applied this to aliens, visitors or whatever they call them.

Kripal continues the thought thusly:
> Perfectly faithful to his double-edged, both-and nature of the sacred, Strieber, as an ego with extensive spiritual training, has known what he neutrally calls "the visitors" as both…

If both angels and demons then it would be just as the horror writer Clive Barker put it in his series *Hellraiser*, "Angels to some, demons to others." And yet, by definition, real angels and demons are ontologically different and one's perception does not change that.

Back to Kripal's text:
> Strieber has read deeply into comparative mystical literature, including into the Asian contemplative traditions of Zen Buddhism, Chinese Taoism, and Indo-Tibetan Tantra…he often invokes categories like the Koan of Zen practice or the Kundalini and "third eye" of Indian Tantric Yoga.
> Has had described to me how, as he became more familiar with the visitors, he noticed that they smelled of soil and he thought of them as miners. He would even sometimes hear drilling below the house—a kind of personal hollow earth.

This goes towards the point made above which is that some think that Strieber was *just minding his own business and all of a sudden they are being accosted by unusual beings. Yet, the fact is that he, just like many others who have similar experiences, had a prior history of engaging in occult practices—by any other name.*

Kripal continues:

> He also describes his early fascination with Egypt and his personal involvement in the early discussion about the Viking discovery and 1982 photographic resolution of the "face of Mars," which he instinctively associated with the ancient image of the sphinx.
> The Hawk-headed Egyptian god Horus, or a visitor posing as the god, even showed up in his cabin one night before a stunned houseguest.

This makes for an interesting correlation to Aleister Crowley who was likewise fascinated with Egypt and had interaction with various beings who pretended to be Egyptian gods.

Kripal then goes back to the point about "alien" versus "visitor":

> Although, Strieber consistently rejects and avoids the language of "the alien" (for its bad sci-fi b-movie allusions), he has written five provocative nonfiction books on his encounters with the visitors, which clearly invoke, even as they resist, subvert, and complicate, the earlier symbolic frames of the alien and the UFO. All of this, moreover, was first signaled in a bestselling book, *Communion*, which featured on its cover a female being, whom Strieber describes as "spider-like."

Ted Jacobs would make this being's huge,
black, wraparound eyes immediately
recognizable through his iconic paintings of
her on the book's famous cover. Whether
understood as 'other' or as some deeper
aspect of "us."

On pp. 296-297 Kripal gets into how Strieber's background
became his foreground:

Strieber's central mystical notion of
"communion" is all about moving from an
awareness that we are being written or
manipulated, even sometimes seemingly
raped or mind controlled...to an active,
shared, fully reciprocal, even loving
coauthorship with the alien other of a shared
supernature.

This is what the *Secret School* is all about; it is one of the
most extreme examples of *Stockholm Syndrome* of which
one could think—he is now encouraging us to just
passively sit back and accept being manipulated, raped and
mind controlled because, hey, the visitors know best so,
just trust that the ends will justify the means.

In this same realized and now authorizing
spirit, he invokes quantum physics again in
order to make sense of the radical
participatory nature of his visitor
experiences, that is, the mysterious ways
that the observation of an encounter event in
the external environment is in some sense
dependent on the subject state of the
observer.

> Not unlike John Keel, Whitely Strieber
> understands deeply that observer somehow
> helps create, literally bring into being, the
> observed. In our secret lives, Strieber
> suggests, we are really and truly
> participating in the authorization of reality
> itself, and in ways that remain largely
> unconscious at our present level of
> evolutionary development....we are,
> together, a giant awakening into our own
> unbelievable powers.

Here are the basics of how Strieber's world was turned
upside down:

> On that night, he experienced a dramatic
> abduction by a group of transphysical beings
> in upstate New York in his own forest cabin-
> home. In Communion (1986), he recreates
> that night, its foreshadowing that earlier
> October, and its various deep threads back
> into his childhood through conscious
> memory, journal entries, and, eventually,
> some hypnosis...

> Strieber in fact had no coherent
> understanding of what happened to him that
> night until he sought out medical attention
> for his intense psychological sufferings and
> physical symptoms, which included, he
> learned to his shock and horror, clear
> physiological evidence that he had been
> raped. According to Strieber, Dr. [Donald]
> Klein [Strieber's hypnotist] originally
> approached his symptoms, which had
> developed into PTSD or posttraumatic stress
> disorder, as signs of a crime.

An early short story entitled simply "Pain" (1986) represents an immediate, largely indirect or unconscious attempt to work through the experience before he began to articulate it through hypnosis, the UFO phenomenon, and his own doubleconcept of the visitors. Strieber wrote this short story in the days immediately after his abduction in what he describes as "a state of extreme terror and excitement that somehow involved a provocative, even devastating, female figure. The story reflects my first attempt to cope with the explosive, profoundly confusing combination of ecstasy and terror that the experience inspired."

This provocative and devastating female figure is the one depicted on the cover of *Communion* and has served as a catalyst for the figure of the gray alien which is so well known within pop-occulture.

In concluding this segment, note that Kripal writes (p. 301):
For Strieber, in any case, what the visitors are probably about is not invasion, but a profound and sufficiently gradual change in our worldview and our souls. He is in some good company here. After corresponding with military officials and contactees in the States, no less an intellectual than Carl Jung had read the flying saucer craze of the 1950s in a very similar light in his classic and still prescient *Flying Saucers: A Modern Myth Seen in the Skies* (1958).

Jung's conclusions were subtle, prescient, profound, and humble. He turned to parapsychology for suggestions-which were never any more than that-that these "things seen in the sky" might be planetary poltergeists manifesting a profound dis-ease or metaphysical imbalance in our present materialist worldview, that they may be, as it were, a manifestation of consciousness setting itself aright after a long night of materialism and mechanism. The crisis for Jung, in other words, was not yet environmental. It was primarily intellectual and spiritual.

So, visitor aliens are here to change our *worldview* and *souls*—think about that. It is important to note that the likenesses between Whitley Strieber and Carl Jung are not solely about their conclusions but the fact that they both engaged in occult practices.

On the Spider Bug-Alien Goddess Ishtar/Kali Mother of the Universe

Kripal notes that Strieber authored works of fiction that were actually based on that which was occurring within him; something which did not manifest until the visitors visited (pp. 203, 296-297):

> Strieber confesses, "I believe my whole body of work-my whole life-has been an unconscious effort to somehow overcome my fears and reach back to the 'secret school' of his childhood occult encounters"…

> Here are the barest outlines of Whitley Strieber's life and nonfiction work. From 1977 to 1983, the author wrote bestselling horror novels like *The Wolfen* (1978) and *The Hunger* (1981). Horror, of course, with all of its depictions of the dead and the monstrous, is a profoundly religious genre, even when it is not explicitly religious, since terror, a close cousin of trauma, can also catalyze transcendence.

> Strieber then collaborated with James Kunetka and wrote two works of social criticism, one about limited nuclear war, *Warday* (1984), and one about environmental collapse, *Nature's End* (1986).

There is a lot more to the relationship of the *visitor* experiences and his childhood. I sometimes heard Strieber referring to certain relationships he had with people in the CIA and the military in general. I suspected that he may have been part of MK-Ultra or a related mind control experiment. Well, finally, Strieber came around to recognizing this and spoke very openly about it. He also specified having undergone *Skinner Box* treatment which is a form of sensory deprivation.

Now, I recall seeing a video about what some claimed was actual footage of an alien that was kept at a military base. It was very obviously a puppet, a fake. Now, the video noted that Strieber had been asked to comment on it but he would not appear on camera due to being quite moved by it (read, freaked out). He did make a statement to the producers however which was that if the being in the video is not real then whoever made and manipulated the puppet knows how they, the real deal, move.

Well, this tells me that indeed, he has had experiences with such *beings* but there were puppets, they were part of undergoing mind control experimentation.

Now, having recognized and admitted that he had been experimented upon, Strieber still maintains that his experiences with the *visitors* are legitimate. This is because, he argues, on days in which he encountered them people noted that he was *agitated.* Well, of course, undergoing the experimentation (read, abuse) to which he was subject by the CIA and/or the military, in general, would certainly have left him agitated.

Now, back to the point about his fiction: Strieber thinks that his perception of the visitors was influenced by fiction and recommends what we may term *predictive programming* or, otherwise, infuse supposed fiction with the actual worldview of the author, director, screen writer, etc.—which is what everyone is already doing, of course (p. 304):

> ...he is absolutely certain that his visitor
> experiences appeared the way they did

because of the sci-fi movies that he watched as a kid and young adult, and that if we could create more accurate metaphysical films ("manipulations of light," as he poetically calls them), future generations might have more accurate visitor experiences.

In short, if we could recreate "the actual energy of the close encounter" on film, this would definitely advance both consciousness and culture, but only if we are willing to abandon our rational denials and current cultural beliefs about invading space aliens.

With further relation to that which I covered in the *The (Alien) Goddess* section, I will now consider further correlations between Strieber's experiences with an alien/visitor female whom he correlates with Ishtar and I correlated yet again with the Catholic "Mary" the Queen of Heaven (pp. 306-307):

The first thing to note about Strieber's *Communion* is that it is an expression of a long and sophisticated spiritual quest. The author tells us, without reservation, that 'my faith was a burning fire in me,' and this despite the fact that he was deeply conflicted about his Catholicism.

And had been so for some time, at least since his childhood, when an essay on the existence of God that he wrote for a catechism class was "declared to be a demonic inspiration." It is hardly surprising, then, that Strieber ranged widely in his spiritual quest, always looking for new resources, new insights, and less conflict.

"For half my life," Strieber writes, "I have been engaged in a rigorous and detailed search for a finer state of consciousness." He notes that he was reading the fourteenth-century Dominican preacher and theologian Meister Eckhart at the time of his abduction (Eckhart's sermons are easily among the most sophisticated, and difficult mystical texts one can read).

He also repeatedly refers to Zen Buddhism and notes that he had made a meditation room in the upstairs of his cabin. Indeed, it was there, while he meditated, that the visitors would come as the encounters developed and deepened. He could hear them landing on the roof, like some sort of occult Santa Claus. He would go upstairs to meditate at around 11:00 each night: "A few minutes later, usually with a great clatter and thudding on the roof, they would arrive....Night after night. I meditated with them."

They entered his mind. They conjured memories. And they left him with two clear happy words: "have joy." Strieber also describes a vision of a brilliant sphere in the sky just outside the cabin. Note the explicitly religious and vaguely sexual nature of his response: "This light had rays that I could feel penetrating my skin with gentle pinpricks....I had something close to a

seizure, a paroxysm as my body responded
with fearsome, tingling pleasure to the most
intimate touch I have ever felt, and I knew
then utter compassion and an ancient love."

Hence the title of the book, Communion.
This was not the first title. Strieber wanted
to call the book Body Terror, for that was
the defining feature of his initial abduction:
pure biological terror. But one night, while
he and his wife were in bed, his wife spoke
to him in a deep voice: "The book must not
frighten people. You should call it
Communion, because that's what it's about."
He looked over to argue for his own title
again.

Note something that is commonly reported with alien
abductees, et al.; the visitor/aliens rape him mentally and
physically, "They entered his mind. They conjured
memories" and they leave him in a stupor by leaving "him
with two clear happy words: 'have joy.'"

How many people out there are having demonic possession
experiences of all sorts but end up referring to benevolent
higher selves, spirit guides, ascended masters, etc. all
because after they were tormented they were hypnotically
triggered, as it were, to dissociate from the experience by
screening it with a *happy, happy, joy, joy* label.

Moreover, besides the obvious occult connections with all
of this note something of numerological interest: 11 is an
important number in occultism and was a favorite of
Aleister Crowley, for example. For whatever reason,
Strieber chose, specifically, to meditate (with alien/visitors
no less) at 11 each night.

Moreover, something that some might miss is that on two occasions Strieber experiences visitations of sorts at, specifically, "3:00 a.m." Well, this is the specific time known as the witching hour when the spells cast and the demons summoned by late night magickal workings are put to work (makes you wonder why American's are asked, at each presidential election, whom they would want answering that, specifically, 3:00 a.m. call).

We will leave off with an elucidating quote which plays off of the fact that "Strieber traces the origins of the alien and the UFO back…[to] possible memories of a past life" (p. 310) and thus, asks (p. 311-313):

> "Do my memories come from my own life,
> or from other lives lived long ago, in the
> shadowy temples where the gray goddess
> reigned?"…Strieber often compares the old
> bald gray goddess who could both inspire
> and sexually arouse him to a bug, and, later
> in his work, to a spider.
>
> Enter the insectoid theme…Maybe, Strieber
> speculates, the visitors are our own dead.
> Maybe they are us in more perfect form:
> "Maybe we were a larval form, and the
> adults of our species were as
> incomprehensible, to us, as totally
> unimaginable, as the butterfly must be to the
> caterpillar."
>
> It is here, with the ancient gray goddess
> Ishtar who looked like a bug or a spider, that
> the iconic almond eyes of the alien find us
> again.…Strieber traces the first appearance
> of the standard alien form back to June of

1957 and the cover of a sci-fi pulp digest,
Fantastic Universe. His own mystico-erotic
experiences of an ancient goddess, however,
point much, much further back and recall, in
striking detail, my own speculations linking
the classic alien eyes to Indian art and
Tantric goddesses.

After all, much like Strieber's erotic union
with an alien Ishtar, the Tantric aspirant in
South Asia traditionally unites, sexually or
symbolically, with a Tantric goddess like
Kali to obtain spiritual insight, cosmic
visions, and yogic superpowers. I am hardly
projecting here, as Strieber himself is clearly
aware of these Tantric resonances. Indeed,
he points them out himself to illustrate what
he calls "the mystery of the triangle."

Here Strieber turns explicitly to Indian
Tantra and the goddess Kali, and especially
to her yantra or down-turning triangle, an
abstract symbol of her genitals, with a bindu
or "seed" in its center: "The object of the
worship of the Yantra is to attain unity with
the Mother of the Universe in Her forms as
Mind, Life, and Matter."

Strieber, in other words, imagines his visitor
experiences as a kind of Tantric yoga or
spiritual practice on the way to "union with
Her as She is in herself as Pure
Consciousness." Sexually uniting with the
Mother of the Universe: the oedipal
dimensions return, again. But he is also, at
the same time, sexually uniting with his wife

as Lover. This is how he put the matter to me in a letter: "In some way, she and Anne [Strieber's wife] are the same person. She is with Anne and within Anne, but at the same time free in ways that no one of us have been free. My sensual relationship with her and my sensual relationship with Anne are profoundly intertwined. This is why, when I tell Anne of my liaisons with her, she is never jealous, for they are also happening within her."

But, at least in Communion, it is finally not Kali but Ishtar to whom Strieber feels the most drawn. It is "Her," he senses, with whom he had really communed. He tells us that her name means "star." And what happens to a human being who unites with a star? He becomes that divinity. He takes on that stellar or astral nature.

Hence the wonderful Ted Jacobs painting on the cover of Conroy's commentary and study, which imaginatively portrays the metaphysical effects of Strieber's erotic communion with Her. Those black cosmic eyes, slightly almond shaped and filled with stars, are now his. As in the Catholic eucharist, the author has been consumed by that which he has consumed...

Early in Communion...Strieber describes having the impression that one of the visitors was wearing "a face mask." There is also that odd, never really explained moment in the book where Strieber sees a visitor rush by wearing a hat, a blue card on the chest, and a mask with eye holes and a round hole-in essence, a superhero costume.

Weirder still, there is what I would identify, inappropriately no doubt, as "the Ghost Rider scene." Strieber sees what he thinks is a skeleton on a motorcycle with "great big eyes that just scare the hell out of you." He realizes later that it is another bug like visitor, a visitor who resembles a praying mantis, which resembles a skeleton on a motorcycle. This is just a bit too close to the Marvel Ghost Rider character of the 1970s. All we are really missing is the flaming skull.

Except that we have that too-sort of. Strieber called his sister and asked her what her strangest childhood memory was. She told him about "the time we were sleeping out in the back lot and the fireball came across the lot." It was big and green. Strieber remembered no big green fireball. But he did remember Ghost Rider "All of my life I have had a free-floating memory of a skeleton riding a motorcycle, a frightful effigy. Now I know the source of that image."

Strieber also shared, in person this time, his vision of a Gray rushing through the forest behind his New York cabin. As he described the being zipping in and out of the trees, avoiding each tree trunk as if it too were physical, with "blinding speed."

As for when the *standard alien* first appeared, as you can see from chapter *On the Fifty Shade of Gray Aliens Template and Images* that via pop-occulture we can go back to 1893 AD for large headed beings.

One can suppose that they have a solid marriage, or something, when Strieber's wife Anne accepts his sexual liaisons with the spider bug-alien goddess Ishtar/Kali-Mother of the Universe.

Alien Wife Swap

Strieber correlates his real life human wife Anne with his alien/visitor/goddess/Ishtar/Kali/ Mother of the Universe, "In some way, she and Anne are the same person. She is with Anne and within Anne."

In the previous section, we noted that Strieber refers to "the mystery of the triangle" which he correlated with the upside down triangle associated with Indian Tantra with regards to the false goddess Kali. Along those lines we continue as Kripal notes:

> Strieber also notes that the trinity is "the most common symbolic structure of the visitors" and dedicates an entire section to "the inner meaning of the triangular shape," that is, on the symbolism of the triangle in the history of religions and in the work of the contemporary mystic Gurdjieff, with whose teachings, which include a clear, if bizarre synthesis of alien intervention and Tantric yoga, he had been involved for some time.

> These reflections climax in a vision another contactee reported of two shining discs in

the sky that discharge an immense arc of
energy between them before they fuse into
one. Strieber takes the vision as symbolic,
pointing again to the mystery of the triangle
and the triadic structure of alien thought:
The fundamental idea of the triad as a
creative energy is that two opposite forces
coming into balance create a third force...
"Are the visitors asking us to form a triad
with them?" Strieber finally asks. This is a
rhetorical question. I take its positive, erotic
answer as the implicit message of the entire
visitor corpus. (p. 319)

So, Strieber was involved in a "bizarre synthesis of alien
intervention and Tantric Yoga" and ends up involved with
what?!?! Non-human beings who engage him in psycho-
sensual/sexual relations ("sacred" sex/Tantric yoga). To
reiterate, one followed from the other: I mean, this ain't
rocket surgery!

I recall that in my life BC I was reading Strieber's books
and noticed that he notes that symbolism common with
abductees is eagles and triangles. Well, for whatever it is
worth; upon getting home I noticed, for the first time, that
the bottle in which my favorite ginger beer/soda came had
an eagle within a triangle upon the glass—whatever that
means.

In the previous section we noted that Whitley Strieber
retold of experiences with "one of the visitors" who was
"wearing 'a face mask'" and one which rushed by him
"wearing a hat, a blue card on the chest, and a mask with
eye holes and a round hole" and what "he thinks is a
skeleton on a motorcycle with 'great big eyes that just scare
the hell out of you'" plus "another bug like visitor...who

resembles a praying mantis, which resembles a skeleton on a motorcycle" and a "vision of a Gray rushing through the forest...zipping in and out of the trees, avoiding each tree trunk as if it too were physical, with 'blinding speed.'"

And this is just a taste of that which Strieber has retold in his various books, talks, etc. Besides the *that's weird* aspect, let us note that one may observe a nuts and bolts UFO/spacecraft flashing colors, moving at blinding speed, etc. (which are most likely secret, black budget, government technology) but what is an individual alien doing wearing strange costumes and running around at blinding speed?

This seems to pertain to the fact that much involving alien encounters—as abductees, contactees, experiencers, etc.—is illusion and delusion. That is to say that the "aliens" are manipulating people's minds so that they will see and therefore, believe falsehoods.

With this in mind, note the following:

> One correspondent [someone who wrote to Strieber], for example, was told this: "My dear, one day you will look just like us." Another woke up in the night to find "that his arms were long and thin, and he felt light and seemed to be pulsing with the delicious electricity that eastern traditions identify as kundalini." The Tantra again.

> He could fly now. He flew up to see his son, who was happy to see him. The next morning, however, this shared occult experience was remembered by the son as a terrible nightmare, with his father as "a monster that had flown around his room like a giant bat"—a kind of paranormal Batman.

> Still another person, after physically
> touching a visitor in Strieber's own cabin
> and being left with "an electrical feeling,"
> reported that she now knew herself as "a
> spiritual being solidified into physical
> form." She realized that, "physical and
> spiritual are not separated whatsoever." (p.
> 323)

Here we have someone being told that they will be like the aliens (condemned like a demon, in other words), someone who sees themselves looking like a gray alien who astral projects (or, something) in monstrous form and someone who has a spiritual revelation upon being infused with the spirit within the alien (the real meaning being the electrical touch).

Here we have come to something which I covered in chapter *Likenesses Between Spirit Channeler Mediums and Alien Contactees/Experiencers* and the title says it all. Here is an example of this point from Jim Wilhelmsen's book *Beyond Science Fiction!*:

> Interesting observations about all UFO
> sightings are the electromagnetic
> disturbances experienced during a sighting.
> These same disturbances are experienced
> with ghost apparitions and demonic
> encounters. The common denominator in all
> of this may be a biological function. This
> biological function then is somehow related
> to electro-magnetic fields.
>
> BUFORIA, a British counterpart of
> America's Project Bluebook concluded in its
> findings that UFO's had more in common

with occult activity than it did with any
extra-terrestrial origin. Their findings were
based in part on these electro-magnetic
disturbances.

I should also include that many people who
have encountered UFOs, Ghosts or demonic
activity, have smelled the ionized air, which
is associated with electrical and magnetic
currents and the smell of sulfur, associated
with everything demonic and subterranean.

Couple all of this with the other thing that spirit channeler
mediums and alien contactees/experiencers have in
common; anti-Christian sentiments (along with a
misunderstanding of traditional biblical theology). Kripal
notes the following about Strieber's theology:

...is fiercely alive and wildly heretical. His
rejection of the traditional God, that "old
greybeard in the sky"; his understanding of
Christ ("all are God, all are Christ. The
difference was that he knew it"); and his
rejection of belief ("belief is always a
lie")—these are all thoroughly and
completely gnostic in precisely the terms
that I have defined the expression here and
elsewhere. (p. 327)

Yet, that God is an old greybeard in the sky is not the
traditional God but a cartoonish depiction. That we all are
God is certainly heretical and shows that Strieber has
bought the original deception in the Garden of Eden, "you
shall be like God" (Genesis 3:5). Lastly, Strieber *believes*
that "*belief* is always a lie" and, to quote Forrest Gump,
"That's all I gotta say about thaaaaat."

Also, note something about occult numerology as Kripal notes one of a few instances of Strieber relating odd occurrences at 3:00 am which is traditionally known as the "witching hour" (makes one wonder why Americans are always asked, during presidential elections, whom we want to be there to take the 3:00 am phone call):

> Such thoughts about the alien body are extended further in a more recent text. The Key, which purports to record the memories of a conversation Strieber had while on book tour with a stranger in a Canadian hotel, at 3:00 in the morning no less. (p. 324)

Another important occult number is 11—a favorite of Aleister Crowley's for example—Kripal writes that Whitley Strieber:

> ...repeatedly refers to Zen Buddhism and notes that he had made a meditation room in the upstairs of his cabin.
> Indeed, it was there, while he meditated, that the visitors would come as the encounters developed and deepened. He could hear them landing on the roof, like some sort of occult Santa Claus. He would go upstairs to meditate at around 11:00 each night: "A few minutes later, usually with a great clatter and thudding on the roof, they would arrive....Night after night. I meditated with them."

On the theme of the free will employment of the will relating to the supposed litigious nature of demonic oppression or possession; note that Strieber told of:

> ...a general who shared with him the rumor that [John] von Neumann, who was allegedly on a committee tasked with

making sense of the Roswell recovery, had
written a three-page paper on how the
visitors might be able to enter our own
dimension in large numbers: through the
tripwire or trigger effect of our own
acknowledgment of their existence. Strieber
takes up this story to tell his own about, in
the narrator's words now, "that last
immortal day, where they speculated about
the monsters in elegant phrases, where they
used the language of physics to babble about
the impossible that had become real."

Such monster speculations boil down to the
central idea that the world of experience is a
kind of quanta, that is, a kind of
indeterminate potentiality that "collapses" or
becomes determinate through our individual
decisions and beliefs (and, more so I
presume, through our collective cultures and
religions). The visitors, whose existence has
recently been rendered definitive in the story
through the recovered remains of the
Roswell crash, are experienced as a kind of
demon species within von Neumann's
Jewish Catholic consciousness. (p. 317)

I began this chapter by noting that Whitley Strieber's first
identification of his *visitors* was accurate as he wrote
(*Transformations*, pp. 44-45, 172, 181):

Increasingly I felt as if I were entering a
struggle that might even be more than life
and death. It might be a struggle for my
soul…so far the word demon had never been
spoken among the scientists and doctors
who were working with me…I worried

about the legendary cunning of demons…I
wondered if I might not be in the grip of
demons, if they were not making me suffer
for their own purposes, or simply for their
enjoyment…I felt an absolutely
indescribable sense of menace. It was hell
on earth…I couldn't move, couldn't cry out,
couldn't get away. I'd lay as still as
death…Whatever was there seemed so
monstrously ugly, so filthy and dark and
sinister. Of course they were demons. They
had to be…

Indeed, he also accurately identified that which he went on
to do (*Transformations*, p. 96):

What if they were dangerous? Then I was
terribly dangerous because I was playing a
role in acclimatizing people to them.

Pop-Occulture: The Psychic (Deep Space) Nine and Gene Roddenberry

In order to unpack the strange case of Gene Roddenberry and the psychic (Deep Space) Nine we will glean from the writings of the self-professed possessed professor, Jeffrey Kripal (from his book *Mutants and Mystics: Science Fiction, Superhero Comics, and the Paranormal* which I review in my book series *The Necronomiconjob*) and a *Fortean Times* article by David Sutton.[56]

The Lab and the Foundation

In 1975 AD Roddenberry "was hired to prepare Earth for an alien invasion" by Sir John Whitmore who was involved with an organization called *Lab Nine* which was a direct descendant of the 1948 AD *Round Table Foundation*. The lab's purpose was, "research into the paranormal and its belief that Earth was soon to be visited by extraterrestrial beings traveling in spacecraft" and Roddenberry's purpose, "was to prepare the ground for the aliens' arrival by writing a movie script that would prime the human race for first contact."

The Foundation had been founded by MD, inventor, and paranormal researcher Dr. Andrija Puharich and continued its work via Lab Nine with the assistance of the medium Dr. Vinod, "who promptly went into a trance and began to channel messages from mysterious entities calling themselves 'The Nine Principles and Forces.'" Subsequently, the Lab "continued to receive communications from 'The Nine', initially via flying saucer cultists Charles and Lillian Laughead" and also by Uri Geller.

Also involved were the psychic Phyllis Schlemmer and the pseudonymous *Bobby Horne* who "became the new channeller of the extra terrestrial communications." He "burnt out quickly; he became suicidal and fled after suspecting that he had become the victim of cosmic jokers." This lead to Schlemmer becoming the Lab's official channeller and the "voice" of The Nine. That is, the human voice as the Nine's usual spokesperson an alien entity named Tom.

What they produced has been described as, not surprisingly to those who read such stuff, "all the usual New Age ingredients… grandiose statements, shaky grammar and unprovable predictions" (as per Lynn Picknett and Clive Prince).

Gene Roddenberry's Background and Worldview(s)

Roddenberry was not exactly the perfect fit for this group as he was a WWII B17 pilot, a commercial aviator, a Los Angeles cop, the television writer and creator of *Star Trek* and most relevantly:

> …an avowed humanist with a deep mistrust
> of all organised religions as well as a hard-
> line sceptic when it came to tales of UFOs
> and alien visitors. He did, though, have an
> interest in altered states of consciousness.
> Psi phenomena in particular fascinated
> him…

Roddenberry was also a compulsive womanizer who experienced *escalating* marital problems; interesting how being a hard-line sceptic (in the sense of rebelling against God) is so very often coupled with womanizing and these two are coupled with marital problems.

Roddenberry wrote:

> I do not reject the possibility that other
> forms of intelligence can be in contact with
> humanity or with certain humans. Nor do I
> reject the possibility that another life form or
> forms might even live among us. It would
> seem to me rather extra ordinary if this were
> the only place in the Universe in which
> intelligent life happened to occur. Neither do

we know the real nature of time and whether
it and space are always linear and constant.

On the other hand, I've never seen any
proof, or at least anything I recognize as
proof, that other intelligent life forms exist,
or are or have been in contact with us. Nor
have I ever seen anything I recognise as
proof that other laws of physics exist.

According to his secretary Susan Sackett, Roddenberry's
interest in Psi phenomena was likely a result of a childhood
out of body experience (see Joel Engel's *Gene
Roddenberry, The Myth and the Man Behind Star Trek*, p.
167).

Note that it is noted that "some of his later pronouncements
on religious matters do diverge from his earlier sceptical
humanism towards more mystical 'I am God' type
statements that might have derived in part from his time in
Ossining."

Indeed, the Yvonne Fern book *Inside the Mind of Gene
Roddenberry* is:

>…based on a series of conversations toward
>the end of Roddenberry's life, reveals a
>curious, deeply flawed, guru-like figure
>whose constantly repeated mantra was "I am
>Star Trek" – a man as identified with, and
>possibly trapped by, his creation as
>MacNorth is by "Time Zone"; as hostile to
>organized religion as ever but increasingly
>certain that his own belief in the future in his
>head could lead humanity to the next level.

We will come to MacNorth and the "Time Zone" in a moment but first, note that the aforementioned Susan Sackett (in her book *Inside Trek: My Secret Life With Star Trek Creator Gene Roddenberry*, p. 38) stated that Roddenberry's:

> …spiritual beliefs were extant, although they were revised frequently. When I first discussed this with him, he believed in what he called the "All", the life force of the Universe. Occasionally he referred to this concept as "God", although it was clear that his was not the Judæo-Christian god concept in any shape or form.

Indeed, not Judeo-Christian at all as it is noted that:
> ...a man who had already, through the growing popularity of the then defunct Star Trek, opened a vast number of minds to the possible existence of extra terrestrial life, superior non-human beings and a future for mankind among the stars.

And most relevantly:
> ...one of Star Trek's major themes is that humankind would rather stand alone and on its own two feet than be guided by anyone (or anything) describing itself as a God – the theme of more Star Trek stories than one cares to count.

As an example, consider the *Star Trek* episode *Who Mourns for Adonais?* "in which an ancient Greek 'god' expecting human worship is sent packing by an indignant Captain Kirk."

The God Thing

As the new-age medium channeling sessions continued Uri Geller, under hypnosis, began "channeling an extraterrestrial intelligence called Spectra, a hawk-headed super computer entity aboard a spacecraft":
> Puharich suspected a connection to The Nine, which Spectra confirmed, claiming that it was they who had "programmed" Geller with his remarkable powers when he was a three-year-old child.

Puharich, by now convinced that Geller was himself an ET, planned to use the Israeli's psychic powers to help bring The Nine's message to the world and prepare humanity for the imminent arrival of their spacecraft.

"The God Thing" is the title of an unproduced Star Trek movie and later unpublished novel by Gene Roddenberry and is premised upon, "God as a malfunctioning spacecraft…an enormously powerful, but malfunctioning, machine entity travelling toward Earth to 'save' humanity" which was written before Roddenberry even met Whitmore:

> …but the vast organic/mechanical entity which is more Great Deceiver than Messiah seems to bear more than a passing resemblance to Puharich's Spectra, and its promises of saving human kind from its own excesses are certainly close to those being channelled through Lab Nine.

William Shatner "recalled the climax of the script as follows":

> As the drama builds and we finally approach the craft, the alien presence manifests itself on board the [spacecraft] Enterprise in the form of a humanoid probe, which quickly begins shape-shifting while preaching about having traveled to Earth many times, always in a noble effort to lay down the law of the Cosmos.
>
> Its final image is that of Jesus Christ. "You must help me!" the probe repeats, now bleeding from hands, feet and forehead. Kirk refuses, at which point the probe begins exhausting the last of its energy in a last-ditch violent rampage, commanding the Enterprise crew to provide the assistance it needs in order to survive.

Shatner noted (in his book *Star Trek Movie Memories*, p. 37) that the script was impressive but that he "couldn't imagine Paramount or any other studio agreeing to make such a controversial, perhaps even blasphemous film…for the first time in history God was gonna be the bad guy."

Wow, how very quaint and how times have changed; nowadays you would be hard-pressed to find any movie at all in which God is **not** the bad guy.

The Lab Nine Script

In short, the whole prep for mass landings, first contact, fell by the wayside as the Nine rejected the script and the draft and the whole project fell apart—man, those aliens are tough movie critics—they gave it three suction-cupped-tentacled thumbs down!!!

What Roddenberry did was to produce a script based on his actual experiences with the being played by a skeptic named Jim MacNorth who is the creator of a canceled but still popular sci-fi show called "Time Zone" (this mirrored Roddenberry's own canceled but popular show).

MacNorth was approached by a mysterious Englishman (Sir John Whitmore was Roddenberry's real-life Brit) who represents a group called Second Genesis (Lab Nine) and who hires MacNorth to write a screenplay about the group's paranormal research, and the ultimate "'landings' of The Nine's representatives, which will take place one year from the release of the film."

"Second Genesis," as in new beginning, makes contact with The Nine through a psychic/medium/channeler and uncover a styled ancient astronaut line which is that "human kind was one of their early, failed, experiments." Also, it was revealed, "that some of us are 'of Altean blood' [as in

Atlantis] and possess Altean 'genetic features . . . mixed with our basic Earth features.' Human-alien hybrids..."

In the meantime, MacNorth's "erectile dysfunction is cured by an aura healer"—yeah, so, well, there you have it.

He ends up "travelling the country to observe research into telepathy, auras, faith healing and theoretical physics" (much like Roddenberry who was "given tours of parapsychological labs").

He ultimately:

>...becomes overwhelmed with fears that he is in fact setting up human kind for an impending alien invasion, has a nervous break down and enters his own "Time Zone" (read Star Trek) universe – which, he discovers, was not so much his own creation as an inspiration emanating from the 'real' extra terrestrials.

As recently as 1993 AD, Phyllis Schlemmer was still at it, publishing a book titled, *The Only Planet of Choice: Essential Briefings from Deep Space.* "Her website claims that Roddenberry's contact with The Nine was part of his research for *Star Trek!*" Thus, *Star Trek: Deep Space Nine* may have been a styled result of this whole sorted affair.

The Nine and the Nines

We have "The Nine" and Schlemmer's reference to "Deep Space." Moreover, there is the 1956 AD Edward D. Wood, Jr. movie, "Plan 9 from Outer Space" the original title of which was "Grave Robbers from Outer Space." Perhaps another loose connection is the 2007 AD movie *The Nines* although, merely going by keywords such as "nine," "lab," "deep space," etc. will lead to a very long list of what movies, books, etc. the connection of which would be nothing but terms.

However, *The Nines* is a three-part (occult ascension?) story each part of which pertains to different characters played by the same actor.

Part one is about Gary who is a masturbating sodomite (the sodomy is only in the deleted scenes where he has homosexual sex with a pizza boy whom he has known for about half a minute) who is an actor under house arrest for living in another person's house after having burned down his own house.

He becomes convinced that he is being haunted by the number nine (occult numerology?), including finding a note saying "Look for the nines" written in his own handwriting (occult automatic writing?). He also sees different versions of himself around the house and has experiences with the number nine cropping up everywhere.

His handler, as it were, ends up telling him, "I can get you out of here" but meanwhile, he is so freaked out that he leaving his house arrest which causes a blip in reality.

Part Two is about Gavin who is attempting to get a TV pilot produced the title of which is *Knowing* (as in gnosis as in Gnostic) that is about missing mother and daughter. A TV executive and producer tells Gavin to look for the nines which he then writes on a piece of paper; the same piece which Gary found in Part One and he states that he thinks he is haunted by himself.

The executive and producer pulled fast one which resulted in the show not being picked up and so Gavin slaps her to which she says, "Do you think you are a man?" Part Two is filmed as if the process of him attempting to get a show produced is, itself, part of a reality TV show starring Gavin.

Yet, after stating to the camera to leave him along, after the slapping incident, pedestrian next to him on a street corner asks him to whom he is speaking and it turns out that there is no camera crew, no show, nothing but a delusion.

He then realizes that everyone human has a number seven floating above their heads, much like a halo, but that he a nine.

Flashing back to Part One, we find Gary's handler telling him he is a god-like being. God is a 10, humans are 7 and he is a 9. It is revealed that he could destroy the world with a single thought and, playing upon multiverse theory it is noted that he exists in many different forms but that none of them are real.

Part Three features Gabriel who is a video game designer (in other words, he creates worlds). His car breaks down in the middle of nowhere and he leaves his wife and daughter to seek help. While a woman leads him off into the woods to her car, the mother and daughter become very confused as they watch video clips on a digital camera of the unreal-reality show of Part Two and a scene from Part One.

Gabriel begins to shows signs of intoxication as some water the woman had given him was drugged. Part of the ongoing plot was different women Sarah, Sierra and Susan (three "S"s) to separate the other three incarnations of this being—Gary, Gavin, and Gabriel (three "G"s) from, the mom, Mary.

In this case, drugging him was the only way to get him to stop long enough to reason with him; she is attempting to help him come home. It is noted that much like a video game addiction, Gabriel has been playing for 4,000 years reincarnating into different roles to play with the humans.

Thus, the 3 nines (an upside down 666?) plead with him to come back home.
We find that the daughter has gone missing but Gabriel returns to the car with her in his arms and they all go home. Mary realizes he is not who he seems, tells Gabriel he needs to go and that the world is not real. He reveals that there were ninety variations of the universe and that the current one is the last one and, via his removal of a green bracelet from his wrist, the universe becomes nothing.

Finally, there is a scene of the woman and the daughter who tells her "he's not coming back...all the pieces have been put together" and the woman stating "the best of all possible worlds."

There does not seem to be a one to one correlation with the whole Plan Nine project with the exception that it proposes multiverse, polytheistic, pop-occulture theology wherein the world is saved/destroyed by a super intellect against which humans cannot counteract.

> In the end, Gene Roddenberry died in 1991 AD and "a small sample of his ashes was launched into space to orbit the Earth for six years before burning up on re-entry."

Joe Firmage: Is the Truth A New Alien Galactic World Order?

Herein we will consider the basic UFO extra-terrestrial alien related views of Joe Firmage as an example of extra-terrestrial alien messages. Firmage is the founder and chairman of the *International Space Sciences Organization.*

The premise on my view of supposed extra-terrestrial alien messages pertains to reading between the lines of alien messages. The basics of it are that regardless of the message, particularly the most peaceful ones about humanity getting along and saving the Earth, we must consider how aliens propose we accomplish such truly good goals.

For instance, Erick Davis notes that "Harvard Medical School psychiatrist John Mack writes that one of the central themes of the alien encounters he studies is the conviction that Gaia is on the brink." Gaia is one of the names given to the Earth when it is conceptualized, anthropomorphized, in a Pagan manner as a living being. Davis also notes that Mack has stated that "There is some kind of intelligence that we are connecting with" and, as Davis puts it, "This intelligence seems particularly obsessed with the ecological crisis."

Call it global warming (or the global cooling scare of the 1970s AD), overpopulation, (the catch-all term) climate change, etc. The answer is always to forgo current governing systems and join together in a one world government and forgo current religious theologies and come together in one world religion which follows the alien gospel (which is no gospel at all).

We now come to Firmage via the article "Alien Views - A profile of Joe Firmage, Silicon Valley UFOnaut" by Erik Davis.[57] Essentially, he was a successful businessman who was laughed out of his position due to his views on UFOs and extra-terrestrial aliens. He states that he is a generalist and explains that generalists "predict the future for the whole of civilization."

His transformation from straight-laced businessman to promulgator of all things alien has, as its midpoint, the following experience:

> As he lay there half-slumbering, an image appeared over his bed, a bearded gentleman with a dark brown head of hair.
>
> "Why have you called me here?" the being asked, clearly irritated.
>
> "I want to travel in space," answered the astonished Firmage, who spoke without a moment's deliberation, as if in a dream.
>
> The fellow remained nonplussed. "Why should you be granted the opportunity?"
>
> "Because I'm willing to die for it!"
>
> Then, says Firmage, the man produced a sphere, an electric blue ball about the size of a cantaloupe, which entered Firmage's body, taking command of his muscles and producing unimaginable waves of uber-orgasmic ecstasy.

Now, of course, one is not just minding their own business and suddenly states to an apparition that they are willing to die for the ability to travel in space. This is why this was the mid-point; there is a beginning point and an ongoing point.

If you read my review of the book Mutants and Mystics (which I published in my book series The Necronomiconjob) by the self-professed possessed professor Jeffrey Kripal, you know that, for example, some think that Whitley Strieber was minding his own business and all of a sudden was getting probed by visitors. Well, just as just about every known contactee, experiencer or abductee (and/or their families) Strieber has a background of involvement in occult practices (by any other name).

Likewise, considering some of his background, it is not difficult to discern why Firmage ends up speaking to an apparition:
Firmage's visionary experience did not exactly appear out of thin air. A descendant of Brigham Young, Firmage was raised a Mormon and grew up hearing tales of the otherworldly humans who led the young Joseph Smith to the golden plates he translated into the Book of Mormon.

> And though Firmage abandoned his faith at age 15, the precociously intelligent boy brought rather religious emotions to his new worldview of science, feelings of cosmic awe that he traces to that defining moment of his generation: Star Wars.

> But SF wasn't enough. What really sealed his galactic passions was Carl Sagan's Cosmos series. "It was beautiful and it was science, and therefore it was real, far more

real than religion to me"…[he also] scarfed
up flying saucer books as a teen.

Even these few details about the beginning and midpoints
give us a lot to work with so, let us consider some points.

Indeed, the Mormon god of Earth (one of an innumerable
number of gods, on their view) was a human-like being
who was born on another planet, lived his life, died and
became a god. This is the very same hope of every Mormon
of good standing with their church (yes, the original satanic
deception "you will be like god" Genesis 3:5 is the very
core of their theology). Thus, the Mormon god is an
extraterrestrial alien.

It is therefore understandable that Firmage "brought rather
religious emotions to his new worldview of science" and
hit upon Star Wars. While many think that Star Wars is
about futuristic space battles that is only the façade. Firstly,
the series began with the statement "A long time ago" and
also "in a galaxy far, far away." This is the basic starting
point of Mormon theology.

Firmage also stated that "It's just like Star Trek: First
Contact." And here we go again as the show's creator was
into the occult, both conceptually and in practice, see
chapter *Pop-Occulture: Gene Roddenberry and The
Psychic (Deep Space) Nine*.

What *Star Wars* is about is hinted at when someone refers
to Darth Vader as practicing "sorcerer's ways." Indeed, the
premise is the same basic premise of any and every mystery
religion, secret society, the New Age, witchcraft, etc., etc.,
etc. and that is that there is no personal God but rather an
impersonal and amoral energy—qi, chi, ki, prana, Vril, the
Force—into which one can tap and which one can then

bend towards one's will. This is why within Star Trek the Sith and the Jedi both consider themselves to be the good guys and the others as the bad guys; because the Force is amoral and thus, lacks a premise upon which to define good and evil.

However, the relation between Mormonism and sci-fi does not really relate to *Star Wars* or *Star Trek* but rather to *Battlestar Galactica* as Richard Abanes noted in his book *One Nation Under Gods: A History of the Mormon Church.* The show was not merely somewhat like but actually premised upon Mormonism along with specific references to the planet Kolob, etc.

The next step in Firmage's devolution was being taken by Carl Sagan's Cosmos series which he thought was beautiful and science. Actually, he was not just taken with it but taken in by it. He claims that since it was scientific "it was real, far more real than religion to me" but Cosmos is religious at its core.
The entire series is premised upon the following unscientific *faith*-based assertion, "The Cosmos is all that is or was or ever will be." What so many people, including taxpayer funded public school children, did not realize is that Cosmos is premised upon Sagan's Atheistic worldview—it was just a vehicle via which to get Atheism not smuggled into the back door of public schools but brought right in the front doors.

The last detail is that Frimage "scarfed up flying saucer books as a teen." And so Mormonism's alien god, Star Wars, and the Atheist Cosmos all coalesced—and we do not know what else he was into; conceptually, in practice or both.

So he ends up experiencing what may be termed sleep paralysis which is when an entity seeks to control a person as they are somewhere between wakefulness and sleep; the person is often left aware but unable to move. The apparition of a bearded gentleman actually claims that Frimage summoned him, "Why have you called me here?" and for whatever reason Firmage implies knowledge that this being had the ability to grant him "travel in space" and Firmage states this, at least according to Erik Davis, "as if in a dream."

When the man asks why such a request should be granted, implying that he did possess the ability to grant it, Firmage makes a statement which is indicative of the litigious nature of demonism, "Because I'm willing to die for it!" In other words, his life in exchange for occult knowledge and abilities (here occult meaning literally hidden that is, presently unknown or obscure).

Then "an electric blue ball...entered Firmage's body"; such spheres are commonly reported, not ironically, by both extra-terrestrial alien contactees, experiencers or abductees as well as spirit channeling mediums.
This styled demonic entity manifesting as a sphere then proceeded in "taking command" of Firmage and sealed the deal by giving him the token sensation of "producing unimaginable waves of uber-orgasmic ecstasy" (ditto with Kripal and Grant Morrison).

Thus, we see that a little tale about interest in outer space has a lot to say between the lines.

Firmage eventually published a 600-page book called *The Truth*. At least in the late 1990s AD, he sent out a statement via mass emails. Therein he stated:

> The Truth represents a rather large
> hypothesis, whose overall conclusion has
> enormous implications for every single
> human on Earth…Welcome to The Truth…a
> story that will go on forever. Print this
> out…and read it through at one time.

The URL to the book is *thewordistruth*: the word is truth.
He may have been answering the X-File motto "The truth is
out there" and stating that his word is "The Truth" but note
that John 17:17 has Jesus stating the following to God the
Father, "Your word is truth."

Actually, this is not a stretch considering that Firmage:

> …holds that the founding myths of world
> religions were created by these teachers in
> order to seed human culture with the ethical
> memes we'll need for our ultimate
> graduation into space.

> For proof, Firmage suggests rereading the
> New Testament, replacing the words heaven
> with space, and angel with teacher. "The
> book ceases to have the mythical quality and
> it begins to have anthropological sensibility.
> It begins to say to you, ah, this is how you
> take a chimpanzee and turn him into a space
> traveler."

Here we come to the point about the alien gospel which is
really alien theology sans a gospel (the good news of
salvation via the sacrifice of the Messiah Jesus). We can
see how all religions can come together on this view as
they are not divinely inspired but alien inspired.

Another point which is typical of, both, extra-terrestrial alien contactees, experiencers or abductees as well as spirit channeling mediums is that the one and only faith which is false, faulty, fake and a fraud is Christianity. In this case, we hearken back to an Erik Von Daniken ancient astronaut/ancient alien style reading of the New Testament (what about the Old?). This was a point about a new one world religion.

Now to a point about a new world order of governance:
> Firmage believes that the aliens in our midst are teachers, here to help us strap on the psychological shoes that we'll need for our birth as galactic citizens…By plugging spirituality into a galactic framework, Firmage hopes to keep the ethical and mystical core of religion alive in a world ruled by naturalism.

> It his own fantastic attempt to heal the rift between science and religion, a rift that he believes must be sutured if we are to avert the environmental catastrophes that loom all about us…" the seriousness of the damage we are inflicting on the biosphere."

Note that the point is not that it is not true that we are badly damaging the planet but the how of the aliens' plans for ending our destructive practices. We are to come together in a new galactic world order so as to become "galactic citizens." Did you note the point about keeping "the ethical and mystical core of religion alive in a world ruled by naturalism"?

Consider that, for example, the celebrity New Atheist Sam Harris is an Atheist Buddhist mystic (who does not like the terms Atheist, Buddhist or mystic) who believes that mystical, spiritual, experiences are merely the stuff of gray-matter; mere biochemical reactions (which he has experienced via drug use and meditation). Thus, one does not have to "believe in God" in order to believe in and have mystical, spiritual experiences. This is what is proposed by Firmage and his alien theology; no need for God, just form a new galactic world order and religion.

Moreover:

> Firmage's ultimate faith is not that the aliens will save us, but that the stone-cold truth about their existence will trigger a massive transformation of human culture.

> "People will instantly and viscerally understand that there is a far grander scheme, that they are part of a Star Wars script. Then they will start to behave in ways that naturally tend to self-organize a new type of vision."

The point about a massive transformation is the breaking down of our theology and worldviews and goes back to ancient aliens; they exist, God does not, they created us, God did not. Thus, we will "self-organize a new type of vision" get it yet?

Davis also notes:

> ...while encounters with these critters are often traumatic, [John] Mack insists they can be transformative as well. "This experience shatters people's constricted worldviews, which can then connect them to a larger reality. It opens their pores to the

divine, to home, to source, to what we once called God."

Thus, the alien theology is no theology at all but an Atheistic energy based manner whereby to establish a new galactic world order; a post-God religion.

In a mass email dated to 1999 AD, Firmage noted:
> As the great scientist Carl Sagan long maintained, the discovery of extraterrestrial life will ultimately become the **single greatest unifying force** ever for humanity. We will need that kind of unity to overcome the next century's challenges. [Emphasis added for emphasis]

Sure, and he is not the only one as Ronald Reagan stated it in 1987 AD (speech to the UN General Assembly, 42nd General Assembly):
> Perhaps we need some outside, universal threat to make us recognize this common bond. I occasionally think how quickly our differences worldwide would vanish if we were facing an alien threat from outside this world.
> I occasionally think how quickly our differences worldwide would vanish if we were facing an alien threat from outside this world. And yet, I ask is not an alien force already among us?

Of course, Reagan called his space-based defense system Star Wars and with regards to the correlation between UFO aliens and the government, it is interesting to note the Joe Firmage:

…found himself longing for the day when this dense fog of official lies and obfuscations would finally dissolve in the light of alien truth.

Such hopes are folly as they will likely get the ultimate disclosure and it will be the ultimate deception which will be that there is no God and we were created by aliens.

In fact, Firmage is already post-God and personifies, anthropomorphized the Saganistic Cosmos:

> …**the Cosmos beckons us**, as if to say "demonstrate the judgment to deserve access to this domain." [Emphasis added]

Thus, overall, Firmage affirms our template of how to discern between the lines of the alien messages…and their messengers.

The Manchurian Messiah: Project Blue Beam, UFOs, Aliens & the NWO

Conspiracy theories, conspiracy theories, oh so much to say about conspiracy theories.

A comedian once stated that his grandpa saw a racist conspiracy behind everything:

> How come green olives come in a jar but
> black olives come in a can!

On Seinfeld, uncle Leo thought that the cook was an anti-Semite because he ordered his burger medium rare but it came medium.

But this is just the fun stuff and there are very frightening conspiracy theories which would lead you to believe that everything will poison you: tap water, the plastic used in bottled water, movie popcorn butter, your fire resistant furniture, processed foods, shadow governments, secret societies, aliens, shape shifters, etc., etc., etc.

The difficulty is that most conspiracies are about those secret things to which virtually no one has any access and thus, are very, very difficult to prove.

Also, if you were involved in those secret things and someone sought to uncover you, you could just call them a wacky conspiracy theorist.

Then there is the conspiracy theory debunkers who could, at least, potentially show that an alleged conspiracy is nothing of the sort.

However, this only solidified in the mind of the conspiracy theorist that it is, in fact, a conspiracy because only someone trying to cover up a conspiracy would deny that there is a conspiracy.

Round and round it goes and sadly, much completely credible information about real conspiracies get buried by mockery, a sold out media, misinformation, etc.

In this series we will get to know the concept behind what I have coined as "The Manchurian Messiah" and how the advent of this figure will relate to Project Blue Beam, UFOs, Aliens and the NOW—the New World Order.

Let us begin with "The Manchurian Messiah." A book titled *The Manchurian Candidate* was written by Richard Condon and published in 1959 AD. This was made into a movie in 1962 AD and again in 2004 AD.

The premise is that during the 1952 AD Korean War a US platoon is captured and taken to Manchuria where they are brainwashed to believe that their very own Sergeant Raymond Shaw had saved their lives during combat. For this, Shaw is awarded the Congressional Medal of Honor.

For years later members of the platoon have reoccurring nightmares for years that the Sergeant had murdered two of his own men whilst under the observation of Russian and Chinese officials.
As it turns out, Shaw was made into a "sleeper" agent who functioned like an everyday person until such time as his programing was tapped into by the showing of a symbol,

the Queen of Diamonds card, at which time he would obey orders and after which he would have no memory of his activities. The bottom line is that he has been placed in a position to be a controlled subconscious who could work, behind the scenes, in attempts to overthrow the U.S. government.

As a side note, the original plot was premised upon a true and present danger of Communism which was replaced in the more recent movie with corporations.

Now, back to our point which is that what will be presented here is neither a confirmation nor a denial but food for thought. I once wrote an article about what Atheists demand of God such as what they demand that God do before they will believe in Him.
The most compelling and seemingly simple demand (note that if God heeded our commands we would be God's God) is that God should just appear in the sky in order to announce His existence to everyone and then it would be a done deal.

Well, this is fallacious for various reasons the first being that it exposes one of the secrets behind Atheism: it is not about evidence and proof but about rebellion. Atheists are in rebellion against God and many actually express, in thought, deed and word, that they despise God (here meaning YHVH).
Thus, if YHVH were to appear in such a manner it would merely solidify in them that their hatred truly is well placed. They would not worship YHVH in such as case but would hate Him even more for truly existing. If they could, they may even murder Him...it has been done, you know.

In any regard, I sought to not only play skeptic's advocate but to show that he is more skeptical than thou, as it were.

The essay *Prove "god"* noted something which truly did proceed forth right from the top of the head:

> I could even argue against a global
> appearance of God by claiming that aliens or
> the Illuminati were attempting to manipulate
> us via holograms or some such thing.[58]

Liking to keep tabs on various issues related to worldviews and science, it was years after penning the above statement that the government program known as *Project Blue Beam* was found.

The premise is actually very succinctly put by Jon Ronson (director of the movie *The Men Who Stare at Goats*) in his book *The Psychopath Test: A Journey Through the Madness Industry* in which "He delves into the fascinating history of psychopathy diagnosis and treatments, from LSD-fueled days-long naked therapy sessions in prisons to attempts to understand serial killers":

> ...the idea that the government may one day
> utilize holograms to mislead a population
> was not quite as farfetched as it sounded.
> Some years earlier I had come across a
> leaked U.S. Air Force Academy report
> entitled "Nonlethal Weapons: Terms and
> References," which listed all the exotic
> weapons in the proposal or developmental
> stages within the U. S. Department of
> Defense. One section was labeled
> Holograms:
>
> Hologram, Death.
>
> Hologram used to scare a target individual
> to death. Example, a drug lord with a weak

heart sees the ghost of his dead rival
appearing at his bedside and dies of fright.

Hologram, Prophet.

The projection of the image of an ancient
god over an enemy capitol whose public
communications have been seized and used
against it in a massive psychological
operation.

Hologram, Soldiers-Forces.

The projection of soldier-force images
which make an opponent think more allied
forces exist than actually do, make an
opponent believe that allied forces are
located in a region where none actually
exist, and/or provide false targets for his
weapons to fire upon. [Emphasis added for
emphasis]

By piecing together some already existing technologies
some have pieced together scenarios such as the following.

Airplanes fly over major cities and lay down *chemtrails*
(chemical trails: looks like the plane's exhaust but takes
much time to dissipate and thus, leaves trails). The
strontium barium niobate which they expel in the
chemtrails is used as a screen upon which, via Project Blue
Beam's holographic projections, images of gods are
displayed.

Note that Yitzhaq Hayutman's vision of a holographic
Temple to be displayed over the Dome of the Rock
includes a fog machine that would create a mist which

would be used as a screen for lasers. Fog/mist dissipates quickly and would be difficult to spread and maintain over a large area. This is why chemicals are preferable.

These gods rebuke the populace for misinterpreting their will, their scriptures, etc. and explain that there is only one god—the images may even merge into one. The communication is not via traditional speaker system driven sound waves but via technology which sends signals directly into our heads (see attached video for a commercial example of this).

Some add that the gods will warn of an impending alien attack which will come along with holographic UFOs and which will further unify humanity against the alien threat. Even in first world countries we have given up certain freedoms in exchange for safety and security. So, imagine what humanity will give up when faced with technologically advanced aliens.

Along with this could come weather related anomalies, earthquakes, etc. —and technologies capable of producing sounds in the atmosphere—as being either indicative of the gods' wrath or alien attacks, etc. Of course, we have already had a pseudo alien attack, a hoax for which many people fell: can you say *War of the Worlds*?

Some also add a pseudo rapture, within the Christian context, whereby holographic humans will be seen being literally raptures, take up into heaven.

Also, the still unbelieving or otherwise disobedient could be, literally, prodded when they experience their skin burning via invisible *microwave* style radiation.

It is noteworthy that Jesus warned us as follows:

> For false Christs and false prophets will
> arise and will show great signs and wonders,
> so as to mislead, if possible, even the elect
> (Matthew 24:24).

> The coming of the lawless one will be in
> accordance with the work of Satan displayed
> in all kinds of counterfeit miracles, signs and
> wonders (2 Thessalonians 2:9).

It is interesting that "counterfeit miracles, signs and wonders" may have been thought to have been real *miracles* performed by beings such as Satan (the "god of this world," 2 Corinthians 4:4).

However, it may be that it is the wonders, the miracles, which are false being rather performed via technology. In either case, these are performed in order to draw people away from YHVH and towards the god of this world.

The point will be to finally establish absolute and unified rulership upon the Earth. One false Christ which is noteworthy is Baha'u'llah who established the *Baha'i World Faith*, the goal of which is:

> ...a world commonwealth in which all
> nations, races, creeds and classes are closely
> and permanently united...a world legislature
> whose members will...ultimately control the
> entire resources of all the component
> nations...A world executive, backed by an
> international Force...A world tribunal...A
> mechanism of world inter-communication...
> A world metropolis will act as the nerve
> center of a world civilization....A world
> language will either be invented or chosen
> from among the existing languages...A

world script, a world
literature…currency…weights and
measures…A world federal system, ruling
the whole earth and exercising
unchallengeable authority over its
unimaginably vast resources.

Well, the technology is in place and there are people who
are certainly willing and able to do such things. What will
come of it all is anyone's guess. Yet, one thing is certain:
And Jesus answered and said to them, "See
to it that no one misleads you. "For many
will come in My name, saying, 'I am the
Christ,' and will mislead many. "You will
be hearing of wars and rumors of wars.

See that you are not frightened, for those
things must take place, but that is not yet the
end. "For nation will rise against nation, and
kingdom against kingdom, and in various
places there will be famines and
earthquakes. "But all these things are merely
the beginning of birth pangs…

"But immediately after the tribulation of
those days the sun will be darkened, and the
moon will not give its light, and the stars
will fall from the sky, and the powers of the
heavens will be shaken.

"And then the sign of the Son of Man will
appear in the sky, and then all the tribes of
the earth will mourn, and they will see the
Son of Man coming on the clouds of the sky
with power and great glory.

"And He will send forth His angels with a great trumpet and they will gather together His elect from the four winds, from one end of the sky to the other (Matthew 24:4-8 and 29-31).

Ancient Aliens and Satanic Gnosticism

*Satan's not such a bad guy...we become who
we are and ultimately that is to be like
our makers; to become gods ourselves*
—David Childress, Ancient Aliens, "The Satan Conspiracy" episode

Very much could be said regarding the TV show *Ancient Aliens* which is basically a slight update on Erich Von Daniken's ideas. Yet, that which follows seems to best fit my context.

Under consideration is Jason Colavito's article "Review of Ancient Aliens S06E05 'The Satan Conspiracy,' in Which TV Tells Us to Worship Satan" (October 29, 2013 AD). This manner whereby to critique the episode also allows us to critique a critique towards the end of resulting a more accurate overall picture.

Let us begin with this statement:
> ...the character of Satan is an artificial construct composed from a range of ancient parts...This story [of Satan's fall] is an old one, but almost certainly one that was assembled from various spare parts...this composite figure, the devil...

It is important to note that systematic theology means just that; we systematize concepts by composing a range of ancient parts assembled from various "spare" parts, etc.

In a manner of speaking, Satan is *an artificial construct* in the same way that the Big Bang theory is *an artificial construct* as it was composed of a range scientific datum from various disciplines and observations (mathematics, thermodynamics, etc.) that were assembled from various "spare" parts.

Add to this the concept of progressive revelation (that we receive certain information about certain topics dispersed through time) and that what was culturally known may be more than what was written (and remains intact) down at any given time.

Colavito notes:

> One of those parts was the Hebrew figure of Satan, the adversary, who in the Hebrew Bible is God's agent, satan, and is sometimes a supernatural figure (as in Job and Numbers 22) and other times a general term for any human God uses to block the actions of another (as in 1 Kings 5:4). In Job and Numbers, this figure is an angel. In Zecharia 3:1-2, the Satan ("the Accuser") stands at the right hand of the presiding angel in the presence of God and the heavenly host.

This statement is somewhat accurate if properly understood and yet, somewhat confused as Colavito refers to the *figure* and also to the *term*. He first states that "the Hebrew figure of Satan" is "a general term for any human…" Well, the *figure of Satan* (or, Satan as a figure) and the term *satan* are different issues. The figure of Satan comes into play within the Bible's context when we recognize a few grammatical facts.

Within the Bible, there are many *elohim* but only one ultimate personification of *Elohim*. There are many *Angels* but one ultimate personification of the *Angel of the LORD*.

Likewise, there are many *satans* but only one ultimate personification of *Satan*. For that matter, there are many *devils* but only one ultimate personification of the *Devil*.

Thus, indeed, any human or other being taking an adversarial action is a *satan*. Also, in "Job and Numbers" the term may be employed as applicable to an Angel, but that does not mean that the Angel is the "figure" as in the ultimate personification of Satan.

In fact, in Job, there are "sons of God" which are, within a larger context, known to be Angels but Satan is not said to be one of them but to appear with them before God.

Colavito writes:

> Another part was the serpent in the Garden of Eden, who tempts Eve into sin. The Hebrew Bible does not identify the serpent as Satan; that occurs only much later, taking shape in last few centuries BCE and taking canonical form in Revelation (20:2), in the New Testament, whose authors were all familiar with the newish fallen angels story.

Again, however long it may take; this is doing systematic theology.

He further notes:

> A third part was the material in Isaiah (14:12-15) about the Morning Star falling from heaven, referring poetically in context to a Babylonian king, but applied as early as the New Testament authors to the emerging idea of Satan.

Isaiah's imagery is in turn likely derived
from a Canaanite myth of a lesser god or
hero who attempts to overthrow El, the
supreme god, and is hurled back to earth,
something on the order of the Greek
Bellerophon attempting to conquer
Olympus.

Since I have done a lot of work on the Isaiah 14 issue, as
well as Ezekiel 28 for that matter, I will simply refer
interested readers to my article "Is Lucifer a Fallen Angel?
(Contra Jim Brayshaw)"[59] which, as the title implies, also
deals with the fact that Satan is not an Angel but a Cherub
(and they are different categories of being who look
different and have different job functions). Note that
Colavito missed the fact that Ezekiel 28 states that the
Cherub was in the Garden of Eden.

Colavito writes:

This composite figure, the devil, emerges
largely thanks to Jewish apocalyptic
literature. Satan does not appear in the
apocalypse of Daniel nor is he a main
character in the fall of the Watchers in the
Book of Enoch (canonical only in Ethiopia),
yet because Satan was among the heavenly
host—one of the benay Elohim, the sons of
God—he could therefore be interpolated
into the apocalyptic narratives once the sons
of God from Genesis 6:4 were firmly
declared fallen angels around the time of the
composition of the Book of Enoch.

Colavito seems to be referring to the Coptic text *The
Apocalypse of Daniel*. The *Book of Enoch* (more
accurately, *Ethiopic Enoch* aka *1 Enoch*) is an apocryphal

elucidation of the Genesis 6 affair in which Satan was not involved. Again, Satan is not a "benay Elohim, the sons of God" and there may be a good reason for his lack of involvement.

Angels look like human males (without wings and without halos for that matter). However, Cherubim are quite different having four wings, hand-like prehensile appendages under their wings, cow-like hooves, four faces (human, lion, ox/bull and eagle/vulture) and while their bodies may be humanoid, we are simply not told.

The Sons of God Angels in Genesis 6 get married and reproduce with human females. It may be that Satan does not have the, shall we say, anatomical features with which to copulate with human women.

Colavito comments:

> From Enoch's chief naughty angels Samyaza and Azazel, our Satan gains his rebellious character and his punishment to be bound beneath the earth until the Last Judgment. The last chapters of Enoch, probably composed long after the first section on the Watchers, significantly replace Azazel with Satan, reflecting the transition and fixing it in time, around 100 BCE.

Of course, "Enoch's chief naughty angels" are "Samyaza and Azazel" (with, as noted above, *Samyaza* being transliterated circa 1,001 different ways in the literature.

Yet, Samyaza and Azazel are not Satan and there is no biblical text that claims that Satan is "bound beneath the earth until the Last Judgment" in fact, the exact opposite is the case. He is loose upon the Earth, will be bound during the *millennial reign,* will then be loosed again and finally thrown into the lake of fire which was created for him and his Angels.

"The last chapters of Enoch" could refer to Ethiopic Enoch/1 Enoch's last chapter or to the last chapter of other versions of the *Book*(s) *of Enoch*. In any case, note that chapter LXIX, generally titled, "The Names and Functions of the (fallen Angels and) Satans: the secret Oath" notes:

> ...the names of those angels [and these are their names: the first of them is Samjaza...The name of the first Jeqon: that is, the one who led astray [all] the sons of God, and brought them down to the earth, and led them astray through the daughters of men. And the second was named Asbeel: he imparted to the holy sons of God evil counsel, and led them astray so that they defiled their bodies with the daughters of men. And the third was named Gadreel: he it is who showed the children of men all the blows of death, and he led astray Eve...

In this case, Gadreel is identified with the being that was eventually, biblically, identified as the ultimate personification of the Satan figure.

In any case, Jason Colavito's point is to discern whether Ancient Aliens is being accurate or not—shocking, I know, but it turns out not! Also, see Chris White's *Debunking Ancient Aliens* beginning with my article, "Sources for re-researching the Ancient Alien issue of Vimana-UFOs."[60]

Colavito notes:

I find it interesting that two weeks ago, in covering the Anunnaki, we were instructed that ancient texts had to be taken absolutely literally, particularly the Book of Enoch, yet here we are told we must take the Biblical texts symbolically and interpret the serpent as Satan and Satan as the victim of anti-satanic propaganda.

What Ancient Aliens is doing is merely promulgating Gnosticism which takes the text of the Bible, particularly Genesis, and turns it inside out, upside down and backward. Gnostics and Ancient Aliens turn Satan into a heroic figure who enlightens humanity in conquering God, the God who would keep us nice and ignorant-like.

Colavito notes, "William Henry tells us that Satan is our benefactor, a Promethean figure giving us much-needed wisdom." Indeed, the story of Prometheus is Gnostic-like with Prometheus literally and figuratively enlightening humanity, against Zeus's will, by giving us fire, etc.

This Ancient Aliens episode identifies Satan as all sorts of things from a man to an Angels and from a Seraph to an alien.

However, this does not mean agreement with John Bathurst Deane's book *Worship of the Serpent* wherein he claims that, as Colavito puts it, "all mentions of serpents in pagan myth were all mistaken worship of Satan from a corruption of the Genesis narrative" and as an example from the show, William Henry claims that Quetzalcoatl is Satan because he is depicted as a (winged) serpent.

Amongst other issues, Colavito covers William Henry's claim that Satan is a Seraph which Colavito notes, "is not canonical but rather a later gloss."

Well, as aforementioned, even the "artificial construct...assembled...composite figure" is not identified in Christian theology as a Seraph but is generally, erroneously, referred to as an Angels but is actually a Cherub.

Henry claims that Seraph means "giant serpent" which it does not. Colavito writes:

> More literally it means "burning ones" and is usually used to mean actual serpents. Only once is it applied to angels (Isaiah 6:1-3), and there it's likely reflecting the golden serpents of Near Eastern cult practice. It's only with Enoch that we see these inflated into heavenly dragons.

True, Seraph refers to "burning" or "burning ones" and "is usually used to mean actual serpents" likely due to the burning of serpent's bite. The correlation between serpents and Seraphim as heavenly beings is not serpentine in nature but burning.

Indeed, in Isaiah 6:1-3 they appear to function as keepers of the heavenly temple's altar upon which is fire (although the text does not apply Seraph to Angels as Seraphim, Angels, and Cherubim are different categories of being, look different and have different job functions: Angels are messengers, Cherubim are throne guardians, etc.).

Colavito has done much to discern Ancient Aliens' claims and has a lot more to say on this episode.

Let us close with his closing statement:

> I can't believe that I just sat through an hour of primetime major cable network television asking me to worship Satan. Where the hell is Pat Robertson when you need him?

> Seriously, Harry Potter novels get burned because religious extremists think they lead kids to Satan and network TV is routinely blasted for being satanically liberal, and nobody cares that the History Channel is all but advocating Satan worship?

Ancient (Atheist) Aliens

Some Atheists are quite taken with the concept of aliens that are more evolutionarily and technologically advanced than humans. Let us review a few such cases.

Much about Atheism is quite misunderstood, for example, they are considered anti-supernatural but they are not; many believe in the supernatural realm known as the multiverse. Atheists are considered anti-imaginary friends, super friends, sky daddies, etc. but they are not; many believe in aliens.

Various atheists have appealed to their imaginary friends/super friends/sky daddies as a final court of arbitration who will decide, in favor of Atheism, were they ever to openly reveal themselves.

For many Atheists, aliens know it all, can do anything and most importantly they are Atheists who will someday grace us with their open presence and refute those wacky theists. The technologically and intellectually advanced alien-nerd-herd takes the place of God; they will someday appear and vindicate Atheism—which is fascinating since at the same time New Age types are telling us that aliens are more spiritually enlightened than thou. Of course, anyone who does not believe in a personal God can be a New Ager and/or an Atheist and claim to be "spiritual" since that term is generic.

In his book *King Solomon's Advice*, Professor of Psychology at Harding University Walter L. Porter notes: Now to Walter L. Porter's statement:

> A number of conferences have been
> conducted by scientists on the subject of life

in outer space. The consensus appears to be that other life forms exist out there (in spite of the total lack of what is currently considered to be scientific evidence) and that they include creatures who are not only non-human and "incredibly alien," but are also "'vastly more intelligent than we."

The director of one conference, sponsored jointly by Boston University and NASA, expressed the hope that contact with these creatures ". . . might also lead us to better social forms, possibly to ways to solve our environmental crisis, even improve our own social institutions."

Another participant hoped that these beings can give us ". . . the means by which we can control the application of our knowledge. This is where we have, I think, lamentably failed."

I find all of this incredibly ironic. Modern science is looking toward heaven for salvation!

As a matter of fact, the ancient Israelites recorded many encounters with non-human creatures of vastly superior abilities who provided them with information vital to their survival and prosperity. Many of their great men told of having personally received knowledge from beyond earth.

For example, Moses credited both his power to lead the people out of Egyptian bondage and all the details of his great law to an ongoing encounter with an extra-terrestrial being.

Joseph was a Hebrew slave who rose to the highest administrative position in ancient Egypt.

Daniel, another captive Jew, was a chief adviser to Nebuchadnezzar, who was king of the great Babylonian Empire.

Both of these men achieved greatness because of special knowledge personally provided to them by non-earthlings.

Ancient Hebrew documents contain many similar reports. Indeed, from the time of their founding father, Abraham, the Israelites were told by heavenly beings that they had been chosen for a special role in the development of the human race.

Through the Israelite people the entire world would gain access to special knowledge needed to promote the progress of civilization and to combat our destructive tendencies…What was revealed includes knowledge relevant for understanding ourselves and for telling how we can live together peacefully-the most critical knowledge we need.

It is, of course, an old familiar story told in an old familiar book-the Bible. The Bible tells of another world in another realm or

dimension in the heavens inhabited by
superior creatures and ruled by a supreme
Being whose unimaginable power and
intelligence created not only this universe
but all things.

From time to time in the past,
communication was made from that realm to
some select citizen. Sometimes these
creatures simply materialized in human form
and were recognized only by their
superhuman powers. But more often the
contact was made through a form of mental
telepathy, by means of a spectacular vision
or a dream.

Atheist are all but forced into such views because Atheism
is thought restricting: it restricts it to the natural, material,
physical, reductionist, etc.

Consider that Francis Crick wrote, "Biologists must
constantly keep in mind that what they see was not
designed, but rather evolved" (*What Mad Pursuit*, p. 138).
Richard Dawkins followed up with, "Biology is the study
of complicated things that give the appearance of having
been designed for a purpose" (*The Blind Watchmaker*, p.
1).
When you train yourself, and others, to deny the evidence
right before your very eyes there is little hope of
ascertaining empirical truth.

Francis Crick

Along with Leslie Orgel, Francis Crick is largely
responsible for popularizing the concept of panspermia.

There are two variations of this concept: undirected and directed. This refers to the view that the fundamental building blocks for life are found throughout the universe. Undirected panspermia refers to the view that life began, such as on Earth, by such fundamental building blocks for life just happening to be on Earth due to having been brought to it by asteroids, etc. and just happening to combine in the right way—basically, life as the result of lightning striking a swamp.

Directed panspermia refers to the fundamental building blocks for life having been brought to Earth, on purpose or by accident, by aliens. Of course, this is an infinite regress since appealing to Johnny Alien Seed does not answer the question of origins, information, consciousness or anything but merely pushed the question backward in time: a long, long time ago in a place far, far away.

Longtime *Scientific American* senior writer John Horgan wrote:

> This theory [panspermia] was proposed at the end of the last century by the Swedish chemist Svante A. Arrhenius, who asserted that microbes floating throughout the universe served as the "seeds of life" on earth.
> In modern times Hoyle and…Sri Lankan astronomer N. Chandra Wickramasinghe…continue to promulgate this notion, even arguing that extraterrestrial microbes are the cause of influenza, AIDS and other diseases.
>
> Most scientists utterly reject these assertions, declaring that microbes have never been found in space and are unlikely

to be, since space is so inimical to life. Yet experiments done by J. Mayo Greenberg, an astrophysicist at the University of Leiden in the Netherlands...concluded that a naked cell could survive for hundreds of years in space-and for as many as 10 million years if it is protected from radiation by a thin shell of ice. Greenberg notes that it is still difficult to imagine how organisms could escape other planets or descend to this one intact. Like most other scientists, he believes life was created on the earth. Nevertheless, he says the panspermia hypothesis, while perhaps improbable and certainly distasteful to many scientists, cannot be ruled out on the basis of his experiments.

About a decade ago Orgel and Crick managed to provoke the public and their colleagues by speculating that the seeds of life were sent to the earth in a spaceship by intelligent beings living on another planet. Orgel says the proposal, which is known as directed panspermia, was "sort of a joke." But he notes that it had a serious intent: to point out the inadequacy of all explanations of terrestrial genesis. As Crick once wrote: "The origin of life appears to be almost a miracle, so many are the conditions which would have had to be satisfied to get it going." [Stanley Miller] calls the organic-matter-from-space concept "a loser."[61]

Note that precisely one year after the publication of Horgan's article, *Scientific American* published another article which featured Crick in the "Profile" section. In part, the feature reads thusly:

> ...he [Crick] adds, people must purge themselves of archaic thinking patters-especially those related to religion. "One of the most frightening things in the Western world, and this country in particular, is the number of people who believe in things that are scientifically false," he says.
> "If someone tells me that the earth is less than 10,000 years old, in my opinion he should see a psychiatrist." Some scientists said the same of Crick in 1981 after the appearance of *Life Itself,* a book on the origin of life that he co-authored with Leslie E. Orgel of the Salk Institute. The book proposed that the seeds of life were sent to the earth in a spaceship launched by beings on another planet.
>
> Called directed panspermia, the theory met with derision from other scientists, and Orgel himself described it recently as "sort of a joke." But Crick insists that given the weaknesses of all theories of terrestrial genesis, directed panspermia should still be considered "a serious possibility."[62]

In the original paper "Directed Panspermia," *Icarus* 19 (341-346, 1973 AD), Crick and Orgel wrote:

> It now seems unlikely that extraterrestrial living organisms could have reached the earth either as spores driven by the radiation pressure from another star or as living organisms imbedded in a meteorite.

As an alternative to these nineteenth-century mechanisms, we have considered Directed Panspermia: the theory that organisms were deliberately transmitted to the earth by intelligent beings on another planet.

Carl Sagan

Sagan was dichotomous and enigmatic or perhaps qualified to perform his duties as a scientist but unqualified when he stepped away from that in which he was trained.

For example, he may have performed just fine within his field but was a very, very poor logician as he tended to non sequiturs. Think for example of assertion that since we live temporarily lives upon a pale blue dot we should all just get along when one could just as easily argue that since we live temporarily lives upon an pale blue dot we should rape and pillage.

In any regard, his worldview was clearly damaged by his adherence to Atheism. However, when it came to his book (later turned into a movie) *Contact* he leaned towards intelligent design.

Sagan actually interacted, directly, with the ancient alien concept, then known as ancient astronauts. As noted above within the chapter on Von Daniken about whom, as you may recall, Sagan stated:

> Every time he sees something he can't understand, he attributes it to extraterrestrial intelligence and since he understands almost nothing, he sees evidence of extraterrestrial intelligence all over the planet.

Of course, Sagan was involved in sending messages out into space and the creation of the "gold-anodized aluminum plaques that were affixed to the Pioneer 10 and Pioneer 11 spacecraft."

So now, to *Contact*; succinctly stated, Carl Sagan wrote of extra-terrestrial aliens sending a message to Earth.
Encrypted within the message are plans for the building of a star gate.

The gate is built and one human travels via a wormhole.
She sees a planet whereon there is an alien civilization.
She ends up somewhere and has a discussion with an alien who, taking information from her mind, appeared as her father—for the sake of not freaking her out with its true form, true nature…whatever that is.
She asks about the technology of the star gate/wormhole and the alien states that while there are many alien races who use the superhighway; it was built long, long before they got to it by well, they know not who (or what?).

There is a lot within this point that ties in, directly, into concepts ranging from demonology and alienology.
Technically, this story was not about the origins of the universe nor of life.

Ancient aliens/ancient astronauts implies two views: 1) aliens created life on Earth, seeded it, intelligently designed it, panspermia (who knows how the aliens came into being) and 2) life developed by unguided, blind, goal-less Darwinian evolution on Earth and the aliens generically manipulated early mammals and thus, created humans.

In short, it is interesting that an Atheist identified higher intelligence in the form of aliens who, in turn, are employing technology that is more advanced than their own and which came from some unknown *whos* or *whats*.

Richard Dawkins

A key statement on this issue was made by Dawkins during his discussion with Ben Stein for the documentary *Expelled - No Intelligence Allowed:*

> Stein: What do you think is the possibility that Intelligent Design might turn out to be the answer to some issues in genetics or in Darwinian evolution?
>
> Dawkins: It could come about in the following way: It could be that at some earlier time, somewhere in the universe, a civilization evolved by probably some kind of Darwinian means to a very, very high level of technology, and designed a form of life that they seeded on to, perhaps this planet.
> Now that is a possibility, and an intriguing possibility. And I suppose it's possible that you might find evidence for that, if you look at the details of bio-chemistry, molecular biology, you might find a signature of some sort of designer.
>
> Stein (narrating): Wait a second! Richard Dawkins thought that Intelligent Design might be a legitimate pursuit?
>
> Dawkins: And that designer could very well be a higher intelligence from elsewhere in the universe. But that higher intelligence itself would have to had have come about by some explicable or ultimately explicable process. It couldn't have just jumped into existence spontaneously. That's the point.

So *that's the point* even though Dawkins himself believes that life on Earth just jumped into existence spontaneously. He has written:

> It is as though, in our theory of how we came to exist, we are allowed to postulate a certain ration of luck.
>
> Some kind of multiverse theory could in principle do for physics the same explanatory work as Darwinism does for biology. This kind of explanation is superficially less satisfying than the biological version of Darwinism, because it makes heavier demands on luck. But the anthropic principle entitles us to postulate far more luck than our limited human intuition is comfortable with.[63]

During his "Royal Institution Christmas Lectures" aka "The Royal Institution Lectures for Children" Dawkins told little kids the following:

> If we ever meet life from another planet... I'd also be prepared to put my shirt on the bet that they will have evolved by the way equivalent of Darwinian Natural Selection... They'll probably find us pretty childish, but they will be quite kind about our science. They'll pat us on the head and say, "Well, what you know about Universe is pretty much correct. You got a lot to learn yet, but you are doing fine. Keep it up."
>
> That's what they would say if they were talking to our scientists. What if they were talking to our best lawyers or literary critics

or theologians? I doubt if they'd be so impressed.

They might be…their anthropologists, the equivalent of their anthropologists might be interested in us, but they would be bound to notice that our cultural beliefs are very local and parochial; not just by their standards, their universal standards, where they certainly would be, but even by our own standards.

Because what people believe on our planet depends so much on whereabouts on the planet they happen to be born, which is a fairly odd thing.

Sam Harris

Number eight of Harris' supposed "10 myths about atheism" regards aliens as he ponders the possibility that there "is complex life elsewhere in the cosmos":
> If there is, such beings could have developed an understanding of nature's laws that vastly exceeds our own. Atheists can freely entertain such possibilities.
> They also can admit that if brilliant extraterrestrials exist, the contents of the Bible and the Koran will be even less impressive to them than they are to human atheists.

"If…could have…if…will be…" got it! Let us play the turn the tables game:
> If there is, such beings could have developed an understanding of nature's laws that vastly exceeds our own. Theists can freely

entertain such possibilities.
They also can admit that if brilliant
extraterrestrials exist, the contents of the
Bible and the Koran will be even more
impressive to them than they are to human
theists.

Let us consider this to be yet another of Atheism's
consoling delusions: the delusion of affirmation via higher
intellects, they adoringly look to their cenobites for
guidance.

Bill Nye

The following discussion took place between the *Answers
in Genesis* organization's Ken Ham and Bill Nye "The
Pseudo-Science Guy" at the *Ark Encounter* in
Williamstown, Kentucky in mid-2016 AD:

Nye: It is not crazy, it's extraordinary but
not crazy, to suggest that Mars was hit with
an impactor…you and I are descendants of
Martians.

Ham: And that's not crazy.

Nye: That's not crazy.

Ham: Is it crazy that you and I are
descendants of Adam and Eve?

Nye: We are descendants from a common
ancestor, I don't know that they're named by
those names.

Ham: Is it crazy that God made the first man
and woman and we're descendants from
them?

Nye: For me there's no evidence of that.

Ham: So is that crazy?

Nye: I wouldn't use that word.

Ham: What would you say?

Nye: I'd say you're betraying your intellect. You're not using your head.

Ham: So you're saying it is crazy.

Nye: [shrugs his shoulders] It's frustrating.

Ham: But you're saying we're descendants of Martians and that's not crazy?

Nye: I say it is not crazy, it's extraordinary but not crazy. And we have a process by which we can prove that.

Ham: ...I want you to do that for all these young people, prove that we're descendants from Martians.

Nye: I can't prove that right now. I don't know where you were the last minute and a half. [FYI: he was face to face with Nye and heard him say "we can prove that"]

Ham: I thought you said we could.

Nye: We want to send spacecraft there, we have a process by which we can make this discovery. And it could be on Europa, there might be something alive.

Someone from the crowd: What if there is no discovery?

Nye: That's also extraordinary, there makes us even more unusual in the universe.

Ham: Are you prepared to take—we have a book called the Bible that says it is the Word of God who made all things, who said, "Here's what happened in the past." Are you prepared to take that and consider it in regard to the evidence you see in the present?

Nye: So, I claim Mr. Ham—but I spend a lot of time [inaudible] read it twice and I follow the guys around on the maps and decided that humans made the whole thing up.

Note that while scientists do propose a hypothesis and then set out to prove it Nye seems to be in confirmation bias mode: "you and I are descendants of Martians...we have a process by which we can prove that...I can't prove that right now...we have a process by which we can make this discovery" so if any carbon-based life is found on Mars, Europa, etc. Nye can just say, "See we came from them" and be done with it much like he appeals to a common ancestor which is a mythological crypto-zoological chimera that is unproven, evidenced, unknown, unobserved, etc.

Fifty Shades of Alien Gray Matter: Science, Fiction and Science Fiction

Within this and the following chapter I will glean from Martin Kottmeyer's articles *Varicose Brains*, part 1 "Entering a Grey Area," part 2 "Heading Towards the Future" and part 3 "Headhunt," which were published in *Magonia Magazine*.

I will attempt to keep things chronologically. Following, I will relate some of the details specifically relevant to the large headed small bodies gray alien archetype in general. These will be from early scientific speculation which leads to early and ongoing science fiction.

Of course, this is not a comprehensive list as, for example, comic books (and many others from fiction to non-fiction) have been saturated with aliens for decades.

The Egyptian image known as "Mortuary House 21," kept at Tuna-Gebel, includes a large headed, diminutive bodied figure. Martin Kottmeyer notes, "the being is the shadow of the deceased represented symbolically as a black emaciated corpse."

In fact, the head is not disproportionally large but appears as such in relation to the body (I included this one within the chapter on images).

Kottmeyer relates that in *Grand Illusion* (White Buffalo, 1994 AD, p. 243) Gregory Little relates:

> ...the watchman at the gates of Sheol in the
> Hebrew Book of Enoch as gray in colour,

short like children, and taking on a
somewhat human appearance…

Well, Kottmeyer does not provide a citation to the Hebrew
book of Enoch aka 3 Enoch which was written by Rabbi
Ishmael Ben Elisha the High Priest.

The relevant portion is found in chap XLIV:5 and states:
And I behold the appearance of their face
(and, lo, it was) as the appearance of the
children of men, and their bodies like eagles.
And not only that but (furthermore) the
colour of the countenance of the
intermediate was like pale grey on account
of their deeds, for there are stains upon them
until they have become cleaned from their
iniquity in the fire.

Those being described are the spirits of the intermediate as
opposed to the spirits of the wicked.

They are gray or like pale gray but not "short like children"
since according to the historical, cultural and grammatical
context "the appearance of the children of men" does not
mean little kids but that they looked human as in
"somewhat human appearance" even with "bodies like
eagles."

In "Ishtar Descendant," (*The Skeptic*, 9, #3, 1995 AD, pp.
12-15) Martin Kottmeyer described, "items from ancient
Denmark and the Congo whose facial features mimic the
exotic facets of Strieber's Visitor."

1800s AD

1838 AD, Pierre Boitard employs the imagery of large
craniums in his book *Musee des Familles*. The beings in

question are otherwise fully human and represent Sun dwelling aliens. The large heads can be seen to be imagery for increased brain size and the supposedly resulting increase intelligence which some authors also take to result in psychic abilities.

1890 AD, Camille Flammarion wrote the following in "Urania" (Estes and Lauriat, 1890 AD, p. 37):

> In short, the head had grown, the body had diminished in size. Giants were no longer to be seen...Four permanent causes had modified insensibly the human form; the intellectual faculties and of the brain, the decrease in manual labour and bodily exercise, the transformation of food, and the marriage system.
>
> The first had increased the size of the cranium as compared with the rest of the body; the second had decreased the strength of the limbs; the third had diminished the size of the abdomen and made the teeth finer and smaller; the tendency of the fourth had been rather to perpetuate the classic forms of human beauty: masculine beauty, the nobility of an uplifted countenance, and the graceful outlines of womanhood.

Kottmeyer notes that within the story:

> By the 200th century, a single race existed. It was small in stature, light-coloured, and suggested Anglo-Saxon and Chinese descent. Differences converged towards one race, one language, one general government, and one religion.

1875 AD, Herbert Spencer speculates of our "Larger-brained descendents" in his "The Principles of Biology" (D. Appleton, 1875 AD, pp. 494-508). The speculation was that of, as Kottmeyer puts it, "higher cerebral development…Of strength and agility."

1895 AD, a student of Thomas Henry Huxley at the Royal College of Science named H.G. Wells sent him a book of fiction titled "The Time Machine" wherein is described "a slight creature – perhaps 4 feet high." Martin Kottmeyer adds that "The lips were thin. The ears were singularly minute. Chins were small and ran to a point. The eyes were large, but mild and indifferent." In fact, the surface dwelling race, the Eloi, were, essentially, androgynous as they had "little to distinguish the sexes" as Kottmeyer terms it.

In the 1898 AD book "War of the Worlds," H.G. Wells envisages aliens thusly, as per Kottmeyer paraphrase:

> The Martians were 4-foot diameter round heads. They had very large dark-coloured eyes, no nostrils, and no ears per se. They had a fleshy beak for a mouth. The internal anatomy was, in a word, simple. They had no entrails and did not eat. Rather they injected blood from other creatures, most notably a type of biped with flimsy skeletons and feeble musculature, and a round head with large eyes set in flinty sockets.

In the 1898 AD book "Ten Thousand Years in a Block of Ice," Louis Boussenard wrote that "a polar adventurer freezes to death in an iceberg and awakens to a group of small men with large globular heads who float about in the air."

1900s AD

1901 AD, from H.G. Wells' "First Men in the Moon":
> His brain grows, or at least the mathematical faculties of his brain grows, and the rest of him only so much as is necessary to sustain this essential part of him…they bulge ever larger and seem to suck all life and vigour from the rest of the frame. His limbs shrivel, his heart and digestive organs diminish, his insect face hidden under its bulging contours…his deepest emotion is the evolution of a novel computation.

Kottmeyer adds:
> Ruling all was the Grand Lunar. Resembling a small cloud, it had a brain case measuring many yards in diameter and was tended by a number of body servants who sustained him. It has intense staring eyes. He eventually saw the dwarfed little body, white, with shrivelled limbs and ineffectual tentacles. "It was great. It was pitiful."

1901 AD, Eden Phillpotts' "A Story Without an End" envisages that "Future man turns out to be cone-heads. The cone-like head extends three-feet above the face. His is pink, pliable, has gills, wings, is telepathic and subsists on odours."

1908 AD, George Raffalovitch's "Planetary Journeys and Earthly Sketches" contains a story titled "Trip to a Planet" which describes a "hairless, macrocephalic [excessively large head] entities in billowing robes are floating above a field and communicating to each other by telepathy."

1909 AD, James Alexander's "The Lunarian Professor":
>...has the narrator on a fishing trip when he encounters a lunarian...It is humanoid with a large, globular head and huge eyes. It also has six wings of various sizes. He got here by manipulation of gravitation...Around the time we develop the ability to choose the sex of children, the Lunarians plan to intervene and enforce the creation of a third sex that is neuter. It will be more intelligent and less passionate. The resemblance to modern ufology's Hybrid Program is hard to miss...

>The Lunarian reveals that by the tenth millennium mankind will be short, large-headed, toothless, and nearly bald. By the hundredth millennium, he shrinks even more and will have no digestive system. The umbilical cord stays after birth and machines infuse nutrition into the creature. It has long arms, but no ears, teeth, or toes.

1910s AD

1911 AD, James Beresford's "The Hampdenshire Wonder":
>...describes the childhood of a future man born to normal parents by apparently spontaneous mutation. The child has a large, bald head...

The same year, William Greene's "The Savage Strain":
>...envisions North Americans as shorter and weaker in the year 2410, but with a more developed mental ability.

1915 AD, Speculating, Harry Keeler "accepts the notion of larger heads and punier bodies for the year 3221" within his book "John Jones's Dollar."

1918 AD, In Aleksandr Romanovich Belyayev's "The Struggle in Space: Red Dream, Soviet-American War" humans are speculated to have "degenerated to pot-bellied, spindle-legged, bulb-heads and use genetic engineering to create monstrous man-machine combinations.

1920 AD

1922 AD, Martin Kottmeyer describes Edgar Rice Burroughs "The Chessmen of Mars" thusly:

> A race called the kaldanes exists that is 90% brain by volume with only the simplest of vital organs forming the remainder…The eyes were hideously inhuman, set far apart, protruding and lidless…A girl abducted by the kaldanes experienced him fastening "his terrible eyes upon her. He did not speak, but his eyes seemed to be boring straight to the centre of her brain…
> They seemed but to burn deeper and deeper, gathering up every vestige of control of her entire nervous system"…The nose was "scarce more than two small parallel slits set vertically" above a round mouth. Most had a skin that was bluish-gray.

They also "have no sex," quoting directly from Burroughs' book:

> Evolution proceeded. The brains became larger and more powerful. In us you see the highest development, but there are those of us who believe that there is yet another step – that some time in the far future our race

shall develop into a super-thing — just brain. The incubus of legs and chelae and vital organs will be removed. The future kaldane will be nothing but a great brain. Deaf, dumb, and blind it will be sealed in its buried vault far beneath the surface of Mars…just a great, wonderful, beautiful brain with nothing to distract it from eternal thoughts.

1923 AD, The movie "Radio-Mania" includes, "a dream sequence in which Martians are depicted as having oversize heads."

1924 AD, John Lionel Tayler book "The Last of My Race" is set in 302,930 AD and has a being with "huge head with tremendous brainpower, big chest, long thin legs, light weight…"

1926 AD, In G. Peyton Wertenbaker's "The Coming of the Ice" people of "the hundredth century" are "men with huge brains and tiny, shrivelled bodies, atrophied limbs, and slow ponderous movements."

1927 AD, Donald Wandrei's "The Red Brain" is set at "the last days of the universe when all that remains are some giant brains with god-like powers."

1928 AD, Ray Cummings "Beyond the Stars" features, "Small huge-headed beings."

The same year had a *Weird Tales* issue which included the story "Evolution Island" relates the fictional "discovery that evolution can be accelerated or reversed by means of an earthly radiation. A mad doctor enters the evolution ray and is transformed into a big-domed superman."

Kottmeyer relates, "Frank R. Paul regularly did cover paintings of spindly, big-domed men of the future for issues of *Wonder Stories* in the early 1930s."

1930 AD, Elwyn Backus "Behind the Moon" includes, "little gray humanoid creatures capture a fair maiden astronaut and plan to use her as breeding material to improve their race."

1931 AD, a paraphrase of Olaf Stapledon's "Last and First Men" is provided:

> Ten million years in the future, the environment acted upon a few human species surviving a disaster to create Second Man. They had a roomier cranium, but this needed a more massive neck, stouter legs, and greater bones. Their eyes were large and jade green. Teeth were smaller and fewer…This is basically sounder architecture and has a good logic about it…
>
> "…the brain of the second human species threatened to outgrow the rest of the body"…Third Man superseded Second Man and this race embarked on a project to create the next race, envisioned as a super-brain. We would call it a genetic engineering scheme with elements of embryo growth acceleration. The brain grew to 12 feet across with "a body reduced to a mere vestige upon the under surface of the brain."

The same year brought us Clifford Simak's "The World of the Red Sun" which includes:

...a Big Brain named Golan-Kirt comes out of the cosmos and rules the Earth five million years hence...Then there were the bald, big-brained humanoids from Alpha Centaurus who abduct Buck Rogers and his cohorts as part of a sampling expedition designed to take specimens of life for interstellar transport.

Also that year, "The Man Who Evolved" by Edmond Hamilton was published which is related thusly:

...[a] biologist learns he can speed up evolution by means of concentrated cosmic rays and decides to submit himself to its effects...reduces the body by half. It is thin and shrivelled. "The head supported by this weak body was an immense, bulging balloon that measured fully 18 inches from brow to back! It was almost entirely hairless, its great mass balanced precariously upon his slender shoulders and neck. And his face too was changed greatly, the eyes larger and the mouth smaller, the ears seeming smaller, also...

He had become simply a great head! A huge hairless head fully a yard in diameter, supported on tiny legs, the arms having dwindled to mere hands that projected just below the head! The eyes were enormous, saucer-like, but the ears were mere pinholes at either side of the head, the nose and mouth being similar holes below the eyes...gray head-thing," wrinkled and folded, two eyes, and only two muscular tentacles. The body is entirely atrophied.

The last one for 1931 AD is From Jack Williamson "The Moon Era":

> Their limbs atrophied, perished from lack of use. Even their brains were injured, for they lived an easy life…facing no new problems…Generation upon generation their bodies wasted away. Until they were no longer natural animals. They became mere brains, with eyes and feeble tentacles. In place of bodies, they use machines. Living brains, with bodies of metal.

As it turns out "Some saw the dangers associated with machines and split away, but those who became the Eternal Ones continued the path of degeneration:

> A soft helpless gray thing, with huge black staring eyes…And their eyes roughened my skin with dread. Huge black, and cold. There was nothing warm in them, nothing human, nothing kind. They were as emotionless as polished lenses.

1932 AD, from Amelia Reynolds Long's "Omega":

> He had shrunken several inches in stature, while his head had appeared to have grown larger, with the forehead almost bulbous in aspect. His fingers were extremely long and sensitive, but suggestive of great strength. His frame was thin to emaciation…He has become a man of the future physically as well as mentally.

1932 AD, Edmond Hamilton also wrote of "bulbous heads and stilt-like legs and arms" in "A Conquest of Two Worlds."

This was not included by Kottmeyer but I am adding it with regards to large headed beings of whatever sort. It may not directly relate to UFOs and aliens but consider the following.

1934 AD, within the Nation of Islam's theology/cosmology a certain scientist named Yacub aka Yakub was born in Mecca over six and a half thousand years ago and was from a branch of the Tribe of Shabazz: Yacub was referred to as "big head" due to literally having a large head and also due to his arrogance.

This was the claim of Nation of Islam founder Wallace D. Fard Muhammad (in "Lost Found Muslim [or, Moslem]" lesson No. 2) and was further elucidated by his successor Elijah Muhammad (see "The Making of Devil" section of his book "Blackman in America" for one such instance).

The Nation of Islam does, in fact, hold to a belief in a UFO, of sorts, known as the Mother Plane or Mother Wheel.

1934 AD, John W. Campbell's "Twilight" is based on "A modern man [that] accidentally time travels seven million years forward":

> They were little men – bewildered –
> dwarfed, with heads disproportionately
> large. But not extremely large. Their eyes
> impressed me most. They were huge, and
> when they looked at me there was a power
> in them that seemed sleeping, but too deeply
> to be roused.

1937 AD, The relevant point of Nat Schachner's "Past, Present, and Future" is described thusly, "ten thousand years in the future…encountered is a little man with a bald bulging forehead. He had a delicate body, spindly limbs, and brain case that could be easily disrupted. The nose was vestigial."

The same year had "Fessenden's World" including "a short description of a world ruled by an oligarchy of living brains."

1939 AD, Kottmeyer also points out that the Wizard of Oz is a "floating disembodied, bald Big Brain." Well, the Wizard had a face but indeed, the head was very oversized.

It is also noted that "The Scully hoax proper starts in the 'Scully's Scrapbook' column for the October 12, 1949 *Variety*. From a crash is pulled 16 men described as the size of Singer midgets." Singer midgets refers to the little people who acted in *The Wizard of Oz* movie.

1940s AD

1940 AD, Henry Kuttner "No Man's World" includes the following description, "bulbous-headed and spindly-limbed."

1941 AD, in the future within Robert Arthur's "Evolution's End" humans are enslaved by *The Masters*. The story states, "Their great, thin-skulled heads and mighty brains...nothing but brain." Kottmeyer adds "the head is set upon a small neckless body, the neck being lost so the weight could be handled by shoulder and back muscles."

A 1945 AD *Readers Digest* article by Roy Chapman Andrews was titled "How We Are Going to Look" and noted:

> Human beings, half a million years from now would be caricatures in our eyes – something out of a bad dream. Big round heads, almost globular, hairless as a billiard ball...Their faces will be smaller. But they will be taller, probably several inches, with longer and only four toes.

1946 AD, In Neil Bell's "Life Comes to Seathorpe" the description is "The head is large and magnificent. The brain is more complex."

A 1947 AD issue of *Science Digest* was titled "The Shape of Men to Come" and included an article titled "Mankind So Far" by William Howell which claimed:

> …the beast in us will continue to recede and the brain to advance, until we have huge bald heads together with spindly legs and wormy little bodies…and live on food pills.

Kottmeyer adds, "He accepts some of Henry Shapiro's ideas and feels the heads will be rounder to economize bone with the face smaller and chin more pointed. He notes baldness is hereditary and common in Whites, but rare in other races. Whether it will become universal is anybody's guess."

1950s AD

I cannot seem to find it but it is related that the illustration by Frank Paul for Stanton Coblentz "Into Plutonian Depths" (1950 AD) "nicely prefigures the Gray form in having a bulbous head, large eyes, no evident nose or ears, a scrawny frame and bony limbs."

1980s AD

1987 AD, "Journey to the Year 3000" Edward Packard depicts people with "bigger heads and slighter bodies."

Fifty Shades of Alien Gray Matter: Close Encounters of Various Kinds

Continuing on from Kottmeyer's articles, I will now focus on the chronology of some reported supposed encounters with aliens.

He notes, "the Airship Waves of 1896/97 where researchers have found 36 detailed CE3Ks [Close Encounters of the 3rd Kind], at least 14 of which are explicitly extraterrestrial."

H.G. Shaw 1896 AD case as reported in Robert G. Neeley, *UFOs of 1896/1897: The Airship Wave* (FFUFOR, n.d.), pp. 46-69, case #1 includes the following description:
>...seven feet high and very slender...The creature was easily lifted with "a specific gravity" (sic) of perhaps an ounce...The faces and head are without hair. The nose is like polished ivory. The eyes are large and lustrous. They are toothless and have so small a mouth it was inferred that their lives were sustained by some sort of gas.

Gray aliens are generally reported to be short but they are said to have tall comrades (leaders?). In any case, aliens are reported to be of every shape and size. Referring to Linda Howe's "Glimpses of Other Realities: Volume 1: Facts and Eyewitnesses" (LMH Productions, 1993 AD), p. 265, it is noted that her "taxonomy allows the existence of 'Taller Gray Beings, No Hair.'"

With regards to height, Neeley's case #6 reports, "7 foot tall Jupiterians."
Case #12 "11-12 foot tall Martians."
#16, "9½ foot tall."
#19, "an unusually large Apollo."
#21 reports a being described as "tall."
#22 "man from Mars is 18 feet tall."
#35 "20 feet tall and weighing 1000 pounds."

1940s AD

In 1947 AD alien / UFO encounters were making it into the newspapers.

A letter to the Nashville *Tennessean* reported "strange little men, 'all heads and arms and legs, and glowing like fireflies.'"
The *Houston Post* published a report titled, "Circle-Silly: Sailor Sees A Sociable Saucerite" which referenced, "A little man, two feet tall and with a head the size of a basket ball."

Curitiba, Brazil's "Diario da Tarde" reported "Jose C. Higgins in the Brazilian state of São Paulo, allegedly encountered some 7-foot tall entities...Described as having huge round bald heads, huge round eyes, no eyebrows, no beards, and indeterminate gender."

Gordon Creighton's "The Villa Santina Case" published in Charles Bowen's "The Humanoids" (Henry Regnery, 1969 AD, pp. 187-99) reports an August 14, 1947 AD encounter with "short, earthy-greenish, big-headed, big-eyed extraterrestrial beings" however, "no document exists preceding his March 20, 1964 letter to a Turin ufologist."

Reference is also made to a certain *Branton*'s "Operation Retaliation" within "The Dulce Book":

> They are "no more than 90 centimetres in height" and his sketch shows them to be slender. Their heads were bigger than a normal human's and "they had no signs of hair." The absence of eyebrows also favours the presumption of hairlessness, but a cap prevents certain knowledge of how bare the skull is. The eyes are enormous, protruding and round; the colour of well-ripened yellow-green plums. They have vertical pupils…a nose, "straight, geometrical, and very long"…the mouth is a mere slit.

1950 AD

Time magazine reported on the Rosenwald Foundation UFO crash according to which the aliens were "three-ft tall and a bit primitive, even monkey-like in appearance."

The Los Angeles *Mirror* published Ray L. Dimmick's "'Flying Saucer' Crash in Mexico Told by L.A. Man" which reported on "a pigmy-sized man, about 25 inches tall…The tiny visitor reputedly had a large head and a very small body."

Kenneth Arnold, "flying saucer" (as the news reported them) witness, was asked about such phenomena, his reply was as follows:

> I don't scoff at reports that "little men" have fled from alleged crack-ups of flying saucers in Mexico and southern California…Who am I to say that no such men exist? My mind is always open to anything. I haven't seen any of the tiny men myself. But I have

letters from persons who have seen them.
And they're serious, too.

"Early tales towing the little man line include an Oxford, England account of a...'...flying saucer...with lots of little men with ginger hair inside having tea'" as Kottmeyer quotes and elaborates upon Loren Gross' *UFOs: A History: 1950: April-July*, p. 2.

June 1950 *Talk of the Times* Dr. E.W. Kay's model saucer that appeared in the press on January 11, 1950.
The other is of two agents holding up a small humanoid with proportions somewhat like a small monkey.
The caption reads:

> As one silver capsule broke: the first Mars
> man was captured! Eyewitness G-man,
> McKenerich, from Phoenix (Arizona),
> reports "I was astounded by the importance
> of this great moment. For the first time I was
> seeing a being from another world. At the
> same time I was equally amazed by the
> desperation of this Aluminum Man. His
> body was covered with a shiny metal foil."
> The observatory in Phoenix, Arizona,
> presumes that this is for protection from
> cosmic rays.

As chronicled in Harold T. Wilkins, *Flying Saucers on the Attack* (Ace Star, 1967/1954), p. 261, 1952 AD has Joe Roher relating his experience with "A little man...The little saucer men have a smaller bony structure than earth men..." and a report of "a little fellow three feet tall."

In 1954 AD, Dorothy Kilgallen asserted that a British official of Cabinet rank related to her an experience with "small men – probably under four feet tall."

1958 AD, psychoanalyst, and occultist Carl Jung noted "According to the rumour, the occupants are about three feet high and look like human beings or, conversely, are utterly unlike us. Other reports speak of giants 15 feet high."

1958 AD, Edmund Rucker reports a being with "bulging eyes and domed foreheads."

I cannot seem to locate it but it is related that a San Diego newsweekly *Point* photo by David Shantz depicts "27 inch Men" as he related witnessing a flying saucer landing the inhabitant of which were "several tiny men...They appeared luminous and ghost-like."

This relates to aliens known as "Etherians" that are said to be "great godlike creatures 9 to 10 feet tall. They live 200 to 300 years. They reproduce like humans. They can think themselves down to 27 inches to facilitate manoeuvrability of the craft, but they can think themselves to the size of mountains."

In 1953 AD we got the Edward Watters photo of an alien or rather, just a "shaved monkey" hoax.
It is noted that "A case in Vallee's Magonia catalogue places 1.5 meter men with oversized heads near Tonnere, France as early as September 4, 1953" and that this is "a backdated tale, a common threat."

1954 AD, Marius DeWilde encountered two humanoid figures "about 80 cm to 1 metre" thus, just over three feet. They appear to have been wearing some sort of helmet as when he pointed his flashlight at them it reflected off of their heads.

UFOlogist Aimé Michel reported the following about this case, "very short, probably less than three and a half feet tall, but very wide in the shoulders, and the helmets protecting the heads looked enormous. I could see their legs, small in proportion to their height."

Martin Kottmeyer references Harold T. Wilkins' "Flying Saucers Uncensored" (Pyramid, 1967/1955 AD, p. 53-4):
> The story was widely disseminated. One newspaper, speaking of George Pal's *War of the Worlds* film then playing nearby wrote, "Marius DeWilde saw a big head protected by some kind of glass helmet." In the Paris paper *Soir*, it was rendered, "Both were little beings with enormous heads."

Kottmeyer also references Jacques Bonabot's "Dossier Quarouble 1954" *Bulletin du GESAG*, #72, Jun 1983 AD which quotes DeWilde thusly, "on the contrary to what some of your colleagues have written, they did not have a big head."

1954 AD, Franz Hoge reports "3½ foot tall – peculiarly shaped creatures with "thick-set bodies, oversized head, and delicate legs."

1954 AD, Aimé Michel's "The Humanoids," pp. 44-45, case #111 reports on Francois Panero and Jean Olivier who reported a "1.20 meters tall" being, "His head was large with respect to the rest of his body, and he had enormous eyes." *Life* magazine printed "A photo of a chalk outline of the Toulouse Martian drawn" by Panero and Olivier "with caption reading "Dumpy little space man they saw land in luminous sphere on basketball court near Toulouse."

The very next month, *Life* published "Astral Adventurers" which reported on "little men of many colours" and "a little whiskered man":
Two photos show men with hands set about a yard above the ground. The caption reads "Martian Men's Height is shown by two bakers. Pierre Lucas of Loctudy was going to a well when, he said, orange ball fell from the sky. Suddenly a small bearded figure with one eye in middle of forehead tapped him on shoulder. Serge Pochet of Marcoing was approached by two small shadows."

1955 AD, "a very strange dwarfish being resembling a gorilla" was reported.

1959 AD, William B. Gill reported "small manlike creatures…the outline of normal human beings."

1970s AD

Otto Binder, in a 1974 article surveying 400 occupant cases, indicated 280, about 70%, involved beings below average in height. There was no consistency.
Of skin and clothing colouring he lists: All black; blue and bearded, green skin and hair, shining yellow eyes, black face, and glowing green torso; Dun, like potato bags; fish-scale skin, legs golden yellow; striped clothing; bright red faces; pure white skin.
Anatomical features showed no consistency either. He lists Dwarfs, hairy bodies; glowing orange eyes; misshapen bald head; no arms; slit mouth, nostril holes; 3-fingered hands; shrivelled face, white hair, pumpkin head; 8-fingered hands; large chests; huge heads; furry, clawed hands; thin, hooked nose; heads like potatoes; one-eyed;

elephantine ears; fingerless hands; twisted legs.
Some walk or run; some float; some can vanish. Some are vicious; some are shy; some are indifferent...

1974 AD, Allen Hynek's "The UFO Experience" (Ballantine, 1974 AD), pp. 184-185 relates, "Large heads, spindly feet, and, generally a head that sits squat on the shoulders without much evidence of neck are often described."

In a 1976 survey of occupant cases, James M. McCampbell similarly reports a clear dominance of humanoids being diminutive. 61 of 81 entity cases with quantitative estimates were dwarves.
Among those with no quantitative estimates, there are another 58 qualitatively considered dwarves. Add them up and there were 119 dwarf cases. The modal value was 3 feet.

Kottmeyer notes that "When MacCampbell offered his analysis of ufonauts he would also notice that big heads appeared repeatedly."

1973 AD, UFOlogist Antonio Ribera notes, "we can already talk about the classic humanoid: the humanoid with big eyes and a big head."

1974 AD, a report by a certain "Monsieur X" notes, "The shape of the head is an inverted pear. It has two perfectly round eyes like marbles. The nose was small."

1979 AD, Eric Zurcher "tried to find some order among 142 entity cases catalogued in France, but ended up with a confusing typology consisting of 8 main groups, but 16 sub-groups. The biggest group were ufonauts of small size":

> …The B group has bald heads that are slightly large. The eyes are bigger than normal. However they have pointed noses and chins. A beard was noted on one…
>
> The C group comes closest to our idea of Grays. The skull is completely hypertrophied in relation to the body. It is bald. It has a flattened nose and an atrophied chin…the skin is very white in this group. There is a hole in the place of the mouth…
>
> One rather striking feature to this taxonomy is the absence of certain generalities of the modern Grays. Beyond the problem of no gray skin, there is no talk of large all-black eyes or long necks. Why does the French version have a mouth hole instead of a slit mouth?

Index

Endnotes

[1] http://www.truefreethinker.com/mormonism-church-jesus-christ-latter-day-saints

[2] Washington D.C.: U.S. Government Printing Office, 1969, p. iv. Prepared under *Air Force Office of Scientific Research Project Order*, 67-0002 and 68-0003

[3] John A. Keel, *UFOs: Operation Trojan Horse* (New York: Putnam's, 1970 AD), p. 215

[4] John A. Saliba, "Religious Dimensions of UFO Phenomena," in James R. Lewis, ed., *The Gods Have Landed: New Religions from Other Worlds* (New York: State University of New York Press, 1995 AD), p. 25

[5] *UFO Magazine*, Volume 14, Number 8, August 1999 AD, Issue #77

[6] Volume 8, Number 1, January/February 1993 AD, Issue #33

[7] Richelle Hawks, "Yabba Dabble Doo: How Aleister Crowley Introduced the Iconic Grey Alien," *Women Esoterica*, Nov 16, 2007 AD

[8] *New York Times Book Review*, July 27, 1975 AD

[9] *Religion*, Volume 34, Issue 3, July 2004 AD, pp. 163-189

[10] Jim Wilhelmsen, *Beyond Science Fiction!* (iUniverse, 2004 AD), pp. 89, 147

[11] *Flying Saucers: A Modern Myth of Things Seen in the Skies* (Signet Books, New York, first ed. 1959 AD)

[12] Jeffrey J. Kripal, *Mutants and Mystics* (University of Chicago Press, 2011 AD), p. 227

[13] *The Intuitive-Connections Network*'s "Conversation with Barbara Marciniak."

[14] "Mind at Large: Knowing in the Technological Age," *Research in Philosophy and Technology*, JAI, 1988 AD, p. 12

[15] For example, all of the top psychics are (or have been, were raised as, etc.) Catholic. Their being taught that prayer to the dead (a style of necromancy) Mary, saints, etc. leads them to conclude that communication with the dead, in general, is perfectly acceptable. See *Appendix B: Catholicism and the Psychic/Medium Connection* in my book *In Consideration of Catholic Doctrines, Traditions and Dogmas* for evidence. That was about spirit channeler medium psychics. As for extra-terrestrial alien channelers, see chapter What Whitley Strieber and Barbara Marciniak Do Not Know above.

[16] Harold Cherniss and William C. Helmbold, trans., (Cambridge, MA. Harvard University Press. London. William Heinemann Ltd. 1957 AD).

[17] Footnote reads, "Alcman, frag. 43 (Diehl) = 48 (Bergk4). In both Quaest. Conviv. 659 B and Quaest. Nat. 918 A Plutarch quotes the line as an explanation of the origin of dew, Cf. Macrobius, Sat. vii. 16. 31-32."

[18] Footnote, "Cf. Aristotle, Hist. Animal. 588 B 4 ff. and De Part. Animal. 681 A 12-15."

[19] Footnote, "See 938 C supra and note d there. On the text and implication of this sentence cf. Class. Phil. xlvi (1951), pp. 147-148."

[20] Footnote, "28 For ἡ ἅλιμος cf. Sept. Sap. 157 D-F; [Plutarch], Comment. in Hesiod. § 3 (vii, p. 51. 14 ff. [Bernardakis]); Pliny, Nat. Hist. xxii. 22 (73); Porphyry, Vita Pythag. § 34 and De Abstinentia, iv. 20 (p. 266. 5 ff. [Nauck]); Plato, Laws, 677 E (where the word ἅλιμος itself does not occur, however)."

[21] Footnote, "Works and Days, 41."

[22] Footnote, "Cf. Epimenides, frag. A 5 (i, pp. 30-31 [Diels-Kranz]), where reference to this passage should be added."

[23] Footnote, "Cf. Aristotle, De Gen. Animal. 761 B 21-23 for the suggestion that animate beings of a kind unknown to us may exist on the moon and [Philoponus], De Gen.

Animal. p. 160. 16-20 for a description of these creatures that do not eat or drink."

[24] http://en.wikipedia.org/wiki/The_Sixth_Finger

[25] http://www.truefreethinker.com/articles/illuminati-occult-fashion-model-photo-shoots

[26] William Ramsey, *ABOMINATION - Devil Worship and Deception in the West Memphis Three Murders* (CreateSpace Independent Publishing Platform, 2012 AD)

[27] "Was Philip K. Dick possessed?: http://www.truefreethinker.com/articles/video-was-philip-k-dick-possessed

[28] http://www.truefreethinker.com/articles/book-review-jeffrey-j-kripal%E2%80%99s-mutants-and-mystic http://www.truefreethinker.com/search/luceneapi_node/%22Christopher%20Knowles%22

[29] "Inside The Church of Scientology: An Exclusive Interview," Penthouse Magazine, 1983 AD

[30] "Quoted from L. Ron Hubbard, Messiah or Madman? by Bent Corydon and L. Ron Hubbard, Jr. (Lyle Stuart, 1987) p. 307."

[31] http://www.truefreethinker.com/articles/l-ron-hubbard%e2%80%99s-son-speaks-out-scientology-or-satanology

[32] "Top 10 Revelations in Steven Tyler's Memoir, Does the Noise in My Head Bother You?," *Vanity Fair*, May 9, 2011 AD

[33] http://www.truefreethinker.com/articles/scientology%E2%80%99s-media-blackout-and-mountain-vault

[34] http://www.truefreethinker.com/articles/free-e-book-aliens-ufos-nazi-cia-mk-ultra-mind-control-high-tech-brain-hacking-etc

[35] See generally *Project MKULTRA, the CIA's Program of Research In Behavior Modification, joint hearing before the Select Committee on Health and Scientific Research of*

the Committee on Human Resources, Unites States Senate (Washington: Government Printing Office, 1977 AD)

[36] Robert Eringer, "Secret Agent Man," *Rolling Stone*, 1985 AD

[37] John Marks interview with Victor Marchetti (Marks files, available at the *National Security Archives*, Washington, D.C.)

[38] In an interview with John Marks, hypnosis expert Milton Kline, a veteran of clandestine experimentation in this field, averred that his work for the government continued. Since the interview took place in 1977, years after the CIA allegedly halted mind control research, we must conclude either that the CIA lied, or that another agency continued the work. In another interview with Marks, former Air Force-CIA liaison L. Fletcher Prouty confirmed that the Department of Defense ran studies either in conjunction with or parallel to those operated by the CIA. (Marks files.)

[39] George Estabrooks, *Hypnotism* (New York: E.P. Dutton & Co., Inc., 1957 [revised edition]), 13-14

[40] Info gleaned from:
Futureofmankind - FIGU Bulletin 002
Futureofmankind - FIGU Bulletin 005
Futureofmankind - gaiaguys/meier.v1p11-20
Futureofmankind - Pleiadian
US.FIGU - A Word to Our Readers: tabid/68

[41] http://federal-circuits.vlex.com/vid/maclaine-marguilies-stoddard-bantam-37284566

[42] http://www.tjresearch.info/tjauthor.htm

[43]

https://www.law.cornell.edu/copyright/cases/907_FSupp_1 361.htm

[44] http://www.truefreethinker.com/articles/video-l-ron-hubbard-immanuel-velikovsky-connection-%E2%80%93-scientologydianetics-worlds-collision

[45] *Mutants and Mystics: Science Fiction, Superhero Comics, and the Paranormal* (University Of Chicago Press,

2011 AD), pp. 118-119 which I reviewed here:
http://www.truefreethinker.com/articles/book-review-jeffrey-j-kripal%E2%80%99s-mutants-and-mystic
[46] http://www.smithsonianmag.com/science-nature/What-Is-on-Voyagers-Golden-Record.html
[47] From his book *Ancient Atom Bombs - Fact, Fraud, and the Myth of Prehistoric Nuclear Warfare*
[48] Kripal, p. 52
[49] http://ancientaliensdebunked.com/references-and-transcripts/vimanas/
[50] Jim Wilhelmsen, *Beyond Science Fiction!*, pp. 49-50, see my review of the book here:
http://www.truefreethinker.com/articles/book-review-beyond-science-fiction-jim-wilhelmsen
[51] *The Origins of the Space Gods - Ancient Astronauts and the Cthulhu Mythos in Fiction and Fact* (Creative Commons Attribution Non-Commercial No-Derivatives License, 2011 AD)
[52] Kripal, p. 179
[53] Ivan Van Sertima, ed. *Blacks in Science: Ancient and Modern*, pp. 27-46
[54] http://www.truefreethinker.com/articles/richard-dawkins-new-book-evolution-delusion and
http://www.truefreethinker.com/articles/richard-dawkins-rules-out-abiogenesis-part-1-2
[55] *Astrophysical Journal*: R. S. Harrington, 82: 753, 1977 AD, I. W. Lindenblad, 78: 205, 1973 AD and H. L. Shipman, 206: L67, 1976 AD
http://www.journals.uchicago.edu/ApJ

Michael Heiser's *Bad Archaeology* site, "The Sirius Mystery"
http://www.badarchaeology.com/?page_id=585

Bernard R. Ortiz de Montellano, "The Dogon Revisited"
http://www.ramtops.co.uk/dogon.html

Carl Sagan book, *Broca's Brain*

François-Marie Arouet aka Voltaire's book, <u>*Micromegas*</u>

Genevieve Calame-Griaule, "On the Dogon Restudied," *Current Anthropology*, 32 (5): 575–577, 1991 AD

George Michanowsky's book, *The Once and Future Star: The Mysterious Vela X Supernova and the Origin of Civilizations*

Griaule and Dieterlen's book, *God of Water: Conversations with Ogotemmêli*

Ivan Van Sertima, ed., book, *Blacks in Science: Ancient and Modern*, pp. 27-46

Ian Ridpath, "Investigating the Sirius 'Mystery'," *Skeptical Inquirer*, Fall 1978 AD
http://www.csicop.org/si/7809/sirius.html

Ian Ridpath's book, *Messages from the Stars – Communication and Contact with Extraterrestrial Life*

Isaac Asimov's book, *Quasar, Quasar Burning Bright*

Jacky Boujou, "Comment," *Current Anthropology* 12: 159 (1991 AD)

James Oberg's book, *UFOs and Outer Space Mysteries – A Sympathetic Skeptic's Report*

Jason Colavito's book, *Golden Fleeced*

Jay B. Holberg's book, *Sirius: Brightest Diamond in the Night Sky*

Jonathan Swift's book, *Travels into Several Remote Nations of the World in Four Parts, by Lemuel Gulliver* aka *Gulliver's Travels*

Luc De Heusch, "On Griaule on Trial," *Current Anthropology* 32 (4), 1991 AD

Lynn Picknett and Clive Prince book, *The Stargate Conspiracy*

Marcel Griaule and Germaine Dieterlen book, *The Pale Fox*

Marvin Luckermann's "More Sirius Difficulties"

Nigel Appleby's book, *Hall of the Gods: The Quest to Discover the Knowledge of the Ancients*

Noah Brosch, *Sirius Matters*

P. and R. Pesch, *The Observatory*, 97: 26, 1977 AD
Paul Lane, "Comment," *Current Anthropology* 12: 162 (1991 AD)

Philip Coppens, *Dogon Shame*
http://www.philipcoppens.com/dogonshame.html

Peter James and Nick Thorpe book, *Ancient Mysteries: Discover the Latest Intriguing, Scientifically Sound Explanations to Age-Old Puzzles*

Ken Ammi, *Pop-occulture: Gene Roddenberry & the psychic (Deep Space) Nine* http://www.truefreethinker.com/articles/pop-occulture-psychic-deep-space-nine-and-gene-roddenberry

Ralph Ellis's book, *Thoth Architect of the Universe*

Ron Oriti, "On Not Taking it Seriously"

Tom Sever, "The Obsession with the Star Sirius"

Walter van Beek, "Dogon Restudies. A Field Evaluation of the Work of Marcel Griaule, *Current Anthropology* 12: 139-167 (1991 AD)

Wikipedia, *The Sirius Mystery*
http://en.m.wikipedia.org/wiki/The_Sirius_Mystery
[56] http://www.forteantimes.com/specials/star-trek/1661/from_deep_space_to_the_nine.html
[57] http://www.techgnosis.com/index_firmage.html
[58] http://www.truefreethinker.com/articles/prove-%E2%80%9Cgod%E2%80%9D
[59] http://www.truefreethinker.com/articles/fallen-angel-just-what-lucifer-contra-jim-brayshaw
[60] http://www.truefreethinker.com/articles/sources-re-researching-ancient-alien-issue-vimana-ufos
[61] John Horgan, "In the Beginning...," *Scientific American*, Vol. 264, February 1991 AD, pp. 116-125
[62] "The Mephistopheles of Neurobiology," *Scientific American*, February 1992 AD, pp. 16-17
[63] Richard Dawkins, *The Blind Watchmaker—Why the Evidence of Evolution Reveals a Universe Without Design* (New York: W.W. Norton & Co., 1986 AD), p. 139
Richard Dawkins, *The God Delusion* (Boston & New York: Houghton Mifflin Co., 2006 AD), p. 158

CPSIA information can be obtained
at www.ICGtesting.com
Printed in the USA
LVHW080758010520
654827LV00018B/1762